THE EMOTIONAL FOUNDATIONS OF LOVING RELATIONSHIPS

THE EMOTIONAL FOUNDATIONS OF LOVING RELATIONSHIPS

John S. Hoffman, Ph.D.

iUniverse, Inc.

New York Lincoln Shanghai

The Emotional Foundations of Loving Relationships

Copyright © 2005 by John S. Hoffman

iUniverse books may be ordered through booksellers or by contacting:

iUniverse
2021 Pine Lake Road, Suite 100
Lincoln, NE 68512
www.iuniverse.com
1-800-Authors (1-800-288-4677)

ISBN: 0-595-34100-4

Printed in the United States of America

To my parents—descendants of the early American pioneers who crossed the Great Plains—for blazing the path of life for me through their hard work, courage, sacrifice, and love

CONTENTS

PART ONE
EMOTIONAL AWARENESS

Part Two
Emotional Responsibility

PART THREE
FULFILLING EMOTIONAL NEEDS IN RELATIONSHIPS

PART FOUR
HANDLING EMOTIONAL STRESS AND TRIALS

PREFACE

Most of us treasure the relationships we have with our spouse, family, and friends. Aside from our spiritual relationship with God, relationships are our greatest source of ongoing happiness and fulfillment in our lives. Relationships have the power to fulfill our most basic human emotional, intellectual, and social needs and desires. Without deeply fulfilling relationships, few of us would consider ourselves to be truly happy.

But the power of relationships can be used for ill as well as for good. Insensitive, uncaring or abusive relationships inflict great personal suffering. Whether this misuse is intentional or unintentional, conscious or unconscious, habitual or reactionary, the resulting damage is the same. Needs go unfulfilled, hope is diminished, dreams are shattered, personal potential remains unrealized, and lives are permanently changed. Everyone has felt the pain inflicted in relationships by those who have made unkind or angry remarks or who have manifested selfishness or insensitivity. Tragically, some forms of misused relationships—those involving verbal, emotional, or other forms of abuse—have seen shattered lives; broken homes; divorce; mental, psychological, and physical illness; or even death.

How we treat others in our relationships and how they treat us does make a difference. Our sense of happiness and well-being, the fulfillment of our emotional needs, and our having the emotional safety nets and support structures we need to help us through difficult times are all greatly dependent on the quality of our relationships. If this is true for ourselves, then it is also true for others.

Because of this, we must learn how to treat those in our relationships well, especially our spouse, our children, our parents, and others. When it comes to our personal happiness, they depend upon us and we depend on them. If we do not use our relationships to build others up—to help them mature, grow, and achieve their divine potential—we are failing in one of our most important responsibilities, and we are strengthening the forces of opposition which are working to destroy both them and us. Sadly, some of us still fail to realize that we cannot neglect or tear down others without ultimately neglecting or tearing down ourselves.

Our happiness in life greatly depends on whether we are working and sacrificing to build up and strengthen those in our relationships.

One reason relationships are so critical to our happiness is their power to fulfill our emotional needs. Whether we feel loved, appreciated, valued, supported, and understood largely depends on how well those in our relationships are helping to meet those needs. Similarly, how much affection, emotional warmth, emotional intimacy, and emotional closeness others feel toward us depends largely on how much affection, warmth, emotional intimacy, and friendship we show them. With few exceptions, the more we address the emotional needs of others, the more likely they are to be motivated to meet our own emotional needs, in ways consistent with the level of understanding and maturity they currently possess. In short, the more love we show, the more likely we are to receive love in return.

But our ability to be aware of and to meet the emotional needs of others is not something that we are inherently born with or instinctively know. To the contrary. Powerful natural tendencies urge us to be selfish, to lash out when we are hurt or injured, to ignore or be insensitive to the needs of others (especially when our own needs are being adequately met), to handle stress and frustration by taking it out on others, to drag others down when we are feeling down, and to express or act out whatever negative emotions we are feeling. These natural tendencies tear down relationships; they do not build them up.

So how do we learn to treat those in our relationships with care, restraint, and consideration to protect both their happiness and ours? It must be taught. Some of us are fortunate enough to be raised in families in which these skills and values were lovingly taught and exemplified. Others of us must learn these things by conscious decision and by our being taught these things from other sources, if we are to learn them at all. Hence the motivation for writing this book.

This book discusses the *emotional* foundations of happy, loving relationships. In this book, you will learn the importance of emotional maturity, why you must become emotionally responsible, and the serious and far-reaching consequences that follow emotional irresponsibility. You will learn how to take emotional responsibility and better manage your emotions. You will learn how to be sensitive to and care for the emotional needs of others and how you can help meet those needs. You will learn about five destructive behaviors that will quickly destroy a relationship. You will learn techniques and strategies for handling emotional trials and stress. In short, you will learn why you must properly manage your emotions and help meet the emotional needs of others so that you and they can enjoy happy, loving, fulfilling relationships.

My hope is that this book will help you achieve just such relationships.

ACKNOWLEDGMENTS

None of us accomplish anything significant in this life without the help, guidance, support, and expertise of others. So it was with the writing of this book.

I express my love and appreciation to my wife and children for their support throughout this entire effort and for putting up with a husband and father who spent many hours working on a project that seemed to never end.

I am also indebted to those who reviewed the manuscript at various stages of development and provided valuable feedback, including Dr. Georgia C. Smith, Psy.D., Donald Conkey, Barry Hall, and Kevin Hoffman. In particular, I would like to thank my brother, Wallace Hoffman, a writer in his own right, for his insightful and extensive review of an early version of the manuscript and for his support and encouragement at a time when they were most needed.

In writing a book such as this, I would feel remiss if I did not acknowledge the powerful influence that many others have had on my life, including my family, friends, teachers, and church leaders. I express deep gratitude to my former college sociology professor, Dr. Reed H. Bradford of Brigham Young University, for the profound influence his teachings, especially regarding the true meaning of love, have had on my life. May I show my appreciation to these profound thinkers and leaders by doing for others what they have done for me.

Finally, I acknowledge the help of John Williams who, during my early work on this book, cheerfully fixed a problem on my very old IBM personal computer when all seemed hopeless and lost. John, you are proof that, in relationships, the little acts of kindness are in reality the big acts that make a profound difference in the lives of others.

PART ONE

EMOTIONAL AWARENESS

CHAPTER 1

WHAT'S SO IMPORTANT ABOUT EMOTIONS?

The quality of your life is greatly affected
by the quality of your emotional life

If you are like most people, you think of success in life largely in terms of money—income, net worth, or accumulated wealth. This is not surprising. You spent years training to earn a living so that you could provide for your material needs. As an adult, you worry about salaries, benefits, investments, loan payments, promotions, bills, and retirement. Through television, radio, billboards, magazines, and newspapers, you are bombarded with scores of advertisements promising to pamper your every desire. The rich and famous are paraded before you as societal role models. People and businesses everywhere measure progress in terms of dollars, profit margins, stock dividends, and standards of living.

Nevertheless, providing for your physical needs, as important as that is, does not in-and-of-itself generate happiness. This is because human beings are more than just *physical* creatures. Unlike cows that are content merely to graze green pastures, we humans have complex social, emotional, intellectual, and spiritual natures, not just physical natures. Our happiness depends on many factors, including our ability to grow and mature in all these aspects of our existence, our anticipating and fulfilling important needs, and our leading a balanced life.

The news is full of examples of financially wealthy people who— despite their money—lead unhappy, unfulfilled, and even desperate lives. From the outside, these people seem to have everything going for them. They dress in the best clothes, live in the finest houses, drive the most expensive cars, do not have to report in to work every day, and can go wherever they want whenever they want. Why should *they* have any problems? Are not *all* of their needs being met?

Obviously, their physical needs are more than being met. But, as you probably learned early in life, appearances can be deceiving. Physical needs are just that— physical needs. Satisfying physical needs does not automatically satisfy other needs. Food is not love, sleep is not a state of intellectual growth, and huddling around a warm fire is not an act of great faith. Just because your physical needs are being met does not mean that your emotional, intellectual, social, and spiritual needs are being met or that you are living a balanced lifestyle.

Wealth does not by itself assure the wealthy of an emotionally happy life. Marriages in Hollywood are notoriously short-lived. Suicides, murders by impassioned assailants, and death from drug overdoses decrease the population of the rich as well as the poor. Alcoholism, drug addiction, depression, and other serious emotional illnesses overshadow the lives of millionaires as well as those who are debtors. These examples conclusively demonstrate that wealth alone is not enough to assure emotional well-being.

Unfortunately, many people overestimate the importance of wealth to their happiness and underestimate the importance that emotions have on their quality of life. The seriously depressed, for example, may lead as restricted a life as those who are confined to a wheelchair. The minds of bitter victims of real or supposed injustices are overwhelmed by thoughts of hatred or retaliation. The quick-to-anger damage their relationships and fail to enjoy the emotional intimacy and support they so desperately want. Teenagers who hate the way they look, shy away from others or develop eating disorders. A wife consumed by the needs of her children may ignore the needs of her spouse and end up divorced. In each of these examples, the individual's quality of life has been dramatically altered by his or her emotions.

Bill had it all. A thirty-something professional engineer, he earned a terrific income, lived in an upscale neighborhood, had three healthy young children, and parked his luxury sedan in his garage next to his wife's brand-new sport utility vehicle. He and his wife dressed well, went out every Friday night, and were always the first to see new movies and big-name entertainment. From all outward appearances, Bill and his family were living the American Dream. In fact, most people thought Bill lived a charmed life.

Privately, Bill knew otherwise. Whenever he drove home from work, he became increasingly tense and anxious the closer he got to home. When he entered his neighborhood, he slowed down, reluctant to drive the last few blocks to his house. By the time he pulled into his driveway, his hands were sweaty, his muscles were tense, and his mind was torn between wanting to go in to see his children and wanting to drive away as fast as he could.

As Bill parked his car, he thought, "I really don't want to go through that kitchen door. In fact, I'd rather be anywhere else in the world right now. But where else can I go? This is *my* house and *my* home. Everything I have worked for my entire life is right here. All I want to do is come home, eat dinner, relax, and enjoy a pleasant evening with my family. Is that too much to ask?" Bill knew that for him, it *was* asking too much.

As Bill cracked open the door to the kitchen, he had a powerful urge to poke his briefcase through to see whether it would be yelled at or warmly welcomed. Just yesterday he had received a severe verbal lashing for forgetting to bring home a gallon of milk from the store, a mistake he paid for throughout the evening.

But that was a relatively minor incident. The previous week, Bill walked into his house to discover that his wife had transformed herself into an emotional shrew. Set off by some earlier, petty event with the housekeeper, she terrorized Bill and the children for an entire day—screaming, belittling, ridiculing, making great false accusations, trumpeting damning but false evidence, treating others contemptuously, glaring, throwing her hands and arms around in wild and exaggerated gestures, making others an offender for a word, harassing, dictating, and threatening.

Episodes like these were nothing new to Bill and the children. Bill had been married to his emotionally abusive, unstable wife for over eighteen years. Although his wife sometimes apologized after these episodes were over, more often than not she could not even remember her emotionally abusive behavior—only that she had been "upset." Bill knew that even though his wife was calm again, the same transformation would occur again, as soon as a few minutes or as long as a few days.

Bill loved his wife and his children. He believed his wife's problems were physiologically based, caused perhaps by some unidentified brain dysfunction or imbalance. His wife had sought professional help from doctors, psychiatrists, and other medical specialists for over sixteen years. Even though she had received many different types of treatment, nothing seemed to work. All Bill could do was cling to the hope that someday medical research would find a cure or a treatment that would help his wife become emotionally stable. In the meantime, he had the reality of her day-to-day emotional instability and abuse to live with.

Jack, Bill's friend from high school, led a very different life. He drove home in a broken-down minivan to his little house in an old, run-down part of town. He was always relieved when he arrived safely, surprised that he had made it all the way home without breaking down on the roadside. Before going inside his modest home, Jack picked up the litter thrown into his yard by passing cars and retrieved the mail from his mailbox while keeping an eye out for the stray dogs that freely roamed his neighborhood. Despite these petty inconveniences, unlike Bill, Jack looked forward to coming home every day. He did not hesitate to enter his house.

As Jack came through the door, his wife greeted him with a warm smile and a loving kiss and inquired about his day. His children ran up to him, hugged him, and begged him to play. After playing with the kids, Jack enjoyed a pleasant evening unwinding from the tensions of the day by talking with his wife and catching up on some reading.

Jack could not afford to take his wife out to the latest movies or big-name entertainment. Nevertheless, he and his wife went out regularly. To keep costs down, they exchanged baby-sitting with another couple and visited friends, parks, ice cream shops, and budget movie theaters.

Although Jack did not see the costly entertainment that his higher-paid coworkers enjoyed, he was always refreshed and energized when he arrived at work every day. His relationship with his wife was one of mutual respect, service, and consideration. His wife's daily dose of love and kindness recharged his batteries and renewed his spirits. Jack's marriage was not perfect, but he and his wife worked out their differences peacefully. They kept their emotions under control, avoided attacking each other's character, and shunned making exaggerated accusations or careless remarks.

Although Jack often wished he had a nicer house, a newer car, and money to spend on exotic vacations and the latest electronic wizardry, he knew that his basic emotional needs were being met, for which he was profoundly grateful. Jack was not wealthy, but he slept soundly at night, looked forward to each day, and enjoyed a rich and fulfilling life.

EMOTIONS WILL GREATLY IMPACT
THE QUALITY OF YOUR LIFE

NO ONE LIVES in an emotional vacuum. The way others manage their emotions will impact your life for good or bad:

- You are feeling happy that your family is finally together for a family outing. The mood is pleasant and fun. But your sons soon begin to fight over who has taken the most potato chips. Talk quickly turns into accusations, then shouting. You try to intervene, but you are ignored and the fighting continues.
- You are enjoying a beautiful sunset on your back patio. Finally, you have a moment of peace and quiet. Suddenly your spouse charges out the back door and administers a verbal lashing because you forgot to take her dress to the dry cleaners that morning.
- You arrive at work Monday morning feeling cheerful and refreshed from the weekend. When you check your e-mail, you find a note from your marketing manager that falsely blames you for a miscommunication with a major client. The note has already been copied to your executive-level manager.

Even if you were to react maturely in these situations, you would probably find it difficult to recapture the original good feelings you were enjoying right before they were so rudely interrupted.

Some situations are far more serious than that of the simple dimming of a pleasant emotional atmosphere. Those who are emotionally irresponsible often inflict intense emotional pain on others. When the emotionally irresponsible are upset, they are *not* content merely to sit in a corner and quietly sulk. Their unchecked Dark Emotions fester and multiply and prompt them to act in immature ways—to seek revenge, to threaten, to make ugly facial expressions, to shout, to accuse, to lash out, and to hurt—and they respond accordingly. They hurt others and pollute the emotional atmosphere for all who are unfortunate enough to be in their presence.

Amazingly, society seems largely unaware and unconcerned about emotional pollution. While many are concerned about the ill effects of secondhand cigarette smoke on nonsmokers, very few are coming forward to complain about the emotional pollution that is being forced upon them by "emotional smokers." Nobody seems to care that the immature emotional behavior of others has effectively made them "secondhand emotional smokers."

The emotions of others affects not only your mood and the amount of temporary emotional grief you might have to endure, but your motivation—and hence your ability to succeed. You have probably been around people who are a pleasure to be with, whose self-confidence, positive energy, and emotionally upbeat disposition are contagious and revitalizing. Likewise, you have probably been around people whose pessimism, quick temper, and unpredictable emotional disposition drain your energy, test your patience, and deplete your emotional reserves.

If Dark Emotions—like hidden skin blemishes or ingrown toenails—simply kept to themselves and only afflicted the person who harbored them, the damage would be limited and contained to a single individual. But this is seldom the case. Those who are angry shout, stomp around, accuse, and stare at others with dagger eyes. Those who are bored stir up arguments or engage in destructive interaction to liven the atmosphere. Those who are jealous put others down or take possession of things deceitfully or dishonestly.

One of the most extreme examples of how the emotions of others can dramatically affect your motivation, your happiness, and your ability to succeed can be seen in the case of emotional abuse. Emotional abusers not only pollute the emotional air that others must breathe—they poison it. They reduce the quality of life of their victims to that of a living hell. Instead of expressing Dark Emotions in the usual immature ways, emotional abusers feel compelled to tear their victims to pieces verbally and emotionally, like wild animals devouring their captured prey.

Emotional abusers, for example, use their position of control or authority to emotionally torture or blackmail others. They distort reality, make great false accusations, trumpet damning but false evidence, force their victims to "walk on emotional glass," scream, denounce, ridicule, glare, taunt, harass, dictate, manipulate, make ugly facial gestures, demand instant results, violate trust, make bold and unreasonable demands, treat small indiscretions as capital crimes, make their victims an offender for a word, laugh devilishly at their prey's supposed mistakes or failures, threaten their victims with their worst fears, radiate pure hatred, revile, bear down unmercifully, attribute offensive behavior or characteristics to those they torture, act and react unpredictably, lay down emotional booby traps, trample upon that which is personal or sacred, and otherwise emotionally corner and torment their victims. Those who are emotionally abused are often so devastated that they are left struggling for survival—physically, psychologically, and emotionally. Such is the awful potential that unmanaged Dark Emotions possess for destroying the quality of your life (and that of your loved ones)!

YOUR EMOTIONS WILL POWERFULLY ALTER YOUR ABILITY TO SUCCEED

MANY OF US start down the road to success, but few of us make it to the end. While the sun is shining, the road is paved, and our enthusiasm fresh, we push forward energetically toward our goals. When storms arise, winds beat down, and stones are tossed across our way, our enthusiasm wanes, our energies diminish, and we become disheartened. We become discouraged, and before long, our goals seem farther away than ever. In our discouragement, we finally give up on our goals and turn our attentions to other things. We conclude that we do not have what it takes, that our objectives were simply too hard to achieve, or that we are just not as lucky or fortunate as others. We base these conclusions largely on emotional—not logical—thought processes.

How you feel makes a difference. It affects your motivation, your energy, and your self-confidence. When you are feeling good, you feel energetic, self-confident, and capable. You approach life with zeal and enthusiasm. You persist when obstacles block your way. You take reasonable risks and draw upon your full creative resources to solve problems. You bounce back quickly from minor setbacks. You actively engage yourself (and others) in working toward your goals. You not only feel effective, you feel powerful.

When you feel down, your energy is low, your motivation is weak, and your determination is shallow. You question your self-confidence and your ability to succeed. You become increasingly vulnerable to discouragement, hopelessness, anger, jealousy, bitterness, and resentment. Small setbacks seem like major catastrophes. Your thinking becomes short-sighted and your behavior turns defensive. You get impatient. Your energy seems consumed by your problems and negative feelings. You feel sickly, even weak. You and your relationships suffer accordingly.

The bottom line is this: Unless you can emotionally survive the trials, hardships, and setbacks of your life, you will become discouraged and give up working toward your goals. To achieve success, you *must* have the help of your emotions.

Still not convinced? Consider the following reasons why your emotions are critical to your success:

YOU WILL HAVE TO GO IT ALONE EMOTIONALLY
MANY TIMES IN YOUR LIFE

Sooner or later, you will have to go it alone emotionally. There will be times when your normal sources of emotional support will be unavailable or cut off. No one will be there to provide you a sympathetic ear, to boost your spirits, to revalidate your self-worth, to cheer you on, or to help you make difficult decisions. Even those who are closest to you may not be there for you emotionally—they may never have experienced what you are going through, or may be too busy to care, or may be consumed by their own problems.

When you go it alone, you are cut off from the emotional support of others and are left to confront the powerful forces of emotional darkness by yourself. Losing someone you love, going through a divorce, struggling to overcome a deep-seated personal problem, leaving home for the first time to attend college, or living with a spouse who is emotionally immature are all situations that may require that you go it alone. Going it alone emotionally is not a rare event; it is something you will have to do repeatedly throughout your life.

The ability to go it alone when called upon to do so is characteristic of all great people. No one reaches the top of a mountain by being pulled up to the summit. Those who have achieved greatness have done so by courageously forging ahead—often alone—against impossible circumstances, fierce opposition, and major setbacks. Great individuals have learned to withstand emotional trials so severe that most people would consider them justified in their giving in to the overwhelming Dark Emotions that beat down upon them.

Going it alone successfully requires advanced and intelligent preparation if the outcome is to be successful. This is especially true with more severe emotional trials. Most of us would never consider kayaking solo down white water rapids, parachuting out of an airplane, scaling sheer granite walls, or skiing down steep mountain slopes without extensive training. We know that these activities require considerable knowledge and skill that is well beyond our natural inborn capability. Nevertheless, many of us do not even think twice about attempting to successfully "solo" through critical emotional rapids in our lives without similar training.

YOU WILL BE SUBJECTED TO EMOTIONALLY
IMMATURE PEOPLE IN YOUR LIFE

Perhaps you will encounter one as you drive down the freeway on your way to work today, wait in line to get your driver's license renewed, interact with your spouse late at night, or observe your company laying off huge numbers of workers while management continues to bask in job security, raises, and promotions. Unless you plan to live your life as a hermit holed up in the mountains (as good as that may sound on occasion), you are assured of being the target of emotionally immature behavior on repeated occasions.

Even if you are able to handle the level of immaturity that you come across in today's society, it will be increasingly difficult to do so in the future. More and more children are growing up in dysfunctional, abusive, or broken homes. Many children are born with permanent mental or emotional problems due to malnutrition, drug abuse, heavy smoking, or heavy drinking by their mothers during pregnancy. Some commentators believe that children in our society are becoming increasing rude, mean, selfish, violent, irresponsible, and insensitive. These are the same children who will shortly become the adults of tomorrow.

Who knows, you may live long enough to have one of them as your boss. You may unknowingly elect one of them to be your mayor or your judge. You may meet one of them someday as the policeman who pulls you over, as your mail carrier, or as your car mechanic.

Even if you do not survive that far into the future, your children will. Your children will have them as their bosses, their spouses, their managers and coworkers, their storekeepers, their manufacturers, their politicians, and their service people. Your children may have to face getting up every day to an emotionally immature spouse; going to work for a selfish, demanding employer; consuming products that look good on the outside but soon fall apart due to shoddy craftsmanship; getting ripped off by deceptive and lying sales or service representatives; electing politicians who say all the right things, but inwardly laugh at how easy it is to manipulate and deceive the people; being tried by juries made up of individuals who lack judgment and are vulnerable to emotional manipulation by skillful lawyers; and paying more taxes to hungry government officials who believe that they can spend your children's money more wisely than your children can.

Your Emotions Will Influence the Outcome of Critical Life Decisions

Most of us like to believe that we make all of our decisions in life on a purely rational basis. We think of ourselves as logical, rational beings who make the best decisions we can under the circumstances. What we often fail to realize, though, is just how much our emotions affect our perception of what is "rational." For example, when we are angry, we feel justified in shouting, screaming, and lashing out at others to get their attention, point out the error of their ways, and show them just how upset we are. After cooling off, we may look back on the situation and see that we were a little "emotional" in our response.

Your emotions can influence the outcome of critical life decisions, such as who you choose to marry. Most of us do not choose a spouse on a purely rational or objective basis. We choose our mates based on their looks, on how much fun they are to be with, on how well they meet our needs, on how they make us feel, and on other not-so-rational criteria. While your emotions should not be ignored when making important decisions, you must be aware of the influence they wield on your ability to make sound judgments. Otherwise, you may make critical life decisions you later regret.

How can your emotions affect your judgment and thus your decisions? One way is through *rationalization*, which is distorting one or more aspects of a situation to justify your actions or make your behavior seem more logical and reasonable. For example, you might rationalize away your having eaten all of the cookies in the cookie jar by pointing out that dinner was late and you were starving. Rather than admitting to behaving in a self-contradictory, socially unacceptable, or irrational manner, you alter your interpretation of the situation to make your actions seem more rational, reasonable, and acceptable. For example, you:

- Focus on only one aspect of the situation (*I was starving*).
- Gloss over or ignore other important considerations, such as others who may also enjoy eating the cookies, the potential weight you might gain, or the time and labor spent by the person who made the cookies (*There weren't enough cookies for everyone anyway*).
- Justify your behavior (*I had a hard day at work*).
- Show how some good came out of the situation (*At least you got to finish your shopping because you didn't have to rush home to fix dinner*).
- Blame your behavior on others (*If you hadn't left the cookie jar out there in the open, I never would have noticed it*).
- Make it look as if it were necessary for some other activity (*We were out of chips, and I had to have something to munch on while I watched the ball game*).
- Point out that others have done the same thing (*You ate all of the chips last night, so I thought it was OK if I ate all of the cookies tonight*).

- Claim that you were overpowered by emotion *(When I saw that they were my favorite, I just couldn't resist!).*

Of course, if the consequences of all your decisions in life were only as serious as a brief scolding and the disappearance of a few cookies, there would be little reason for concern. Obviously, such is not the case. Many life decisions have very serious consequences. Consider the following scenarios (the words in italics indicate where emotion is involved in the decision):

- A young teenager is urged by his peers at a party to try drugs. The teenager knows how dangerous drugs are, but wants to *feel accepted* by his peers.
- A college graduate did well in her pre-med program and was accepted to medical school, but when she learns that her boyfriend just left her for another coed, she is *devastated* and *feels like committing suicide.*
- Your sister has fallen in love with a guy she believes is a shining knight on a white horse. At first, you were impressed too, but as time went on, you and others began to have serious doubts about his integrity and character. When you try to discuss your feelings with your sister, she *defensively* brushes them aside, insists that her shining knight is "practically perfect in every way," and accuses you of being jealous of her "catch."
- A gifted high school student *feels rejected* and *feels like giving up* his career interest in computers when others call him a nerd and make fun of him.
- A wife who has caught the Christmas spirit *feels* like surprising her spouse with that big screen television he has been dreaming of, even though she knows they cannot afford it.
- A high school student *feels* like dropping out of school when he gets an offer to work for a few dollars an hour more than minimum wage.
- A discouraged husband *feels* like encouraging the advances of a young, attractive woman at the office.

There Are Those Who Are Willing to Take Advantage of the Emotionally Ignorant

If you are not aware of the influence that your emotions can have on your thoughts, perceptions, and decisions, you will be vulnerable to being manipulated by those who would take advantage of you for their own selfish purposes. The world is full of voices that cry out for your attention, your vote, and your pocketbook. These voices appeal to you largely on emotional grounds, because this is what they have found to be the most effective in achieving their desires. Salespeople, politicians, advertisers, scam artists, and others take advantage of you through subtle or not-so-subtle emotional manipulation. Not only do you stand to lose your hard-earned money, you may suffer other, more serious consequences.

A woman who has long-term, unfulfilled needs for love and companionship, for example, may be led on by the romantic advances of a handsome man who she thinks is truly interested in her, but who is only using her for his own self-gratification. A teenager's strong need for acceptance by his peers may leave him vulnerable to emotional manipulation when his buddies pressure him to use drugs and be one of the gang.

Consider the following story:

A newly married couple attending college received an advertisement in the mail claiming they would receive either a free television or some other expensive gift for merely attending a presentation on a timeshare located at a nearby ski resort. The young couple could not believe their good fortune at being offered something nice for free, especially because they were living on a shoestring and could not afford such luxuries, so they eagerly made an appointment and drove out to the resort. When they arrived, they asked to see the prize they had won. They were told that they would have to attend a "brief" presentation before they would find out.

Agreeing to the presentation, they were whisked into a fancy office by a beautiful, expensively dressed sales agent. She sat the couple down around a table and began a highly polished marketing pitch. Using glossy marketing brochures, newspaper articles, and other documents, she explained how quickly the couple could make a fortune by using the timeshare as an investment (even though the timeshare was at a ski resort and all of the available time slots were for midsummer). She related one testimonial after another of how she and other intelligent people had made a small fortune in a very short time by buying and reselling their time-shares.

The sales agent also tried to pitch the timeshare as a great vacation spot for the couple's future family, even though they were not expecting to have children for some time. She assured them that they could easily swap their time slot with other couples using a national timeshare trading network, although she was careful to avoid explaining why anyone would want to vacation at a remote ski resort in the middle of the summer.

Next, the couple were brought into a small theater, complete with surround sound, where they were shown a professionally produced, emotionally persuasive marketing film. After the movie, the couple hardly noticed that over two hours had passed by since they had walked in the door.

The husband and wife were next escorted into a "bull pen" where dozens of other couples were sitting around small round tables, listening intently to their sales agents. Every fifteen or twenty minutes, one of these agents would jump up, ring a deafening bell, and proudly announce that *their* couple had just made the smartest decision of their lives by signing a contract to purchase one of the few remaining time-shares.

The hype was thick. The emotional appeal of the presentations was almost irresistible. When the young couple's agent popped the big question, they simply nodded to each other across the table and immediately signed on the dotted line.

Because the couple did not have enough money in their bank account to cover the down payment, their sales agent agreed to allow them to send another check a few days later, after they received their tax refund (which they were counting on to pay for their upcoming college tuition).

After a brief celebration and exchange of congratulations, the couple left the noise and bustle of the bull pen feeling jubilant that they made a wise investment that would return huge profits in just a few years. They didn't even seem upset that the free gift they received as they walked out the door could have easily been thrown in the garbage, given its true value.

When the couple arrived back in town, they decided to stop by the home of the husband's older sister to share their excitement. But rather than being happy, the husband's sister was shocked. She and her husband had responded to the same mailing a few years earlier and had been trying unsuccessfully for over a year to sell their contract. They finally sold it at a huge loss, but felt fortunate to do so because they had been paying hundreds of dollars a year in mandatory "maintenance fees."

The young married couple's ecstasy quickly turned into turmoil and anguish. With churning stomachs, they returned to their one-bedroom basement apartment deeply hurt and depressed by what had initially been an exciting journey. For the first time in their married lives, they had been taken advantage of by people who thought nothing of deceiving others through lies, distortions, and carefully crafted emotional manipulation. It was a hard lesson to learn that they would not soon forget.

OTHERS DEPEND OR WILL DEPEND ON YOUR
EMOTIONAL STABILITY AND MATURITY

As a child, you relied on others to fulfill your needs. As an adult, others now rely on you for the same. Your children, for example, rely on you for self-esteem, encouragement, mentoring, guidance, support, discipline, mental stimulation, and social skill development. If you are emotionally crippled, immature, or consumed by your own problems, how will you meet the needs of those who depend on you? If you fail to meet the needs of those who depend on you, how will you affect their growth and their hopes, dreams, and future lives? Whether you realize it or not, you are helping to mold the destiny of those around you and even the future generations yet to be born. How well you discharge this responsibility will affect you, your loved ones, and your posterity's future society.

YOUR MODERN LIFESTYLE WILL PUSH YOUR
EMOTIONS TO THE LIMITS

You live in a unique era of human history—one marked by rapid change, unlimited mobility, and an explosion of information and technology. Perhaps as late as a few hundred years ago, it was still possible for one person to master all that was known to mankind. Today, you are probably struggling just to stay current within the narrow specialty of your profession or trade. A few decades ago, a college degree was a fair guarantee of a good life. Now, college students must master two and three times the amount of knowledge that their predecessors did to graduate and are often required to obtain advanced degrees or work more stressful jobs to achieve the same standard of living.

Not only is preparing to make a living more difficult, making a living itself is more stressful. Employers are demanding that employees work longer days, stay abreast of the latest developments in their fields (largely on their own time), and take on responsibilities that used to fall under the domain of highly paid managers and senior-level staff. Workers are being pressured to produce more and more, regardless of their current productivity, as if there were no limit to human capacity. Job security is a thing of the past. Relocation, unemployment, and change seem to be the new norm.

Not only are employers expecting more, you yourself are expecting more out of your life. Like everyone else, you too want to enjoy the American Dream. By today's standards, the Dream includes a nice house, two late-model automobiles, the latest electronic wizardry, stylish clothing, and money for travel and entertainment. Because one salary typically does not support this lifestyle, both partners in a relationship must if they want to achieve the Dream. The result is that *two* people come home at the end of the day exhausted. Yet dinner still has to be cooked, the dishes still have to be done, the kids still are clamoring for attention, and the lawn still needs to be mowed.

And if this were not enough, modern living requires that you be constantly on guard against crime, no matter where you live, work, or shop. You must worry about letting your kids play in the front yard; choosing child care centers that will not physically or sexually abuse your children; shuttling your children to music lessons, art lessons, and dance lessons; losing more of your spendable income to taxes and inflation; and providing for your children's education. In an attempt to keep up, you push yourself beyond your limits to meet your unrealistically high expectations. Soon you are operating on vapors instead of gasoline—not getting enough sleep, eating too much junk food, putting off exercise, neglecting adequate rest, and taking on too many commitments. Under these conditions, it is no wonder your native emotional coping skills are overwhelmed.

THE CONSEQUENCES OF UNCHANNELED DARK EMOTIONS ARE SIMPLY TOO DEVASTATING

Not all decisions in life are equal. Failing to clean up your room, to wear fashionable clothing, to go to bed on time, or to floss your teeth have very different consequences than failing to drive defensively, to resist peer pressure to use drugs, or to restrain young children from running into the street. Although making incorrect decisions in some areas of life may result in only minor irritation or inconvenience, making incorrect decisions in other areas can lead to severe injury, pain, or even death.

Because of this, you must learn to distinguish between decisions that have relatively minor consequences and decisions that have very serious consequences. Obviously, you want to give your highest priority and most careful attention to those that have serious or far-reaching consequences. Your safety, well-being, and happiness (and that of your loved ones) depend on it!

Stephanie's parents had done all they could to raise their daughter to be the fine individual she was when they sent her off to college. But Stephanie was shy, not as pretty as the other girls, and less socially skilled. By her senior year, Stephanie had not been asked out even on one date.

Most of the guys with good, solid characters had already married by the time they were seniors or they were looking for younger prospects. Stephanie felt lonely and isolated.

To fill her emotional void, Stephanie started hanging out with a different crowd. There, she was given attention, accepted, and asked out on dates. The only thing she had to do in return was lower her standards. She began using drugs, drinking heavily, and sleeping with her dates. Within a year, Stephanie had died from a lethal combination of drugs and alcohol.

How you decide to manage your emotional life can seriously affect your life and the lives of your companion and loved ones. Unmanaged Dark Emotions can lead to serious consequences such as drug abuse, sexual abuse, physical abuse, emotional abuse, alcoholism, mental and emotional illness, criminal activity, divorce, hopelessness, depression, despair, and suicide. The toll on human potential and on human life itself is very high indeed.

EMOTIONAL WELLNESS IS NECESSARY FOR PERSONAL AND INTERPERSONAL HAPPINESS

MANY OF US joined the physical fitness movement of the last decade, much to our overall improved health and well-being. We benefited from this movement in several ways:

- We learned that we cannot live a carefree physical lifestyle and assume that we would enjoy good physical health. For example, we learned to reduce our total fat intake, to avoid foods high in cholesterol and saturated fat, to eat in moderation, to exercise regularly, to reduce stress, to eat more fresh fruits and vegetables, to eat high-fiber foods, to recognize the early signs of cancer, to get adequate rest, and to take advantage of preventative health care measures such as regular physical checkups and screenings.
- We learned that certain activities, such as smoking, are extremely harmful to our physical health and should be avoided altogether.

- We changed our attitude from that of relying on the surgeon's knife and doctor's prescriptions to restore health after the fact to that of proactively preventing disease and injury. We also learned to promote fitness and good health through education.

- We learned that physical fitness and health is our responsibility, not our doctor's. This means, among other things, that it is our responsibility to educate ourselves in matters of physical fitness and health and our responsibility to subsequently live in accordance with the knowledge we have learned.

To summarize, we learned to take responsibility for our own physical nature; to educate ourselves in the areas of nutrition, exercise, and disease prevention; and to live by important values. We learned that we cannot recklessly do whatever we physically please and then expect to be physically strong and healthy. We learned that physical fitness and health are the earned rewards of those who take responsibility for their physical lives, who learn the principles upon which physical fitness and health are based, and who apply these principles through appropriate self-discipline and lifestyle management. In short, we learned that physical fitness and health are not free gifts after all.

Now, if your physical nature requires so much care, forethought, and disciplined self-management, then what about your emotional nature? Can you expect to be emotionally healthy when you have taken no thought for your emotional life? Can you expect to enjoy Happy Emotions when you do not understand the principles upon which emotional happiness are based? Can you expect to enjoy deeply fulfilling relationships when you express Dark Emotions without hesitation or restraint? Can you wait until you are clinically depressed, alcoholic, or suicidal before you take your emotional health seriously?

The answer, of course, is no. To achieve emotional health and vitality, you must understand and practice the fundamental principles on which emotional wellness is based.

What we need is an emotional fitness and wellness movement, patterned after the physical fitness movement of the last few decades. This movement would have similar objectives as did the physical fitness movement—to raise our understanding of our emotional nature, to teach us emotional responsibility, to promote education on emotional wellness, to show us the happiness that comes when we properly channel our emotions, and to heighten our understanding of the seriousness of emotional abuse and neglect.

Unlike the so-called "hippie" era of the sixties which promised to increase emotional awareness through the free expression of all emotion, this movement does *not* promote the uncontrolled, free expression of all emotion. Such an approach would only repeat the mistaken notion of physical "freedom" professed in that era—that one should be free to do whatever one physically desired in life, whether that be smoking pot, taking LSD, sleeping with another person, or what have you—regardless of the consequences. A recent documentary on public television showed some of the not-so-well-known consequences of the so-called "free 60s": nonenduring relationships, self-centeredness, outbreaks of childhood diseases in communes, sanitation problems, inattentiveness to common health problems, primitive standards of living, sexually transmitted disease, and people physically impaired by drug flashbacks, stunted mental capacities, and permanent hearing loss. Clearly, the freedom to do as one physically pleases does not mean that one can do whatever one chooses without any consequences. Such physical free-for-all attitudes and behaviors lead to physical addiction, physical limitations, permanent injuries, disease, suffering, and even death.

Rather, the emotional wellness movement would embrace the same values promoted by the physical fitness movement of the last two decades; namely, individual responsibility, awareness, education, preparation, prevention, daily self-management, self-discipline, and the adoption of important values.

It would be difficult today to find anyone who does not believe that we have benefited from the physical fitness movement. As a whole, we are physically healthier and in better shape than ever before. We are living longer and feeling better. These benefits are obvious to all. Whether we have experienced them ourselves or have witnessed them in the lives of others, they cannot be denied.

Now, if you know firsthand the benefits that come from physical self-management, then it should be easy for you to understand and believe that similar benefits will come from proper emotional self-management. If we humans are emotional as well as physical beings, then the parallel between the two movements is obvious. If we gained so many terrific things through proper physical self-management, then we can also expect to achieve great things through proper emotional self-management.

At age twenty-eight, Barney was meticulous in caring for his body. He ate only healthy foods, checked his weight every day, and swam, jogged, and lifted weights at the local health club. Through this disciplined regimen, Barney radiated health and fitness. He became muscular, energetic, and attractive. His pride in his physique and high level of physical fitness were obvious, even to strangers.

Unfortunately, Barney was not so careful about caring for his emotional health and fitness. He frequently yelled at his wife and children, said whatever he felt like saying when he was angry or upset, was rude and uncaring about the feelings of others, and was reactionary, manipulative, and critical of those around him.

Although Barney was physically fit and attractive, emotionally he was diseased. If people saw Barney's emotional being instead of his physical body, they would see a disfigured, overweight figure covered by cancerous growths and self-inflicted diseases.

Five years later, Barney's emotional ignorance and irresponsible behavior cost him his marriage and his children. Barney brushed the whole thing off by blaming the breakup on his former wife. To this day, Barney continues to work out six times a week, cut his hair twice a month, and study his physique every morning in the mirror.

YOU ARE THE AUTHOR OF YOUR EMOTIONAL DESTINY

EMOTIONS ARE AN inherent part of your nature. How well you understand, manage, and take care of your emotions will affect the very things you care about most—the quality of your life, the happiness of your relationships, the extent of unnecessary pain and suffering you will have to endure, your ability to cope with unavoidable opposition and trial, and your ability to succeed.

By educating yourself on your emotions and your emotional nature, you are taking the first step toward achieving these things. Knowledge brings enlightenment, and enlightenment bring the power of intelligent choice. You no longer need to be a victim of your emotions. You can become their master. By continuing the journey you have begun toward emotional maturity, *you* can become the author and finisher of your emotional destiny.

Thoughts to Ponder

- Are you happy with the quality of your emotional life? Just as importantly, are those closest to you just as happy about theirs? In what ways can the latter question possibly reveal things about *your* level of emotional maturity?

- Think about instances in your own life in which the emotional behavior of others dragged you down or boosted your spirits. Consider how the way they handled their emotions affected your own emotions. What can you learn from these experiences?

- What affect do you have on the emotions of others? Are you brightening the emotions of those around you or polluting the emotional air that others must breathe? How do you know?

- Are those who harbor Dark Emotions (anger, jealousy, greed, hatred, lust for power, and so forth) naturally content to keep them to themselves? Moreover, are Dark Emotions harmless to those who harbor them?

- What percentage of the great tragedies and human suffering throughout history can be attributed to the way people managed their emotions?

- If your success in life requires long periods of sustained and difficult effort, will your ability to succeed be significantly altered if you suffer chronic depression, hopelessness, bitterness, apathy, or some other debilitating emotional problem?

- Have you ever had to go it alone emotionally? Were you able to do it successfully? If so, what kinds of things prepared you to be emotionally courageous and self-reliant?

- Do you like being subjected to the emotional immaturities of others? Why? What can you learn when you are subjected to such people about how *not* to treat others? Have you applied that knowledge to your own life?

- Have you ever made a critical life decision you later regretted based largely on the emotions you were feeling at the time? How would your life have been different if you would have been aware of the influence that your emotions was having on your decision-making process? How can you recognize critical, important, or far-reaching decisions so that you can take a more structured and rational approach to decision making? Is it safe to let some decisions be made strictly on the basis on your emotions (like where you want to eat out Friday night)?

- Have you ever been taken advantage of because of your emotions? How did it make you feel? Will taking advantage of others through emotional manipulation, distortion, or emotional blackmail bring you long-term success and happiness? Why not? (For example, consider what happens to the relationship when the other party realizes that they have been taken advantage of because of their emotions.)

- What would become of those who depend on you for financial support if you were to neglect or abuse your physical health by taking illegal drugs, abusing alcohol, or becoming physically inactive and obese? What would happen to those who depend on you for emotional support if you were to neglect your emotional health by failing to manage your Dark Emotions, by becoming emotionally disabled or diseased, or by emotionally abusing those around you?

- During times of extreme stress, does emotional survival depend more on your ability to apply brute emotional force or on your prior emotional preparation, training, and habits? Do you sometimes expect to successfully paddle through Class 5 emotional rapids without any prior emotional training? Can stress push your emotional coping mechanisms beyond their limits? Is society becoming more or less stressful? What, therefore, must you become more successful at?

- Is it possible to devote too much attention to one area of your life at the expense of other areas that are just as important (or more important)? How much of your life do you spend thinking about, worrying about, and working for financial success? Your physical health and wellness? Your emotional wellness?

ACTIVITIES FOR SELF-IMPROVEMENT

1. Everyone uses the ego-defense mechanism of rationalization (see page 12) to one degree or another. Rationalizing away small, minor misdeeds (such as eating all the cookies in the cookie jar) is usually no big deal and may even add an element of humor or playfulness to a conversation or relationship. Where we get into trouble with this and other ego-defense mechanisms is when we (1) resort to

them *automatically* and *extensively* to justify ourselves whenever our behavior is called into question, and (2) use them to justify gross misconduct or irresponsibility, such as lying, infidelity, gross insensitivity or outright neglect of the needs of others, abusing or taking advantage of others, or otherwise denying responsibility in important matters.

Create a checklist of common ego-defense mechanisms (see page 12 and pages 161 through 162) and carry it around with you. After you interact with someone, pull out your checklist and place a mark beside any ego-defense mechanisms you used during your interaction. At the end of the day, review your list and notice which ego-defense mechanisms you used in your interactions with others. Were you trying to deny responsibility for your actions (or inactions) or deflect or avoid the negative consequences of those actions?

Reflect afterwards on the following questions: Does your character grow when you use ego-defense mechanisms? Are your relationships strengthened when you use them? Does their use justify your actions? Does their use short-circuit your motivation to make necessary changes your life?

2. Commit yourself to devoting an hour or more a week to your *emotional* health and fitness. Use this time to educate yourself on emotional matters, to ponder or discuss emotional principles with others, and to set goals to improve your emotional life.

CHAPTER 2

WHAT YOU SHOULD KNOW ABOUT YOUR EMOTIONAL NATURE

I feel, therefore I am

Most people give very little conscious attention to their emotional health and well-being. This is not entirely their fault. Little has been written on the topic of emotional health. Classes in emotional self-management, emotional responsibility, and emotional wellness are not part of the curriculum of our nation's schools, even though health and physical education have long been required subjects from kindergarten through college.

If you are like most people, you probably spent twelve to sixteen years of your life in formal schooling preparing for a profession or vocation so that you could become financially self-reliant and meet your physical needs. Assuming that you attended school five hours a day, five days a week, thirty weeks a year for sixteen years, this amounts to 12,000 hours of classroom instruction, not to mention the thousands of additional hours you spent in study and preparation.

Not only did you invest years of your time and energy preparing to become financially self-reliant, you also invested large sums of money. A college education today, for example, costs tens of thousands of dollars. To get your degree, you probably took out a student loan—a privilege you later paid for by making years of monthly payments to the bank. Not only that, when you finally became financially established, you discovered that you would have to continue paying for your previous training for the rest of your life—in the form of property taxes that fund public education.

Although society has long recognized your need to be educated so that you could earn a living and take care of your *physical* needs, society has largely ignored your need to be educated on how to become *emotionally* self-reliant and *emotionally* successful, even though your emotional needs are just as much a part of your nature and existence as your physical needs. Your emotions affect the success and happiness of your life as much as your physical health and well-being.

To demonstrate this point, consider how many of hours (or even minutes) of formal education you spent:

- Discussing the emotional aspects of your existence?
- Learning how to recognize and be aware of your emotions?
- Understanding your emotional needs and their effects on your life?
- Distinguishing positive emotions from negative emotions?
- Understanding emotional responsibility?
- Discussing the consequences of failing to manage your emotions?
- Preparing for and anticipating major emotional events in your life?
- Developing and practicing techniques for managing your emotions?
- Learning to use your emotions to help you succeed?

Most likely, you received very little or no training at all in these areas of your formal education. No investment was made in your emotional future, even though your emotional health is just as important to your overall happiness as your ability to provide for your physical wants and needs. For you, at least, this is about to change.

MEET YOUR EMOTIONS!

AS HUMANS, WE are emotional creatures. Our capacity to experience emotions in all their variety is one of the key characteristics that distinguish us from all other forms of life on earth. In fact, emotions play such a prominent role in our existence that if we were to advertise our species to other forms of intelligent life in the universe, we might very well post an interstellar billboard that simply read, "Human Beings—Emotions 'R Us."

LIFE IS EMOTIONAL

LIFE IS FULL of emotions and feelings. Emotions give life substance, depth, breadth, and meaning. Consider just how much emotions have enriched and deepened your life. Remember, for example, how you felt when you:

- Attended your first day of school.
- Opened presents on your birthday.
- Were embarrassed in front of your peers.
- Were treated "unfairly" by your parents.
- Gave or accepted a proposal for marriage.
- Traveled to an exotic new place.
- Gave birth to (or witnessed the birth of) your first child.
- Interviewed for your first job.
- Attended the funeral of a family member.

These events have meaning to you not just because they altered your life, but because they were punctuated by powerful feelings.

But emotions are not just associated with extraordinary events. They are a part of even seemingly trivial activities. A casual conversation with a friend, for example, may seem rather ordinary. But it is actually a highly emotional event. A conversation is more than just a simple verbal interchange of ideas and information; it is an intimate, personal exchange of feelings, emotions, and reactions to one's experiences. It is also one of the ways in which our emotional needs are made known and addressed. For example, you would not tell your close friend, "My dog was nearly killed this morning" and leave it at that. You would express your disbelief and anger that your son left the screen door unlatched when he went out to play, allowing Champ, your beloved St. Bernard, to bolt out of the house and run into the street in wild pursuit of a neighbor's cat to a near-death encounter with a speeding car full of reckless, crazy teenagers.

EVIDENCE OF YOUR EMOTIONAL NATURE

YOU ARE BIOLOGICALLY "hard-wired" to experience emotions. Inside your brain is a special group of dedicated brain structures—the limbic system—that play a central role in your ability to feel emotions. Your body releases certain chemicals (such as hormones) that dramatically influence your emotions, as anyone who has gone through adolescence or raised teenagers can attest. Your mind reacts to specific types of sensory stimuli automatically with pleasant or unpleasant emotions. Your memory stores the feelings you have with your experiences, not just cold, hard facts. Even newborn infants cry, giggle, kick their legs, and otherwise express their emotions, even though they have not yet had time to learn to be emotional. Just as modern television sets are built "cable ready," we humans are born "emotion ready."

THE PRICE YOU PAY FOR YOUR EMOTIONS

EMOTIONS ARE SO important to you as a human being that you will even seek them out when you feel they are lacking in your life. In fact, you will even *pay* to experience certain emotions:

- We pay to see movies. But the visual and aural stimulation associated with a movie is not the main reason we are willing to part with our hard-earned cash. We pay for movies because of the way they make us feel—because of the humor, romance, suspense, drama, or adventure. Quality cinematography and realistic special effects are great, but without their emotional appeal, movies would be disappointing. We are unlikely to recommend a movie that did not move us emotionally or satisfy at least some our important emotional needs.

- As parents, we take our families to major theme parks, where we exchange pricey entrance fees for a few days of family fun. In return, we hope to experience excitement, thrills, laughter, adventure, and discovery with our loved ones. Parents hope this experience will strengthen family bonds and create treasured, lifelong memories.

- We pay to attend sporting events, such as football, basketball, and baseball games. Again, what we are paying for is the emotional experience. We like the packed stadiums crowded with thousands of noisy, foot-stomping fans. We enjoy the companionship and camaraderie of family and friends. We savor the excitement and unpredictability of the game. We shake our fists, jump up and down, and shout until our voices fail. Sporting events are not just calm, objective competitions. They are highly emotional social occasions that satisfy personal emotional needs.

- We buy things largely for emotional—not rational—reasons. Merchants know this well. They do all they can to influence our decision-making process by influencing our emotions. Visit a modern department store at a major shopping mall. Notice upon entering how you leave the harsh realities of the outside world and proceed into a masterfully crafted artificial world designed to appeal to your emotional needs and desires. Look at the mannequins with their perfect builds, sleek waistlines, and smooth complexions. Listen to the soft, soothing music playing in the background. Note the trendy wall coverings and theme-laden artifacts hanging from the ceilings. Walk across the plush carpets and black marble tile floors. Talk to the attractive, high-society models disguised as jewelry and perfume sales assistants. Look at the giant posters and displays that invoke visions of how good you will look when you buy the clothing and other items set before your eyes.

Such an environment is designed not only to invoke an overall pleasant emotional state (we buy more when we feel good), but to appeal to our emotional needs and desires, such as the desire for excitement, popularity, admiration by peers, or self-esteem. We buy things not just to satisfy our material needs, but to satisfy our emotional needs. After all, how large of a wardrobe do we realistically need to cover our nakedness?

LIFE WOULD BE HOLLOW WITHOUT YOUR EMOTIONS

SOMETIMES WE TAKE our emotions for granted. We do not fully appreciate how valuable they are in our lives. We fail to realize just how empty life would be without our emotions.

What would be the pleasure of hugging a loved one, for example, if you did not experience feelings of closeness, love, and appreciation? What would be the satisfaction of building a house, mastering a musical instrument, or leading a failing business to profitability if you did not feel self-fulfillment, personal growth, and triumph over opposition? What would be the joy of marrying if you had no feelings, no attraction, no obsession for your spouse to be? What would be the joy of anything in life without your emotions?

Indeed, what price can you put on your capacity to feel? Insurance companies compensate victims of accidents for the loss of physical senses, such as hearing or eyesight. Although the loss of a physical sense is a great tragedy for which *no* amount of money can compensate, imagine what it would be like if you were involved in an accident that caused you to lose your ability to experience emotions. What dollar value could be placed on the loss of that part of your being that gives your life feeling, depth, and meaning?

Some of the most frightening crimes in history have been committed by those who seemingly have lost their ability to feel basic human compassion and normal human emotion. Stalin, for example, coldly ordered the execution of millions of innocent people without showing any sign of human empathy or compassion toward his victims. Mass murderers often kill their victims as coolly and calmly as if they were having a casual conversation. We consider such people as past feeling, past compassion, and past love. Indeed, we rightfully refer to them as inhuman and to their acts as inhumane. Without natural affection, human beings can degenerate into deadly emotional corpses capable of wreaking havoc and destruction upon large numbers of their fellow beings.

On a more positive note, life would be hollow without your feelings and emotions. Even Mr. Spock (of the television series *Star Trek*) would be less popular and less believable were it not for his human side. Notwithstanding Spock's brilliantly logical mind, it would be difficult for us to relate to him were he never to "slip" into occasional "illogical" emotions of anger, fear, and love. Even Spock "mind melded" with others to experience their emotions. In fact, much of our apparent intrigue with Mr. Spock's character centers around our fascination with his struggle to resolve the conflict between pure logic and its seeming opposite—pure emotion.

EMOTIONS ARE A CONSTANT AND CONTINUOUS PART OF YOUR BEING

EMOTIONS ARE NOT just intense, punctuated displays of feeling that surface from time to time when you are angry, overjoyed, depressed, or upset. You react to life with feelings, not just with physical gestures, spoken words, and actions. Even boredom, a seemingly empty, emotionless state, is uncomfortably emotional. We say that we hate to be bored, that being bored will drive us crazy, or that we have got to get out and do something exciting. We get emotional just talking about boredom.

Even though you might not be conscious of your emotions from moment to moment, your emotional mechanisms are alive and active. You react emotionally to everything you perceive. The reason you are unaware of the continuous nature of your feelings is that you tend to see life through your emotions, not just through your senses. In short, you feel your way through life. You do not just see or smell or taste life.

Even though your emotional mechanisms are continuously engaged, they are normally transparent until you consciously think about what you are feeling or until your emotions become so intense that they force their way into your consciousness. At that point, you suddenly realize that you are bored, excited, sad, joyful, angry, or depressed. This is no different than your being unaware that you are breathing or blinking your eyes until you consciously think about it or until someone brings it to your attention.

Imagine observing a group of students sitting in a high school history class that is being taught by a boring instructor. From the blank expressions on the students' faces, you might think that these students were not experiencing any particular emotion at all. Nevertheless, their emotional mechanisms are alive and fully functioning. If you could tune in to the instructor's and students' minds, you might hear such things as:

Student 1: "When is that bell going to ring? This class has been going on for an eternity."

Student 2: "I can't wait to tell Mary about my date with Joe last night."

Student 3: "Look at that stupid T-shirt that guy is wearing."

Instructor: "When is that deadbeat slacker on the first row ever going to shape up and pay attention?"

Even though your emotional mechanisms may be outwardly undetectable, your emotions are always active. They are an integral part of your makeup. Under normal conditions, you cannot escape them. As long as your brain is alive and healthy, so are your emotions. Indeed, a continuous emotional response to life is part of the very definition of consciousness itself. In a very real sense, as humans, we can conclude, "I feel, therefore I am."

ARE EMOTIONS GOOD OR BAD?

IN ONE SENSE, we have already answered this question. We have seen that emotions bring depth, meaning, and fulfillment to our lives. We use words such as joy, happiness, love, and delight to describe such moments. Emotions allow us to feel and experience the very best moments of our lives. Surely, then, emotions must be good.

On the other hand, uncontrolled hatred, jealousy, greed, and anger have brought about much destruction and human suffering. Murders are often committed by those who are full of rage or anger. Millions are killed in wars fueled by passions such as greed, hatred, religious intolerance, racism, or desires for domination and power. Emotional abuse transforms the lives of many into a living hell. Surely, then, emotions must be bad.

Of course, emotions themselves cannot be good and bad at the same time. The explanation for this seeming paradox is *not* found in emotions *per se*, but in how you choose to handle and react to your emotions. Emotions can be both good and bad in the same way that so many other things in life can be both good and bad. Consider the following examples:

- Fire can cook, purify (as when refining ore into metal), and make an otherwise freezing room cozy. It can also blacken, ravage, choke, level great forests, and inflict agonizing physical pain.

- Drugs can cure diseases, alleviate pain, and enable those afflicted with serious health problems to lead normal lives. On the other hand, drug abuse and drug addiction have physically and emotionally destroyed thousands of lives. Drug-related crimes, the government's War on Drugs, and drug rehabilitation programs collectively cost taxpayers (you and I) billions of dollars a year.

- Our power to speak and understand a spoken language provides us the unique capability among the animal world to exchange vast amounts of knowledge, share our feelings, and participate in complex, pleasant social interaction. Speech can build, uplift, educate, strengthen, edify, enlighten, and inspire. On the other hand, speech can tear down, demean, deceive, slander, ridicule, depress, and abuse.

In each of these examples, whether the power in question is good or bad depends on how that power is used. Each power possesses a dual potential—namely, the power to build and the power to destroy. Whether that power results in one or the other depends on how it is used.

Similarly, whether emotions are good or bad ultimately depends on what you do with them. You can use anger as an excuse to lash out and hurt others, or you can use anger to motivate you to work constructively to resolve a problem, such as writing a letter to your Congressional representative expressing your viewpoint or cleaning up your garage so you do not stumble over the garden tools again. Ultimately, what determines whether emotions are good or bad is what you do with them.

HAPPY EMOTIONS VERSUS DARK EMOTIONS

ALTHOUGH THE QUESTION of whether emotions are good or bad ultimately depends on how you handle them, not all emotions are equal. *Dark Emotions* are emotions that, left unchecked, *naturally* lead to damaging or destructive acts and consequences. These are emotions such as anger, hatred, bitterness, revenge, depression, fear, hopelessness, domination, and despair. *Happy Emotions* are emotions that uplift, inspire, and prompt you to do good. These are emotions such as appreciation, accomplishment, caring, self-worth, understanding, forgiveness, hope, joy, and love.

To take charge of your emotions so that they do not take charge of you, you must learn to recognize the difference between Happy Emotions and Dark Emotions. Because Dark Emotions naturally lead to destructive acts and consequences, if you fail to recognize them when you are feeling them, you might fail to take action to manage them and thereby suffer destructive consequences. If you do not consciously recognize when you are angry, for example, you might take your anger out on others in ways that you and others later regret.

Learning to consciously recognize Dark Emotions when they occur is not a natural-born talent. It is a skill that must be learned. Just as we teach our children to recognize threats to their physical well-being (such as an approaching semi-truck or a suspicious stranger), we should teach them to recognize threats to their emotional well-being (such as those posed by unchecked Dark Emotions). For example, we should not only help young people recognize threats to their financial security (such as failing to prepare for a trade or profession or spending beyond their means), we should also teach them to recognize threats to their emotional well-being (such as behaving in emotionally irresponsible ways or expressing Dark Emotions unrestrained). If we teach our children to be vigilant in other aspects of their lives, then why not in their emotional lives?

In learning to distinguish Happy Emotions from Dark Emotions, you must be careful not to mistake one for the other. A teenager indulging in physical lusts with her date may feel pleasurable sensations and powerful emotions and wrongfully conclude that lust is a Happy Emotion. But the long-term consequences of her actions, both on herself and her partner—such as unplanned pregnancies, abortions, sexually-transmitted disease, loss of self-respect, and feelings of abandonment or of being used—show unrestrained lust to be a Dark Emotion. Neither do Dark Emotions become Happy Emotions in a relationship just because two people enter into a collusion to help each other perform self-destructive acts. Unfortunately, love, romance, and lust are treated as interchangeable words and concepts in today's society.

Sometimes we mistake Dark Emotions for Happy Emotions because we evaluate our emotions in narrow time frames and contexts. A surge of emotion or excitement cannot, out of context or in a narrow time frame, be taken as evidence of a Happy Emotion. Judging emotions in narrow time frames leads to the common belief that "whatever feels good at the moment is good." Taken to its logical extreme, such a philosophy would lead to the absurd notion that jumping off a high cliff is good because it is invigorating to feel the air rush by, to enjoy a bird's-eye view of the natural surroundings, to have complete freedom of bodily movement, and to feel the rush of adrenaline.

Sometimes, we label Dark Emotions as Happy Emotions in order to rationalize our own selfish motives and desires. Consider, for example, how executives of cigarette companies denied for many years that the pleasures of smoking were harmful or that there was sufficient scientific evidence to prove that smoking was hazardous to your health. This denial was made in the face of hundreds of scientific studies from around the world that clearly demonstrated that smoking was harmful to health. According to the recent findings of researchers from Britain's Imperial Cancer Research, the World Health Organization, and the American Cancer Society, about three million people a year are killed by cigarette smoking. According to this report, if current trends continue, by the time today's young smokers reach middle or old age, there will be ten million deaths a year from tobacco, or about one death every three seconds. It does not take a mathematician to see that, if these trends continue, the death rate due to smoking will far exceed that of all the wars in recent history.

In judging emotions, you must learn to consult your head, not just your heart. Just feeling that something is right at the moment does not make it right or indicate that an emotion is a Happy Emotion. When you become angry, for example, you may feel that it is right to administer swift and decisive justice (at least, your interpretation of justice) on the perceived cause of your anger, but that feeling alone cannot justify your actions.

During the Dark Ages and even into the Seventeenth Century, many thousands of women were accused of witchcraft, mercilessly tortured, and put to death. The fears and superstitions of commoners ran rampant through villages, countries, and even across entire continents. These fears were often inflamed and manipulated by those in power to accomplish sinister and selfish purposes. Many publicly justified their actions by claiming they were doing God justice by persecuting, torturing, and putting to death thousands of (innocent) people whom they deemed to be evil witches. Many commoners believed their assertions and felt they were doing good by identifying the "witches" in their midst. Their victims, of course, knew what was really happening, but they were helpless to avoid their awful fate.

Today, anyone who has seen the instruments used in their torture (as I have) can only turn away in utter shock and revulsion. These gruesome artifacts stand as sullen reminders of the awful—and often inhumane—consequences of unrestrained, unchecked Dark Emotion.

DISTINGUISHING HAPPY EMOTIONS
FROM DARK EMOTIONS

WHEN DISTINGUISHING Happy Emotions from Dark Emotions, you must consult your mind, your experience, your wisdom, your spiritual values, and the wisdom of those who are mature. You must weigh your feelings against important criteria by asking questions such as:

- "Do both the short- and long-term consequences of the actions I feel like pursuing lead to constructive, positive outcomes? Would these actions uplift, strengthen, and build others over the long haul?"
- "Am I thinking this through clearly or is my thinking clouded by rationalization or by the powerful emotions I am feeling? Do I need time to cool off?"
- "What has my own experience and the experience of others taught me concerning emotions in situations like this? What did I learn? Do I need to ask others whom I respect and trust for their opinions?"
- "What do my religious convictions, my personal code of ethics, and my conscience say about the situation?"
- "Have I considered all of the short- and long-term consequences that may follow if I fulfill this emotional desire?"
- "Is this situation taking advantage of my emotional weaknesses?"
- "Is my motivation proper? Can I describe my motivation to others without using rationalization or deception?"

If a careful self-examination of these issues leads you to conclude that the emotion you are experiencing at the moment does *not* lead to constructive, uplifting, or morally acceptable actions and consequences, then you must treat that feeling as a Dark Emotion, even though it may feel like a Happy Emotion at the time. As an unfaithful husband who had lost his family, his trust, his self-respect, and all that he valued lamented, "I wish I had pondered five minutes *before* I was unfaithful to my wife how I would feel five minutes *after* I was unfaithful."

Your feelings by themselves may or may not tell you what is right. It takes more than feelings to discern truth. This simple fact is portrayed in the children's movie *Pinocchio* when Pinocchio follows his feelings (desires for fun and excitement) to Pleasure Isle where he becomes ensnared in an insidious trap. Emotions do not in and of themselves tell you what is right and wrong. For that, you have to draw upon all of your faculties—intellectual, moral, and spiritual—as well as consult experience, wisdom, insight, spiritual values, and other standards of truth.

THOUGHTS TO PONDER

- What emotional qualities does your partner (or friend) bring into your life that you miss when he or she is temporarily away? Suppose your partner were involved in an automobile accident that took away his or her ability to feel emotion. How would this affect your life? Do you truly appreciate and value the emotional assets your partner brings to your relationship?

- Would you ever consider marrying a person who, like Spock, had no passion or feeling and could only interact with reason? Why not? Would you consider marrying a person who is totally driven by his or her emotions? If not, what is an appropriate balance between reason and emotion and how does a person achieve that balance?

- Think about one of your most cherished memories. What makes that memory so precious? How big of a part did your feelings and the feelings of others play in making that memory?

- How much money do you spend to fulfill your basic needs (bare-bones food, clothing, and shelter—without the embellishments)? How much money do you spend on products that bring excitement or make you feel more fashionable, adventuresome, classy, special, socially elite, or financially successful?

- Should you spend time berating yourself or feeling guilty when Dark Emotions come into your being uninvited? How important is it to your life that you channel Dark Emotions into constructive outlets and activities to dissipate, nullify, or counteract their destructive force? What happens when you delay the proper management of powerful Dark Emotions?

- Can you generate Dark Emotions? How can the intellectual conclusions you draw about a situation (such as other people's motives) affect your emotions? Is it possible to change your conclusions (judgment) about a situation and thereby change your emotions? If so, is this one of the keys to successful emotional self-management? Is being "slow to judge" critical to happy relationships? Is also learning to make accurate assessments of a situation?

- Can emotions simply be "turned off?" If not, then what is left for us to do with our emotions?

- Are all emotions equal? Do some emotions have a greater potential for destroying your life and the lives of your loved ones than other emotions? If so, is it important to learn to distinguish potentially highly dangerous or destructive emotions from those that are of little danger or are relatively harmless? Is the proper self-management of certain emotions more critical than that of others?

- How important is it to use all of your faculties and resources (heart, mind, personal experience, spiritual values, inspiration, correct principles, and the wisdom and experience of others)—not just your emotions—in judging situations and making important decisions in your life?

- Do you believe that humans are emotional creatures, not just physical creatures? If so, how much time have you spent in your life learning about your emotional nature, understanding how to identify and address emotional needs, anticipating and planning for future emotional needs, developing effective emotional coping mechanisms, learning proper emotional self-management, internalizing important emotional values, and developing emotional courage?

ACTIVITIES FOR SELF-IMPROVEMENT

1. Keep a diary of your emotions for a day. On one page, list the Dark Emotions you experienced that day, how they affected your emotional disposition, where you think these Dark Emotions came from, and what you did with them. On another page, do the same for the Happy Emotions you experienced. At the end of the day, review your lists. Did you experience more Happy Emotions than Dark Emotions? How important were your Happy Emotions in helping you through your day and in bringing satisfaction, fulfillment, and happiness to your life? How can you increase the number of Happy Emotions you experience in your life and decrease the number of Dark Emotions you experience?

2. Try to create Happy Emotions in someone you know. Reflect afterwards, if you were successful, on how it made you feel. Does this experience point out one powerful way you can increase the number of Happy Emotions you feel in your life?

3. Would you like to save more of the money you earn and reduce your monthly expenditures? If so, track your current spending for a period of time (such as a month). Afterwards, highlight each expense according to the following instructions, using red, yellow, and green highlighting markers. Highlight absolute bare necessities (such as your water bill, food staples, and necessary, no-frills articles of clothing) with green. Highlight nonessential items that you purchased for emotional reasons (fashion ties, cool electronic gadgets, extra or high-fashion clothing, junk food, entertainment expenses, and so forth) with red. Finally, highlight purchases for important necessities that could have been fulfilled in less expensive ways (such as big house payments, luxury car or sport utility vehicle payments, high-fashion clothing, prepared or convenience foods, dining out, and so forth) in yellow, and write beside each of these items how much more you spent on the item because it was more expensive than the no-frills version.

   Now analyze the result. Using a calculator, add up all of items highlighted in red and yellow. Your grand total represents money spent to uphold a *lifestyle* rather than to uphold *life*. Lifestyle is defended on emotional grounds, not on financial grounds. Divide that number by the total of all the money you spent during that time frame. This is the percentage of all the money you earn that you spent upholding your lifestyle, not your life.

   Now for some tough questions. Are you trying to live a life-style, for emotional reasons, that you simply cannot afford? To ask it another way, Can you afford your emotional habits? Even if you can, would you be better off saving at least some of your "lifestyle money" for future needs, such as your children's education or your future retirement?

   If you have concluded that you are spending too much money for emotional reasons, what can you do to change your habits? One way is to fight the emotional manipulation of advertisers by using your own form of emotional strategy: (1) pay for everything you buy in cash. Studies have shown that emotionally it is much harder to part with cold, hard cash in your wallet than to hand over a plastic credit card that simply and invisibly adds the total to an invisible charge account; (2) substitute less costly ways of meeting your emotional needs (and desires!) in place of more expensive ways. For example, many of your deep emotional needs can be satisfied through service, through the pursuit of worthy goals, through planning and carrying out fun family activities, by going on less expensive dates, and by caring for your body and your environment.

CHAPTER 3

UNDERSTANDING YOUR PARTNER'S EMOTIONAL NEEDS

Emotional hunger is bounded only when others care

Bonnie had been married to Jack for sixteen years. They were the parents of three young, beautiful children. Jack made a good living as an engineer at one of the local high-tech companies. He and Bonnie lived a moderate lifestyle in a typical middle-class neighborhood. By careful budgeting, they even managed to satisfy some of their wants, such as putting in an above-ground swimming pool in their backyard.

Still, Bonnie was unhappy. She grew up as the youngest child in a family of eight in a home where love and affection were simply not shown. She carried the need for emotional intimacy into her adult life, but it had never been adequately fulfilled—not even in her marriage.

Bonnie had met Jack the year after she graduated from college. They were married after a five-month, whirlwind romance. Not long after the honeymoon, Jack fell back into his daily routine at the office, where he often stayed late to work on his many projects. A few years later, he was traveling extensively for his employer, leaving Bonnie at home to attend to their three, young, active children.

When Jack was at home, he helped Bonnie by doing housework, playing with the children, and shuttling them around to music lessons and soccer practice, for which Bonnie was grateful. He pitched in as much as he could to lighten Bonnie's day-to-day burdens.

Although Jack was a good father and provider, he wasn't physically affectionate or emotionally intimate with his wife. He refused to kiss her, cuddle her in bed, take her hand in public, give her hugs, tease her, or otherwise show little acts of love and affection. Jack thought these things were childish and a sign of emotional vulnerability and weakness. "I grew up and became a responsible, hard-working adult without doing all this mushy stuff," he reasoned, "so it can't be that important." Meanwhile, Bonnie's deep-seated need for emotional intimacy and affection continued to grow.

One day, Bonnie met a single man about her age in her part-time work as an interior decorator. Bonnie was physically attractive, and the man quickly took a strong interest in her, even though she was married. She knew it was wrong to become involved with another man, but he offered her the qualities she longed for—sensitivity, affection, laughter, emotional intimacy, and physical affection. Soon she began seeing and sleeping with this man whenever Jack was out of town and she could find a baby-sitter.

Jack was unaware of his wife's affair. As far as he knew, everything was going along just fine. Then one day, Bonnie shattered his world by telling him she wanted a divorce. The sudden announcement sent Jack into shock. Angry, confused, and deeply hurt, he eventually fell into a serious depression. He was wounded even more deeply later when he found out that his wife was having an affair with another man.

Jack won custody of his children in the final divorce, but he never fully recovered from his wife's betrayal. He remains a broken man.

WHAT ARE EMOTIONAL NEEDS?

IF YOU ARE an emotional creature as well as a physical creature—if emotions are hard-wired into your very physiology, if emotions are a continuous part of your existence, if you are even willing to pay to feel certain emotions—then you must have emotional needs, not just physical needs.

Moreover, if your physical self has so many complex and interrelated systems (such as your respiratory system, circulatory system, and nervous system) that must function perfectly for you to enjoy physical health and well-being, then you should not be surprised to discover that your emotional self is equally intricate, complex, and balanced. And just as your physical body is sustained by meeting a variety of physical needs, your emotional being is sustained by meeting a variety of emotional needs.

Take, for example, emotional needs such as the need to feel accepted, to be understood, and to feel good about yourself. The fulfillment of these needs is frequently left to chance or to automatic, reactive, or self-destructive mechanisms that have been learned over long periods of time. This does little to promote deep emotional fulfillment or happy relationships.

Many people are unaware of their emotional needs until their needs go largely unfulfilled. Moreover, too few are consciously working to understand and fulfill their (and their partner's) emotional needs in constructive ways. This has resulted in a large percentage of individuals and couples who suffer unnecessary emotional pain and deprivation instead of deep emotional fulfillment and happiness.

TWENTY OF YOUR PARTNER'S MOST IMPORTANT EMOTIONAL NEEDS

YOUR PARTNER IS a living, breathing, emotional being—whether he or she appears to be or not. Your ability to understand and meet your partner's underlying emotional needs is key to your enjoying a happy, enduring, and fulfilling relationship.

The rest of this chapter is devoted to helping you understand your partner's critical emotional needs. You will learn how you can best meet those needs in chapter, *Ten Secrets of Emotionally Fulfilling Relationships.*

Emotional needs are universal. Your partner's fundamental emotional needs are your fundamental emotional needs. What changes is which needs are most pressing and urgent from moment to moment and which ones may not have been met long-term. Because of this, as we discuss your partner's twenty most important emotional needs, we will phrase them as if they were your own to aid in their comprehension and make them more personal.

THE NEED TO FEEL LOVED

The need to feel loved is the most universally recognized human emotional need. From the beginning of recorded history, mankind has centered much of its conversation, entertainment, and literature around its need for love. We talk about seeking love, falling in love, losing love, giving love, and receiving love. We spend significant sums of money dating and courting to find a loving companion. Children and parents even use love as a measure of character when they try to manipulate each other with statements such as, "If you really loved me, you would…" Merchandisers exploit the high value we place on love during the Christmas and Valentine's Day shopping seasons. Arguing couples bear witness to the importance of love when they hurl accusations at each other such as "You don't love me any more" or "You never *really* loved me."

Your need for love is multifaceted. It is the need to feel that others care about you, to feel understood and accepted, and to feel recognized as a valid, important, worthwhile human being. It is the need to feel supported during times of trial and opposition, to feel emotionally close to another human being, and to feel that you are treated with kindness, respect, patience, and sensitivity. It is the need to feel special and appreciated. It is the confidence you have that your needs will be cared for and looked after.

Contrary to what is often depicted in popular entertainment, love does not have to involve physical or sexual intimacy. Sexual intimacy, for example, can be motivated for a variety of reasons, none of which has anything to do with love, as we have defined. Marriages break up all the time, even though the partners were having regular sexual relations. Physical intimacy by itself does not *prove* that love is present in a relationship.

True love is permanent, enduring, uplifting, other-serving, stable, long-suffering, sensitive, kind, empathetic, committed, and purely motivated. True love makes sacrifices to provide the other person with the opportunities they need to reach their full potential.

THE NEED TO LOVE

It may seem strange to include the need to love in a list of human emotional needs. You are probably most aware of your need *for* love, not of your need *to* love. Nevertheless, the need to love is a powerful emotional need. Parents will often admit that their need to love their children is as great as their children's need to be loved. Across the world, volunteers and benefactors give love by offering their time, talents, and means to serve those who are less fortunate. Indeed, many of our deepest joys and satisfactions in life come only as we love others. Your need to love is your need to care for others, to help others in need, and to sacrifice for the welfare of others.

THE NEED TO FEEL ACCEPTED

We humans are social animals. We need to interact with our fellow beings and feel accepted by them. Few want to live the life of a mountain hermit who has no human contact. Those who try generally get bored after a few weeks or months and return to rejoin the human race, despite all its accompanying problems and burdens. Even Thoreau returned to civilization.

The need for acceptance is real. Teenagers have been known to subject themselves to cruel, illegal, or sadistic initiation rites just for the privilege of becoming members of a gang. School children who are consistently rejected by their peers suffer severe emotional trauma. High school students who were rejected by their peers have even shot themselves in front of their classmates.

Your need to feel accepted exists at both an individual and a group level. At the individual level, your need to feel accepted is the need to feel that your partner views you as an important human being, listens to you, seriously considers your opinions, and respects your unique talents and abilities. It is the need to feel included in your partner's life and activities, to feel accepted despite your weaknesses, and to believe that your partner's body language, posture, and actions are friendly.

Your emotional need to feel accepted at the group level is your need to feel that you are accepted as a member of the group—that you are treated equally as "one of the gang," that you are valued by the group as an important member, and that you are included in important group activities.

The Need for Affection

Children who grow up in environments where they are never given any sign of affection, are always kept at an emotional distance, are consistently "brushed off," or given an emotional "cold shoulder" frequently develop serious physical, mental, and emotional problems. Affection is necessary for normal human development. Extreme emotional deprivation in infants, for example, is severely debilitating. Couples divorce over one or both partner's lack of affection.

Your emotional need for affection is your need to feel "mothered"; to feel emotional warmth; to receive hugs, smiles, sympathetic words, and friendly gestures; and to be treated with kindness, love, and sensitivity.

The Need for Emotional Intimacy

Even though physical intimacy is paraded everywhere about us in movies, television shows, books, and advertisements as the ultimate sign of love in a relationship, is not the same as emotional intimacy. Emotional intimacy is rooted in the emotional world, not the physical world.

Your need for emotional intimacy is your need to feel that your partner understands your dreams, hopes, fears, aspirations, and struggles. It is the need to feel that you can share important feelings and confidences with your partner without worrying that those feelings will be mistreated, misjudged, divulged to others, or otherwise misused. It is the need to feel that your partner knows you so well that he or she can "read" your emotions and respond to your changing emotional needs, often even without your expressing those needs.

Emotional intimacy is an earned privilege, one that is built over time as trust and a safe emotional climate are established and consistently honored. Newlyweds, for example, cannot assume that just because they are wearing a wedding ring, they will enjoy emotional intimacy. Emotional intimacy is built on a personal record of trust, stability, love, and sensitivity. It cannot be mandated, forced, or pronounced by a clerical authority.

Emotional intimacy is violated when you are emotionally insensitive, emotionally volatile, or inconsiderate. It is violated when you spend little time thinking about how your partner feels, when you embarrass your partner in front of his or her friends, and when you exploit your partner to get things you want.

THE NEED FOR EMOTIONAL SUPPORT

We all experience times in our lives when we are challenged by opposition, trial, or serious discouragement. During these periods, our partner's encouragement, vote of confidence, helping hands, hugs, sympathetic ears, and expressions of appreciation can go a long way toward boosting our morale and soothing our tattered emotions. Even day-to-day living, with its tedious drudgery and test of endurance, calls for regular doses of emotional support.

Your need for emotional support is your need to be lifted up when you are feeling down or discouraged, to receive encouragement, to have your self-confidence strengthened, and to have your burdens lightened. It is your need to know that you can turn to your partner and receive help during times of need.

Emotional support is the fertile soil that promotes personal growth. It is the critical factor that often helps others make correct decisions during crucial junctures in their lives. Smart parents, for example, know that children accomplish far more in life through positive encouragement than through criticism or dictatorial demands. Sports teams play more vigorously on home fields where they have the visible support of family, friends, and cheering fans. Great historical figures frequently attribute their success to a single person who gave them needed emotional support and encouragement during certain critical times in their lives.

Wise spouses know that the success of their companions in the outside world is often determined by how much support they receive at home.

THE NEED FOR COMPANIONSHIP AND FRIENDSHIP

Is is difficult to imagine a rich, fulfilling life without family or friends. After all, what other source is there of companionship, friendship, and support? Your emotional need for companionship and friendship is your need to have someone with whom you can confide, socialize, and have fun. It is your need to share your interests, dreams, challenges, and frustrations with those who care about you and are empathetic toward you.

THE NEED TO BE UNDERSTOOD

Understanding another person is more than simply comprehending what the other person is saying. It is understanding the messenger himself—how he thinks, perceives, and feels and what he or she has been through—not just interpreting the person's speech. Many arguments are rooted in misunderstandings.

Your emotional need to be understood is your need to feel that the other people who are important to you understand you—who you are, where you are coming from, what your background is, what trials you have endured, what setbacks you have experienced, and what victories you have celebrated. It is your need to feel that others understand your total life situation and what you are currently going through.

The need to feel understood applies not just to interpersonal situations, but to any situation involving human beings. For example, in business, employees have a need for their employers to understand them—to recognize and view them as human beings who have needs, struggles, and challenges—not as so many "head count" (that is, head of cattle) that can be herded about at will without regard to individual situations, talents, needs, or abilities.

THE NEED TO FEEL VALUED

Humans have a strong need to feel valued and appreciated. Spouses who regularly express appreciation to their mate for his or her companionship and contribution strengthen the bonds of their relationship. Parents who regularly let their children know that they are appreciated and valued build self-esteem and inspire the best in their offspring. Employers who recognize the talents and skills of their employees and regularly show their appreciation to them enjoy higher morale, loyalty, and productivity.

Your emotional need to feel valued is your need to feel recognized and appreciated for your contributions and for who you are (your character and personality). It is your need to feel that your ideas, suggestions, and efforts are appreciated and are important. It is your need to be given credit and recognition for your ideas, inventions, creativity, and contributions and to be treated with courtesy, respect, and dignity.

THE NEED TO FEEL HOPE

If certain animals are placed in a painful or aversive situation in which nothing they do—no matter how hard they try—has any effect on the intensity or magnitude of a painful stimulus, they eventually stop trying to end the painful stimulus. From a human point of view, it is as if they have given up hope. This condition, called "learned helplessness" by psychologists, is found in humans as well as in animals and can lead to severe consequences.

What happens, for example, if rats that have attained a state of learned helplessness by being placed in tanks of water where they cannot swim to safety are suddenly placed in tanks of water in which they *can* swim to safety? They simply give up and drown, even though they could have easily saved themselves by swimming to the side of the new tank. A human example of this occurred a few years ago, as reported in the news. Several shipwrecked passengers swimming in the ocean gave up hope and drowned moments before others who were still swimming were rescued.

When you think that your efforts are not getting you anywhere, it is easy to give up hope and stop trying, regardless of whether your perceptions are accurate. Although the decision to give up may have seemed very logical at the time, in reality, you might have been very close to achieving your goal. For example, there may be possible solutions or actions that you never thought of, that you previously dismissed, or that you failed to discover. As Albert Einstein once said, "Imagination is more important than knowledge." This seems to be exactly what is needed in many problem-solving situations. Other situations, like the one with the shipwrecked passengers, just require that we hang in there a little bit longer.

On the positive side, when you think that your efforts are moving you closer toward your goal, you feel encouraged and keep trying, whether or not your perceptions are true. One of the reasons that television infomercials on new exercise gadgets and diet programs will always be around is *not* because science is constantly reaching fantastic new breakthroughs in the areas of weight loss or exercise machines. Many of the fundamental principles of health and fitness have been known for years and remain relatively constant. Rather, these commercials are effective because they convince individuals that there is hope for *them* to lose weight or to get back in shape—if only they will buy the merchant's products. These companies make their fortunes selling hope—not diet, exercise, or physical fitness.

Your emotional need to feel hope is your need to believe that your goals are attainable and that you are progressing toward your goals. It is the need to feel that your future is bright, that things will shortly improve if they are not going well, and that your deepest dreams will someday come true.

THE NEED TO SUCCEED

Most of us seek out success, however we define it. Success can bring more than just financial rewards. Success can bring emotional and social rewards, including a sense of accomplishment, increased self-esteem, and the praise and admiration of others. Your emotional need to succeed is your need to achieve at least some of your important goals, hopes, and aspirations. It is your need to feel successful in what you do and to feel that your efforts are moving you closer to your goals.

THE NEED TO AVOID FAILURE

Companion to your need to succeed is your need to avoid failure. Although these needs are just flip sides of the same coin, they are important enough to be treated separately. Your emotional need to avoid failure is your need to avoid feelings of inadequacy, incompetence, disappointment, and defeat. It is your need to avoid damaging your self-esteem and to avoid the social embarrassment and stigma that often accompany defeat.

Your need to avoid failure can grow to the point that it dominates your emotions and inhibits your growth. For example, fear of failure can cause you to withdraw, to be overprotective, or to pass by opportunities. Fear of failure can cause you to avoid taking the reasonable and necessary risks that are necessary to succeed.

THE NEED TO FEEL IN CONTROL

Think about the last time you sat in a roller coaster or in some other adrenaline-producing amusement park ride. These attractions not only subject you to suddenly changing G forces, they put you in convincing situations where it appears that you might at any moment fly out of control to certain death or injury. The feeling of being out of control in a situation you perceive as dangerous can be as terrifying (or more terrifying) than the actual danger itself. Theme park rides play on this fear, but in a "safe" way.

Your emotional need to feel in control is your need to feel that *you* are in control of your life, not other people or other forces. It is your need to feel that *you* possess the power to reach your goals and that *you* are in control of your destiny. It is the opposite of feelings of helplessness.

THE NEED FOR VARIETY AND STIMULATION

Researchers in human sensation have demonstrated that your physical senses rely on physical variety and stimulation in order to function. For example, the light-sensing cells in your retina depend on constantly changing light stimuli for you to see. To provide for this change of stimulus, the eye makes small, rapid, normally imperceptible movements as you look at things—no matter how hard you try to hold your eyes steady. If you were to put on special equipment that compensates for these small eye movements so that the visual image falling on your retina does not change, you would soon report a loss of eyesight and experience temporarily blindness.

Your need for emotional variety and stimulation is equally important to your emotional health and well being. Retailers capitalize on this fact by periodically changing their displays to keep their stores fresh and exciting. Large, indoor shopping malls spend thousands of dollars on decorations and other special attractions during the holiday season to create an aura of excitement, discover, and stimulation. Some have even made those attractions permanent. The Mall of America in Minneapolis and many other mega-malls even have indoor amusement parks, elaborate swimming parks, ice skating rinks, multi-story movie screens, and other major attractions. These all-out efforts by retailers not only provide physical stimulation, but emotional stimulation as well—excitement, suspense, variety, surprise, entertainment, and fun.

Your emotional need for variety and stimulation is your need to experience a variety of emotions, to avoid boredom, and to experience excitement, stimulation, variety, and fun.

THE NEED FOR BALANCE

Who has not heard about the need for moderation and balance in life? We are told to eat a balanced diet, balance aerobic exercise with stretching and strength-building exercises, take history classes as well as computer science classes, balance our work lives with our personal and family lives, and balance short-term goals with long-range goals. Balance is a universal concept. Every area in life requires a proper balance.

Your emotional need for balance is your need to experience a variety of emotions in their proper proportion, to avoid undue obsession with any one aspect of life, and to lead a balanced life—physically, emotionally, intellectually, socially, and spiritually.

Emotional balance is a natural side-effect of living an overall balanced life. When you lead a balanced physical, intellectual, social, and spiritual life, you automatically experience a balanced variety of healthy and wholesome emotions. On the other hand, when you focus too much of your life on a single area, such as your need for financial success, you burn out, become emotionally lopsided, and feel unhappy about your life.

THE NEED TO FEEL GOOD ABOUT YOURSELF

We all feel guilty about something at one time or another. Although guilt serves a desirable and important purpose, it is an uncomfortable emotion, and people often resort to a variety of methods for dealing with it in their lives. Guilt threatens your self-esteem. It attacks how you feel about yourself.

Your emotional need to feel good about yourself, though, is more than just an absence of guilt. It is the need to feel that you are progressing in skill, wisdom, and character; to feel that you are basically good; and to feel that you are acting with integrity, in accordance with your personal code of ethics. It is the need for positive self-esteem.

THE NEED TO MAKE A DIFFERENCE

Most of us want to make a difference in the lives of others. Spouses need to feel that they make a difference in the lives of their mates. Employees need to feel that their contributions make a difference to the success of the business or organization. Children need to feel that they contribute in important ways to the family. Scientists need to feel that their discoveries further the understanding and cause of human kind. Your emotional need to make a difference is your need to feel that you have made a difference in the lives of others and that you have made the world a better place.

As it turns out, making a difference in the lives of others also makes a difference in our own lives. When we see that our actions have blessed the lives of others, we feel good. Those who suffer from mid-life crisis are struggling not only for self-identity, but to know if their life has made any real difference.

The Need to Be Fairly Treated

Fairness is a human concept that is found everywhere in the world, at an individual, group, and societal level. We are keenly aware of the idea of fair play and are quick to point out even small differences in treatment to us or to other groups and individuals. Children fuss over who was given the biggest piece of cake or over who received the most presents at Christmas and are quick to notice if parents play favorites. Students gripe about being graded on the curve, sensing that not every class of students are identical in their intellectual capacity or performance. Workers carefully monitor salary increases, promotions, and work demands to see if they are administered fairly. Our concern over prejudice is based on the unfair treatment of certain groups of people, based on their gender, race, religion, or some other criteria. Countries have even gone to war because they think that they or another country has been treated unfairly. Fairness is not just an intellectual assertion. It is an emotional issue—one for which individuals will fight and for which countries will even go to war.

Your emotional need for fairness is your need to be treated equitably, to work in a system that is fair and impartial, and to be given comparable *opportunities* (not the same possessions) as others.

The Need to Feel Safe and Secure

Your need for safety and security is greater than just your need for shelter and protection from bodily harm (as important as that is). Feeling safe and secure is an emotional need, not just a physical need. You may be in no immediate physical danger and still not feel safe. For example, you may feel insecure when you are at home alone in your house at night, or you may feel threatened because you think you might be laid off your job.

In relationships, the need for emotional safety and security is the need to feel safe from emotional abuse, emotional manipulation, emotional instability, and emotional volatility. Relationships riddled with unpredictable hostility, sudden outbursts, or malicious accusations produce emotional fear and insecurity. For example, nobody likes to be around people who make you "walk on pins and needles" for fear of offending them or making them angry.

Your general emotional need to feel safe and secure is your need to feel safe and secure in your person, possessions, source of income, position, and lifestyle.

THE NEED FOR AN EMOTIONALLY STABLE ENVIRONMENT

Imagine trying to build a magnificent skyscraper on unstable soil or shifting sand. You could not even build a simple house on that kind of foundation, let alone a Sears Tower or a World Trade Center. Yet that is what many of us try to do in our emotional lives.

Your need for an emotionally stable environment is your need to live with others who are emotionally predictable and stable, to have emotionally stable relationships, and to avoid those who manifest wild mood swings, unpredictable emotional reactions, and disturbing emotional volatility.

Emotional stability is a requirement for healthy and enduring relationships. Parents who are grossly inconsistent in the way they treat and discipline their children often have offspring who grow up with serious emotional, psychological, and behavioral problems. Spouses who are happy one minute, angry or hateful the next, and smiling the next often suffer alienation and divorce. Coworkers who are unpleasant and unstable are shunned. The emotional climate others create for us largely determines whether we look forward to being around them or whether we are anxious to get out of their presence.

EMOTIONAL NEEDS VARY FROM MOMENT TO MOMENT

WHEN YOU ARE swimming, air is your greatest concern. When you are traveling across a hot desert, water is your highest priority. When you are traversing a rugged mountain range, food, water, and shelter are uppermost in your mind. Your physical needs vary from moment to moment, depending on your situation.

Likewise, your emotional needs also vary from moment to moment. When you lose someone close to you, love, sympathy, and emotional support are your most important needs. When you finish a long, hard week at work, variety, escape from stress, and a change of pace are your top concerns. When you hear strange noises in your house, the need to feel safe, secure, and protected suddenly take center stage. When you were a teenager, feeling understood, accepted, and part of a peer group were critical to your happiness.

IDENTIFYING EMOTIONAL NEEDS

IF MEETING YOUR partner's important emotional needs is a key to your enjoying a happy, lasting, and fulfilling relationship, then you must be able to identify those needs. Even though emotional needs vary from moment to moment and across developmental stages of your life, the following two techniques can be used to identify emotional needs in both yourself and your partner.

EMOTIONAL MONITORING

The first technique is *emotional monitoring.* To use this technique on yourself, consciously monitor your feelings throughout the day and periodically ask yourself the following question:

- What am I currently feeling?

When you can describe what you are feeling, try to identify the emotional needs these feelings reflect. The following questions may help:

- Why am I feeling this way?
- When do I feel this way?
- What led to my feeling this way?
- How often do I feel this way?
- How intense are my feelings?
- What do I think would help me feel better?

To use this technique on your partner, have your partner perform this analysis independently and then jointly discuss the results. You might even lead your partner through the analysis whenever you sense that he or she is feeling emotions that you suspect reflect underlying unmet emotional needs (to do this, rephrase each of the questions to the "you" form—for example, "What are you currently feeling?" and so forth).

Many of us never stop to consciously reflect on our feelings. We react to situations on emotional autopilot without giving them conscious thought. We will gain greater insight into our underlying emotional needs only when we consciously identify and analyze our feelings.

Sam hated Sunday nights. As the evening progressed, he always became increasingly anxious, worried, and tied up in knots. A multitude of thoughts kept racing through his mind.

"How am I going to go back to work tomorrow. I don't know if I can pull this off any more. What if they give me a project I can't handle? What if I can't meet my deadlines? Maybe I'm just not smart enough for this job. I feel like I am always faking it. What if I make a stupid mistake? Then I'll get fired. I'll lose my house, my car, and everything I've worked hard to achieve the last twenty years. My kids will have to drop out of college. My wife will divorce me. I bet my boss is just waiting for an excuse to get rid of me."

Thoughts like these made Sam even more tense and anxious. Sleep became difficult. He arrived at work Monday mornings with little or no sleep at all, which impaired his performance and added fuel to his belief that he might be fired.

In reality, Sam was one of his company's best employees. He was conscientious and hard working. He kept his skills current. He performed quality work. His peers looked up to him and viewed him as knowledgeable and competent. He had made many significant contributions in his fifteen years with his company. Sam's boss thought very highly of him and did not want to lose him.

After reading about emotional analysis, Sam decided to give the technique a try. He consciously thought about the emotions he was experiencing and asked himself the following questions:

"What am I currently feeling?"

"Intense anxiety, fear, worry—maybe even terror."

"When do I feel this way?"

"Every Sunday night. Also, whenever I return from vacation or three-day weekends."

"Why am I feeling this way?"

"Because I am afraid of losing my job."

"What led to this fear?"

Sam paused. This was a tough question to answer. He thought about it for a long time and even explored the question with his wife.

As a result of this introspection, Sam began to realize that his anxiety was a larger emotional pattern carried over from his childhood. Sam was the youngest in a large family. His two older brothers always seemed to be smarter and more successful than he. They were physically taller and stronger and were permitted to do things that Sam was not. His brothers often pointed out their superiority and called him "stupid" and other derogatory names. Sam ultimately believed his brothers' negative statements about himself.

Sam had few friends. Although there were a few other boys his age in the neighborhood, they had completely different interests and personalities. Because of this, Sam did not get an opportunity to socialize like the other boys his age. He felt self-conscious and socially awkward at school. He assumed that others viewed him as inferior or defective. This perception affected his actions, which in turn reinforced others' negative perceptions of him. Sam never felt like he was "one of the guys."

When Sam married and entered the job market, he carried this emotional baggage with him into the workplace. He soon realized that his shyness was a liability, and bravely worked hard to overcome it and become more sociable. Although he achieved a measure of success, he felt like he was faking it and was not being his real self.

Through introspection, Sam realized that he was viewing his boss in the same way he viewed authority figures his entire life—as older brothers who were out to get him and who looked down on him as an inferior being. Sam also realized that he was attributing thoughts and feelings to his coworkers that they simply were not having and that he automatically dismissed the many positive comments his boss and others made to him.

Sam decided to consciously change this negative thinking and frame of reference that had gripped his mind so long. For the first time in his life, Sam began to interject positive thoughts and accurate interpretations of reality into his thinking. This new view of life was liberating. Sam now saw himself for what he was—a valued employee with substantial talents and job skills.

Sunday nights are no longer agonizing long or sleepless. Sam currently views going back to work in a positive light and sees his boss and peers as equals and as professional colleagues.

HOT-BUTTON ANALYSIS

The second technique is *hot-button analysis*. To use this technique on yourself, identify your "hot buttons" (situations that provoke emotionally *immature* behavior) and then analyze them to see if they are prompted by unmet emotional needs. For each hot button, ask yourself the following questions:

- What types of situations trigger my behavior?
- What feelings are aroused when my hot button is pressed?
- Which of the needs listed in this chapter was my behavior trying to address?
- What are the consequences of my current approach to fulfilling those needs?
- What am I expecting others to do that they are not doing?
- What rationalizations do I use to justify my behavior?
- Are there other circumstances in which I react this way?
- How often do I act this way?
- How intense is my behavior?
- Why did I choose to act that way?

To use this technique on your partner, have your partner perform the analysis independently and then jointly discuss the results. Alternatively, make a note of your partner's hot buttons and analyze them with your partner when your partner is calm and in a good mood (again, rephrasing each question to the "you" form). If this is not possible, try your best to analyze your partner's hot buttons yourself.

By analyzing situations that cause you or your partner emotional trouble, you will undoubtedly identify important unfulfilled emotional needs. When you consciously understand these needs, you can more intelligently seek their legitimate fulfillment.

If you realize that you or your partner is attempting to fulfill an emotional need in an inappropriate way, make a conscious effort to address that need in a constructive way. To help you and your partner with this task, reflect on the following questions:

- Why was the way I undertook to fulfill this need improper?
- What was my rationalization for excusing my behavior and why is it faulty?

- What are the ultimate consequences of my emotionally immature behavior? Is that what I really want?
- What would have been some better ways of addressing my need?
- How can I assure that a legitimate means of fulfilling this need will be available and accessible to me in the future?
- Was this a situation where I should have simply endured a temporary state of emotional deprivation?
- Who is an outstanding example of maturity in this area? What do they think and do in these situations?
- Are there any books or other sources of information that I can turn to that will teach me appropriate ways of handling my needs?

Susan and Mike had been married for twenty years. They were the parents of two children: Michelle, age 16, and Chad, age 13. Susan had always wanted more children, but, for medical reasons, was unable to have a larger family.

Although Susan loved each of her two children, she treated them differently. Like most first-time parents, she expected her firstborn, Michelle, to grow up more rapidly and accept adult responsibilities more quickly. At the same time, she viewed Chad as the "baby of the family" and wanted him to mature more slowly so that she could enjoy mothering him for as long as possible. Susan gave in to Chad's requests more readily and allowed him to remain a child much longer than Michelle.

Michelle resented this differential treatment. She viewed her younger brother as lazy, irresponsible, and irritating and was appalled at how easily he seemed to get what he wanted. Michelle felt that she was being treated unfairly. She often accused her mother of spoiling Chad and giving in to his "manipulations." Because of these perceptions, she avoided interacting with her younger brother as much as possible and often treated him coldly or accusingly.

Occasionally, Michelle's resentment broke to the surface in a fight between her and Chad over Michelle's interpretation of something Chad said or over his apparent neglect of one of his household responsibilities. Michelle typically accused Chad of being irresponsible, lazy, or mean, after which she immediately left the room in a bodily display of anger.

One day, Michelle's father, Mike, witnessed this interaction. When he tried to intervene and investigate the scuffle, his daughter burst out in tears, accused her father of always siding with her brother, and ran up crying to her room. Michelle's crying quickly got the attention of her mother, who became instantly alarmed. After hearing her daughter's side of the story, Susan marched out, yelled at Mike in a loud voice, and demanded to know, "What did you do to cause your daughter to cry and fall to pieces?"

At that point, no matter what Mike tried to say, he was guilty of wrong-doing. His wife likewise accused him of always siding with their son and of hurting his daughter's self-esteem. She then demanded that he "go straight up and apologize and make things right" with his daughter.

Mike's second attempt to try to explain the situation only made his wife more angry and outraged. Viewing his desire to discuss the issue as pure stubbornness, she continued her offensive: "How can you be so stubborn? How can you be so unfeeling? I can't believe I married a man who is so heartless and cruel. No, you're definitely *not* the man I married. Can't you see that your daughter is bawling her eyes out? Don't you care about her? Don't you love your daughter? How can you be so blind? Can't you see you're ruining her life. You get up there right now and apologize to her and make things right."

Mike could tell that this was no ordinary demand. He could tell that his very marriage was at stake. Although he was concerned about the long-term consequences of his daughter's distorted perceptions of both himself and his son, Mike complied with his wife's demands, even though he felt emotionally blackmailed into doing it. Later that week, he tried a third time to discuss the incident with his wife—again unsuccessfully.

One day, Susan read about hot-button analysis in a woman's magazine as she was getting her hair done at the beauty shop. She decided to see if the technique really worked and to give it a try.

The first step was to identify her emotional hot buttons. She began by writing down what *she* thought were her hot buttons. Then she asked her husband and children to write down what *they* thought her hot buttons were (without showing them her list).

Next, she monitored her emotions for two months and recorded every incident in which she emotionally blew up at others.

Using this approach, Susan identified several of her hot buttons, some of which she was previously unaware. She decided to work on the one involving her blowing up at Mike whenever she felt her daughter's self-esteem was being threatened.

Next, she asked herself the following questions:

"What situations trigger my behavior?"

"Any situation in which I perceive that my daughter's self-esteem is being severely damaged, threatened, or crushed, as evidenced by my daughter crying her eyes out, withdrawing, or becoming depressed."

"What are my emotional reactions?"

"Anger, hatred toward the person responsible for bringing this on, righteous indignation, and a desire to protect my daughter and extinguish the threat."

"What underlying needs do I have that might be motivating these reactions?"

This was a tough question for Susan to answer. After several days of repeated reflections, she wrote down the following:

"When I was a teenager growing up, I had terrible fights with my own father. My feelings were deeply hurt, and I would run up to my room and cry for hours at a time. I thought my father was cold, insensitive, and cruel. I was emotionally devastated by these incidents and am now determined not to let this same thing happen to my own daughter—I know how it feels and just how damaging and painful those emotions are to a young girl's life."

"I am determined to be a good mother. It is my highest priority in life. Anything that threatens my perception of being a good mother threatens my self-esteem, and therefore me. My self-esteem is too fragile to take that kind of threat. Unless my daughter succeeds, I am a failure, and whenever I see her in such an emotionally devastated condition, I see her future life hanging in the balance. How can she succeed if her self-esteem is destroyed? I must protect my children from this kind of attack. Threats like these are serious life-and-death threats and must be handled swiftly and forcefully."

From these insights, Susan realized that her hot spot was an attempt to fulfill several of her own emotional needs: the need to succeed (as a mother), to feel good about herself (by ensuring that the needs of her daughter were being met), to avoid failure (by making sure her daughter succeeded), to look after her daughter's safety (by making sure that her daughter's self-esteem was protected), and to feel in control (by demanding that her husband "make things right" with her daughter).

"These are certainly praiseworthy needs to want to fulfill," Susan thought to herself as she moved on to the next question.

"What are the consequences of my approach to fulfilling those needs?"

This question required more than introspection. To answer this question, she needed feedback from others. When she talked to her husband about the consequences of her actions, she learned some things that surprised her.

When Susan refused to hear Mike out and demanded that he apologize to his daughter, she violated his emotional trust. By resorting to ultimatums and emotional blackmail, she coerced Mike to comply with her desires and violated his sense of agency. By making these demands in front of the children and by treating him like a naughty child who had to be forced by his mother to apologize, she humiliated him and demeaned his role as father. By refusing to discuss the incident or see things any other way, she shut down the lines of open communication and damaged her relationship with her husband.

Mike felt deeply disturbed and betrayed by his wife's treatment and harsh judgment of him. Because Susan had reacted similarly on a number of other occasions involving Michelle, he was considering giving up trying to actively parent his daughter. If this happened, Susan would be left by herself to provide all of the guidance and parental training her daughter would receive before leaving home the next year for college.

Moreover, Susan's reactions during such incidents sharply reinforced Michelle's negative perceptions of her father and brother, setting up destructive thought and behavioral patterns that, left unchecked, would set Michelle up for the very failure that her mother was trying to avoid in the first place.

And Mike wasn't the only one hurt by these incidents. Chad was also negatively affected. He often commented that his older sister always seemed to be "mad at me." Susan blamed Chad as well as her husband for these incidents and forcefully unloaded heavy guilt trips on Chad. Chad felt unfairly accused, blamed, misjudged, and misunderstood. His own self-esteem had taken a severe beating.

As difficult as it was to continue in light of this information, Susan went on with the next question: "Are these the consequences you want?"

"No. They are just the opposite of what I want. I want to have a close relationship with my husband, I want my daughter to grow up to become a mature adult, and I want my son to have high self-esteem as well."

"Are the means you are using to fulfill your needs immature or inappropriate?"

Susan concluded that the way she was trying to meet her needs was inappropriate and destructive to almost everyone involved.

Deciding to act on her newfound insights, Susan took several positive steps. She read several good books on parenting and learned that she needed to govern her children by principles, not by passing emotions, quick judgments, and unmet personal needs. She realized that she could not play favorites or take sides and favor one of her children and accomplish anything in the long run. She realized that she must be consistent in her decisions and in her administration of the family rules. She began to rebuild emotional trust with her husband, support his role as father of the family, and appreciate the complementary and rounding-out influence he had on the children. She identified a friend as an excellent role model of mature emotional behavior in this area and tried to follow her example.

As hard as it was for her to admit, Susan realized that her emotional needs to love, protect, succeed, feel good about herself, avoid failure, and feel in control did not justify an emotionally irresponsible way of fulfilling those needs. By persistent and intelligent effort, Susan ultimately eliminated her hot spot and narrowly avoided the long-term damage that surely would have followed her prior course of action.

WHAT HAPPENS WHEN YOUR PARTNER'S EMOTIONAL NEEDS ARE NOT MET?

WHEN WE DO not eat, we become physically weak and faint. When we do not sleep, we lose our ability to concentrate and risk lapsing into sleep while driving down the highway or working on the job. When we stay out unprotected all day on the beach, we suffer painful sunburn. In short, when we ignore important physical needs, we are subject to physical injury and distress.

Similarly, when we ignore important emotional needs, we are subject to emotional distress, emotional pain, and sometimes even to emotional illness. Those who possess deep, unfulfilled needs for love, acceptance, and affection, for example, often feel intense emotional pain. These individuals sometimes turn to drugs, alcohol, or illegitimate physical relationships in an attempt to fulfill those needs and reduce their pain. Those who do not feel good about themselves often suffer guilt and feelings of inadequacy that affect their entire outlook on life. Employees stuck in an unfair compensation or work environments often suffer increased stress, apathy, and job-induced illness.

Unmet emotional needs can also lead to other life-altering consequences. For example, engaged couples may overlook serious defects in their potential mates because of their own powerful internal needs for love and affection. Teenagers in inner cities often join street gangs and participate in criminal behavior in their attempt to fulfill their needs to feel accepted and valued. Marriages often break up not because couples fail to communicate, but because they fail to meet each other's emotional needs. Emotionally unstable homes often produce emotionally disturbed adults, who then mistreat their own spouses and children. Those who are seriously depressed fail to make their unique contribution to life and sometimes even take their own lives.

Emotional needs are real. Those who suffer serious emotional deprivation suffer real pain and real consequences.

Emotional needs cannot be swept aside or wished away through positive thinking, denial, or inattention any more than a hungry man can wish away or deny his need for food by force of thought. For example, those who are deprived of love cannot wish away their need for love, deny that they need love, or satisfy their need for love by dreaming about what it would be like to be loved. Their need for love is real, and their deprivation is real.

In the movie *Back to the Future*, we laugh at Marty's inability to handle his being called a chicken ("*nobody* calls me chicken"). While it is obvious to us that Biff is simply using Marty's emotional weakness to manipulate him, we are all like Marty in some way. We all have unmet emotional needs in our lives that make us vulnerable to doing dangerous or stupid things we later regret. Because of this, we must monitor our emotions, understand our emotional needs, and practice fulfilling those needs in constructive ways. Otherwise, our emotional needs will pressure us to seek their fulfillment through any means possible—proper or not.

In an infamous case of espionage during the last few years of the cold war, a CIA agent who had given the Soviet Union top U.S. military secrets for years in exchange for large sums of money—a betrayal that authorities later called the worst breach in U.S. security ever—was quoted as saying that he did not believe that he had done anything that would seriously harm the security of the nation, that the CIA was a sham anyway, and that he had done nothing worse than what politicians do all the time in government. To understand how a person's judgment can become this distorted, we cannot look only at that person's basic physical needs for food, clothing, and shelter (which were already being met, even on his salary). Rather, to understand his motivation, we must look at his *emotional* needs and how he chose to address them. Only then can we begin to comprehend in the slightest degree how a person could consciously choose to betray his country, sentence several of his fellow CIA agents to certain death, and risk destroying his own life and family.

Left unchecked, unfulfilled emotional needs can sometimes prompt self-destructive thoughts and actions. For example, those who have an unfulfilled need for love may conclude that "nobody cares" or that they are defective, unlovable, or incapable. These thoughts can then motivate other Dark Emotions, such as hopelessness, despair, and discouragement.

Young children are particularly vulnerable to serious emotional consequences when their emotional needs go unmet. Children are dependent on adults for everything they need in their lives and do not have other sources of emotional fulfillment to turn to when their emotional needs are neglected.

Neither do they have the intellectual or emotional capacity to understand and manage serious deprivations. We are rightly shocked when we hear of parents who starve their children to death by withholding food (as occurred a few years ago in Texas). We ought to be similarly outraged when we hear of parents who seriously abuse or deprive their children of important emotional needs, such as the need for love, affection, and an emotionally stable environment.

Your emotional needs (and those of your partner) fall on a continuum from completely unmet to completely met. Even partially unmet emotional needs, while not as serious as their completely unmet counterparts, can prompt a person to take action, especially if that person's need has gone unfulfilled for some time. Teenagers, for example, who do not feel completely accepted by their peers may do things that violate their personal code of ethics in an attempt to win their peer's acceptance. Dieters often fail to stay on their diet—not out of hunger—but because they miss being able to soothe their feelings of rejection, isolation, or loneliness by eating pleasurable foods.

What does this all mean to relationships? When you ignore your partner's important emotional needs, you place your partner under significant emotional stress. If your partner's overall emotional coping mechanisms are weak, your partner may seek to fulfill their unmet emotional needs in undesirable, harmful, or destructive ways. Even if they don't, they run the real risk of developing serious emotional disorders or illnesses, sometimes against their will. If you do not address your partner's emotional needs, you will not enjoy the emotional closeness and intimacy you desire, and your partner will view you as emotionally insensitive and uncaring. Your partner may seek to terminate the relationship and seek fulfillment of their needs with someone else. Emotional needs are too great to be ignored.

Just Having Needs Does Not Justify Any Means of Their Fulfillment

One of the most dangerous ideas that exists today is the notion that just because you have an emotional need, you are justified in fulfilling that need, regardless of how or when it is satisfied. Such an argument may seem sensible on the surface, because it is understandable for people to want to fulfill their needs, but it is seriously flawed, as the following examples demonstrate:

- You have a biological need to take in food and water and to eliminate waste. However, just having these needs does not mean that you are free to take whatever food you see or to eliminate waste whenever and wherever you feel like it.

- According to some experts, rape is a crime of rage, violence, power, and control, as much as it is a crime of passion. Is rape justified just because the rapist has unfulfilled needs for power, control, or domination? In cases in which domination is not the issue, is rape justified just because a man feels sexually attracted to a woman?

- In many neighborhoods, the chances of having your home burglarized is very high. Police and judges, who are in daily contact with criminals, are quick to point out that most burglaries are committed by drug users who are looking for a way to pay for their next fix. Does a drug addict's need for a fix justify his breaking into your house, threatening your personal safety and security, or stealing your possessions?

- Your boss may have unmet emotional needs to feel important, to succeed, or to feel physically attractive. Does that give your boss the right to sexually harass you on the job, to treat you as a personal slave, or to make you miserable through frequent emotional outbursts, gross insensitivity, or autocratic behavior?

- Gang initiation rites have included almost every form of crime or violence imaginable, including random shootings and murders. Does a young person's need to feel accepted, important, and powerful justify his committing crimes and destroying the property, lives, and the peace of the community?

- Your auto mechanic may have a need to feed his family and pay the bills that are piling up. Does this need justify his ripping you off on your auto repairs?

- Does being hungry, cold, wet, sleepy, ill, or physically miserable give you the right to break into your neighbor's house and steal his food and parka or to demand a prescription from a pharmacist at gunpoint?

These examples demonstrate that needs alone do not justify any means of their fulfillment. Needs are *not* a license to commit crime or to be greedy, selfish, insensitive, angry, domineering, abusive, or anything else. Although everyone has a need for love and acceptance, your being deprived of love does not give you the right to hate, take revenge, commit murder, abuse drugs, commit rape, or anything else. Unfulfilled emotional needs do not give you the right to seek their fulfillment through any means you desire any more than unfulfilled physical needs justify your taking any action you desire.

Although most of us readily accept this assertion in the physical realm, we find it much harder to accept in the emotional realm. For example, in the physical realm, we readily recognize that temporary physical deprivation is a natural and unavoidable part of life. If we get caught outdoors without a coat, we adapt the best we can—we walk around and shiver, ask someone for an extra sweater, or go inside. Likewise, we accept as a normal part of life having to go hungry or skip a meal due to travel, medical tests, or busy schedules. We all accept the fact that temporary physical deprivation is a natural part of life, and we adapt and make-do the best we can.

Yet, we tend to be less willing to accept the fact that short-term emotional deprivation is likewise a natural and unavoidable part of life. When we face temporary emotional deprivation, we expect our needs to be immediately met and get upset if it looks like we will have to endure a period of temporary emotional deprivation. For example, when things do not go our way and our needs are threatened, we get angry, we lash out, we trample over the emotions of others, we pollute the emotional atmosphere, and we otherwise impose emotional pain and hardship on our fellow beings. If we don't have the right to fulfill our physical needs in any way we like, then why should it be different with our emotional needs?

One explanation as to why the illegitimate means for fulfilling emotional needs is so easy to accept (at least in ourselves) is that emotional needs are not as visible and tangible as physical needs. This makes it easier to rationalize away our behavior and to ignore and trample over the emotional needs of others without being seen. It also makes it easier to justify our behavior by pointing our finger to our (invisible) pressing, unfulfilled emotional needs as the real cause of our behavior.

Unfaithful husbands, for example, often justify their infidelity by claiming that their needs for love, affection, excitement, or understanding were not being met by their wives. Immature, abusive parents often blame their children for their own unacceptable behavior by saying that "my children make me angry when they disobey me or defy my authority." Of course, such rationalizations are no more valid than those of drug addicts who claim that breaking into your house and stealing your possessions is necessary to meet their need for money to pay for their next fix.

Another explanation as to why the illegitimate means for fulfilling emotional needs is so easy to accept is social visibility. The damage we impose on others when we illegitimately fulfill our own emotional needs at their expense is often not immediately visible and may be removed in time or space from the offending incident. When we *physically* injure another person, the pain and suffering we inflict is immediately visible and obvious to all—gashes, torn flesh, black eyes, bright red blood, and bruised, broken, or dead bodies. Such visibility quickly draws attention and calls for immediate accountability. On the other hand, *emotional* pain and suffering is not so highly visible or spectacular at the time it is inflicted. We think that others will not see what we have done and that we can get away with our behavior without any negative social consequences.

Yelling and screaming at your child, for example, may appear only to result in a frown or a physical withdrawal, but the real damage to your child's self-esteem and future potential is invisible and remains to be realized. Being a "crank" during vacation over trivial matters may feel good at the time, but may seriously injure your relationships with your spouse and children (as well as your likelihood of going on future vacations). Demanding that your employees double their pace, shoulder even more stressful responsibilities, and work overtime to increase productivity and meet deadlines may fulfill *your* pressing needs to feel in control and be successful, but does so at the expense of your employees.

In the latter case, employers seldom see (or personally suffer) the real consequences of their irresponsible actions on the lives of their employees—strained interpersonal relationships, neglected children and spouses, dangerously high levels of stress, unhealthy anxiety, insomnia, increased on-the-job injuries, increased illness and disease, "burnout," demoralization, and a loss of job satisfaction. These consequences are easily hidden or covered up, at least to upper management and the public at large. Perhaps society would not accept or tolerate such behavior if others visibly bled a little each time we inflicted emotional pain or injury on them to fulfill our own needs or to further our own selfish purposes at their expense.

Yet another reason why the illegitimate means for fulfilling emotional needs is so easy to accept is because such behavior is easy and feels good (at least at the time). Behaving irresponsibly is natural, easy, and often brings immediate pleasure and satisfaction (although a counterfeit means of addressing our needs will ultimately not satisfy us). It does not require any self-control or conscious, disciplined effort. Becoming angry and lashing out when things are getting out of control is easy and requires no self-control or self-restraint.

A final reason why the illegitimate means for fulfilling emotional needs is so easy to accept is because we feel that we can get away with our actions without incurring any significant personal consequences or public sanctions. For example, we take our anger out on our spouse and children when we are frustrated because our children cannot fight back and our spouse may have no other reasonable option but to put up with us. "Besides," we think, "no one will ever know about it—the people at church will continue to befriend me and think of me as a kind, patient, and loving person." Perhaps if, like Pinocchio, our noses grew longer every time we fulfilled one of our emotional needs at the expense of others or grossly ignored their important emotional needs, we would be more reluctant to give in to self-ishness and emotional irresponsibility.

Thoughts to Ponder

- Do emotional needs vary depending on a person's developmental phase (childhood, adolescence, young adulthood, middle age, late middle age, late adulthood)? Are some needs more important at certain times than at other times? If so, what happens when you focus on meeting the wrong set of needs at any given moment with your spouse, children, or others?

- Would you buy a house that does not have a kitchen, bathroom, and bedroom where you could meet your basic physical needs (to eat, bathe, and sleep)? Would you marry someone who was unwilling to help meet your basic emotional needs? Did your spouse marry such a person? Should you have children if you are unwilling to attend to their emotional needs? What have you done in the last week, month, and year to help meet the emotional needs of your spouse and children?

- Can you determine your partner's emotional needs simply by identifying your own needs and assuming that your partner has the same needs, or should you observe your partner's behavior and interact with your mate to understand his or her needs and life situation?

- When your partner or children say, "You don't understand me," could they be suggesting that you are unaware of or uncaring about one or more of their important emotional needs?

- Do your own emotional needs influence what you expect out of your relationships? Is it reasonable to expect your spouse to assume *complete* responsibility for fulfilling all of your needs, or should you shoulder significant responsibility for fulfilling your own emotional needs? If your partner is not mature enough to meet an important emotional need, are you justified in cutting off the meeting of one of their needs, or should you seek to fulfill your need in some other legitimate way?

- Emotional needs are too important to ignore or neglect. How important is it to accurately identify those needs? What are you doing to identify your partner's emotional needs? Will your partner feel deeply loved if you are grossly insensitive or apathetic toward his or her most pressing emotional needs?

- Can unmet emotional needs prompt a person to fulfill those needs in inappropriate ways? If so, are people still free to choose how they will fulfill those needs? Does just having unmet emotional needs justify any means of their fulfillment?

- Do people sometimes seek to fulfill their long-term unmet emotional needs in nonlegitimate, destructive ways when appropriate methods are not readily available? If so, what can loved ones do to help avert such tragedies? Conversely, can people choose an unwise course of action in their lives even though their needs *are* largely being met?

- Is temporary emotional deprivation a necessary part of life? If so, how should you handle these periods of temporary emotional deprivation? Is the ability to properly handle periods of temporary emotional deprivation a sign of emotional maturity?

- People who are healed of long-term, unmet emotional needs often proceed to make great contributions to society and to the lives of others. How can you identify a person who is suffering from serious emotional deprivation? What can you do to meet the long-term, unmet emotional needs of your partner and your children? How can you become an emotional healer and help unleash the positive potential that exists in others?

- One of the most damaging things you can do in a relationship is to be grossly insensitive or apathetic toward the needs of your partner. Conversely, one of the most powerful things you can do to strengthen a relationship and endear your companion to you is to understand your partner's emotional needs and work to fulfill those needs. What are you doing to actively understand and meet the emotional needs of your partner?

ACTIVITIES FOR SELF-IMPROVEMENT

1. Create a list of the twenty emotional needs discussed in this chapter (or use Appendix A). At a convenient and appropriate time, ask your companion to rate how well each of his or her needs is being met on a scale from 1 to 5 (where 1 is "completely met" and 5 is "completely unmet"). Review your partner's answers, making particular note of the answers that are closest to the 5-end of the scale. If your partner is willing, jointly discuss each response to gain additional insight.

   When you feel that you adequately understand your partner's needs, form an action plan for how you will better help address those needs (particularly the ones that are not being met very well). Review your plan with your partner to confirm that your action plan will be effective in addressing his or her most urgent needs. Then carry out your plan and evaluate its effectiveness to determine if your partner's needs are being met. Repeat this exercise regularly to identify and address new needs as they arise.

2. When you see others misbehave, instead of immediately condemning their actions, ask yourself, "What unmet emotional needs are they trying to fulfill?" If certain needs come to mind, ask yourself, "What can I do to help them address these unmet emotional needs in more legitimate ways?" and "How can I help them achieve greater emotional understanding and maturity in this area?" Follow up on your insights.

3. A physician who is stricken with a debilitating physical disease is unable to heal others. Likewise, a person who is suffering a debilitating emotional illness brought on by long-term emotional deprivation is not in a strong position to heal the emotional wounds of others. To become emotionally healthier yourself so that you can more powerfully address the emotional needs of your partner, use the emotional monitoring and hot-button analysis techniques described on pages 54 through 58 to identify your most serious emotional needs and hot spots. Then work to legitimately fulfill your unmet emotional needs and to eliminate your emotional weaknesses.

4. Ask your partner to identify a few occasions in which you fulfilled your own emotional needs in illegitimate ways or at the expense of others. How might you have fulfilled those needs in legitimate ways? Should you have endured a period of temporary emotional deprivation while seeking more constructive ways of meeting those needs?

PART TWO

EMOTIONAL RESPONSIBILITY

CHAPTER 4

WHAT IS EMOTIONAL RESPONSIBILITY?

Just because you have emotions does not mean
that you are helpless to manage your emotions

Darryl lived his life from moment to moment, crisis to crisis, both at work and at home. He seldom anticipated or planned for his future needs, nor anyone else's, for that matter. He simply went to work each day, did as little as possible to get by, came home at night, and sat down in front of his television set with a bag full of snacks. Only occasionally did he interact with his children, and when he did, it was to yell at them for being too noisy or to demand that they bring him another bag of chips from the kitchen. Darryl seldom interacted with his wife either. He viewed her as a substitute mother whose duty was to attend to his every need.

Darryl neglected to maintain his car, house, and other possessions. Because of this, he incurred frequent repairs, major inconveniences, and unexpected expenses. Darryl's health was not good either. After his last heart attack, the doctor told him to stop smoking, lower his cholesterol, and start exercising, but Darryl continued to smoke, lead a sedentary lifestyle, and eat a fat-laden diet.

Darryl's apathy toward his family's emotional needs led to an increasing number of family crises. Over time, his children turned to peers outside the family for all their interaction. Without parental guidance and oversight, his children soon fell into the wrong crowd. Later that year, his sixteen-year-old daughter became pregnant and his oldest son was arrested for possessing illegal drugs. Darryl's wife, who worked full-time herself and carried the entire brunt of raising the children, became seriously depressed herself.

Although Darryl sensed that there were an increasing number of major crises in his life, he failed to see the connection between his behavior and the consequences that soon followed. Darryl blamed everything and everyone for his problems—everyone except himself. He continued to do nothing to take responsibility for his life.

Mary, a friend of Darryl's wife, approached life quite differently. Recently divorced, she understood that people have emotional needs, not just physical needs, and she did all in her power to anticipate and meet the emotional needs of herself and her children.

Mary was positive and proactive. She took care of health. She exercised regularly, ate a healthy diet, and made sure she received a good night's rest. She appreciated what she had and focused on opportunities rather than on deprivations or restrictions. She worked to turn her challenges into opportunities and to model after others who were emotionally mature.

Through careful organization and daily routines, Mary minimized the little frustrations in her life. She kept her house neat and clean and made her environment as uplifting as possible. She kept a reserve of food and household items on hand so she would never be wanting when she needed something. In her free time, she read uplifting books, listened to good music, and worked on special projects and favorite hobbies.

Mary also stayed involved in her children's lives. She went on fun activities with them, celebrated special occasions, helped them with their schoolwork, read to them at bedtime, and gave them love and affection. She set up age-appropriate responsibilities for her children and held them accountable for fulfilling those responsibilities. Through love, encouragement, praise, example, parental guidance, and a system of fair rewards and consequences, Mary taught her children right from wrong, sensitivity to the needs of others, service, self-reliance, and personal responsibility.

Mary did not sacrifice her own growth, either. She improved her character by reading good books and applying the principles being taught to her own life. She took advantage of opportunities to improve her job skills. She developed her own unique talents and interests.

Over time, Mary began to radiate a power in her personality—a power that attracted men of similar caliber who were also responsible, caring, and sensitive. One of these men later proposed to her, and Mary began a new life of even greater happiness and fulfillment.

What Is Emotional Responsibility?

EMOTIONAL RESPONSIBILITY is accepting responsibility for the way you handle your emotions. It is accepting the fact that you have the freedom to choose how you will deal with your feelings, even though these feelings may have come into your life uninvited, undesired, or from origins unknown. It is recognizing that this choice exists not only in easy-to-handle circumstances (such as when you are feeling good), but in difficult times when you are being challenged by powerful Dark Emotions.

Emotional responsibility is more than just an intellectual recognition that you are accountable for your own emotional behavior. It is becoming aware of your emotions and your automatic emotional response mechanisms so that you do not react to your emotions unthinkingly or according to undesirable past conditioning. It is recognizing your emotional weaknesses and owning up to them, rather than denying them or projecting responsibility for them on others. It is recognizing the influence that others may have had on your willingness to assume emotional responsibility—not so that you can place blame—but so that you can step forward and take greater responsibility for your behavior. Emotional responsibility is becoming aware of the arguments made against it and understanding why they are false. Finally, emotional responsibility is actually behaving in emotionally responsible ways, not just owning up to the importance of doing so.

What Emotional Responsibility Is Not

EMOTIONAL RESPONSIBILITY is *not* an attempt to label all emotion as inherently bad or evil and therefore something to be suppressed or exterminated from our lives. Some people view anyone promoting emotional responsibility as puritan "stiffs" who are out to take away emotional happiness from everyone's lives. This, of course, is a gross misrepresentation of emotional responsibility. As we demonstrated previously, emotions are an important part of our existence, necessary to our capacity to enjoy life to the fullest and to experience joy. Emotional responsibility does not deny emotional fulfillment; rather, it promotes it through the only means by which it is enduring—through intelligent emotional self-management. Promoting emotional responsibility will not diminish your good feelings in your life any more than promoting physical fitness will diminish your physical health and vitality.

During the "hippie" era of the sixties, one of the accusations made against "The Establishment" was that society had cast a dark shadow on emotions and looked down on them. "Society" was portrayed as trying to get people to suppress their emotions. Indeed, freedom of emotional expression was one of the heralding calls and most cherished ideals of the sixties. "Free Love" and "Let It All Hang Out, Baby" were typical slogans of the time. Meditation and mind-altering drugs were promoted as a means of getting in touch with one's innermost feelings. Art became anything a person felt like expressing, and one person's painting was as good as another's.

The free expression of all emotion seemed to offer the promise of greater physical and emotional fulfillment. Many people were attracted by this philosophy and attempted to live it. As it turned out, both their accusation against society regarding emotions and their proposed alternative were wrong. Their accusation was wrong because it was untrue. Society, in general, was not advocating across-the-board suppression of emotion or a belief that emotions were inherently evil; rather, they were advocating the mature and wholesome management of emotions and the promotion of uplifting, constructive, and positive emotions. Their proposed alternative was wrong because the unchanneled expression of all emotion cannot lead to enduring emotional happiness nor to stable, lasting, fulfilling relationships (as this book has emphasized throughout).

Emotional responsibility is *not* a thinly disguised attempt to deny people their happiness; rather, it is a recognition that deep emotional fulfillment in life comes only as people learn to handle their emotions in responsible ways.

Neither is emotional responsibility an idealistic attempt to deny the reality that emotions are powerful forces in people's lives. Spouses absorbed in the newspaper know the difference between simple requests and emotional ones. Dictators manipulate the masses through emotional speeches and propaganda. Marketers influence consumers by appealing to their emotional needs and desires. If people did not respond to these emotional appeals, spouses would never use emotion in their voices, dictators would forego giving emotional speeches, and advertisements would consist of nothing more than a printed informational message on a screen or billboard.

But just because emotions are powerful does not mean they are always used for good purposes. In the case of emotional abuse, for example, they are used to destroy and inflict pain and suffering on the lives of others. Raw energy—such as lightning, fire, or uranium ore— is destructive and potentially lethal. Only when energy is harnessed and properly channeled is it productive and beneficial. Why should it be otherwise with human emotional energy?

Moreover, accepting that you have an emotional nature does not imply that you are emotionally helpless. If this were the case, you could draw some other equally erroneous (if not ludicrous) conclusions. For example, you could argue that, as a biological creature, it is part of your nature and existence to eat food and eliminate waste; therefore, you should be able to take food whenever and wherever you see it and eliminate waste whenever and wherever you desire.

Some of us may want to believe that we are emotionally helpless because it places the responsibility for our actions on sources beyond our control. If we are our emotions, then how can we be held responsible for the actions they provoke? If we believe this philosophy, then we *can* blame our actions on our emotions:

- He hit the man because he was *angry*.
- She would not speak to him because she *felt neglected*.
- He shoplifted because he *wanted to be part of the gang*.

Even the structure of our language implies a direct causal relationship between emotions and the consequences that follow:

- He hit the man *because* he was angry.
- She would not speak to him *because* she felt neglected.
- He shoplifted *because* he wanted to be part of the gang.

This commonly used sentence structure hides the fact that *we* are the ones who choose how we will respond to our emotions. A more correct way of saying these same sentences would be as follows:

- When he was angry, he *chose* to hit the man.
- When she felt neglected, she *chose* not to speak to him again.
- When he wanted to be part of the gang, he *chose* to shoplift.

These sentence structures make it very clear that it is the person deciding the course of action, not the emotion. This distinction is critical to the understanding of emotional responsibility; you should not continue reading this book unless you fully understand it.

Unfortunately, we witness immature emotional behavior so frequently that we have come to regard such behavior as normal and to be expected. Nevertheless, just because people frequently express their emotions immaturely does not mean that emotionally mature behavior is impossible or out of the reach of the average person on the street. Just because people who get angry express their anger in abusive ways does not mean that abusive actions are acceptable or to be expected. If this were true, we could argue that it is impossible to keep a car running smoothly because so many car owners regularly neglect maintenance of their automobiles and run them into the ground.

Finally, just because an angry person cannot think of any other ways of dealing with his anger does not mean that proper and constructive ways for handling anger do not exist. This "I have not thought it, therefore it cannot exist" mentality is inherently arrogant and obviously flawed.

Before you can become emotionally responsible, you must accept the fact that even though you are an emotional creature, you are still free to choose how you will handle your emotions.

Jane went grocery shopping with her three young kids. Soon after she arrived at the grocery store, the children were taking items off the shelves, running around, pulling on each other's hair, and otherwise causing a commotion.

Using her sternmost voice, Jane told her children to "shape up and stop—or else" and "you had better not make me angry." This worked for a moment, but soon they became bored and once again resumed their play. Jane repeated her threats with decreasing effectiveness until finally she grabbed her youngest son by his shirt and exclaimed, "I'll teach you to disobey your mother." She then spanked him and told him what a terrible child he was and how he was making her life miserable.

Michelle, another mother who frequented the same store, also had children who acted rambunctiously while she was shopping, but she chose a more creative and mature solution. First, she tried to understand why her children were behaving the way they were by looking at things from *their* perspective. "To young children," she thought, "everything in the grocery store is new, novel, or exciting (after all, marketers design them that way)." She deduced that their attempts to grab and cling onto bags of cookies or boxes of cereal were, in their mind, tangible evidence that they would soon be eating these exciting treats.

Armed with these insights, Michelle planned how she could make her future shopping trips more pleasant and uneventful. She came up with several creative solutions that she then tried out. For example, sometimes she exchanged baby-sitting with another mother so she could go to the store by herself. If she did take the kids to the store, she fed them before they left home, shopped early in the day before everyone was worn out, allowed the kids to push their own children's cart (provided by the store), had each child fill their cart with a few items on their own grocery list (which they had created by cutting and pasting pictures), brought storybooks for them to read, and reminded them about acceptable behavior as they arrived at the store and the reward they would get if they behaved properly (such as cookies and milk or playing a special game with them immediately after arriving at home).

Some of her ideas worked well, others worked with partial success, but Michelle continued to try out new ideas and approaches to the problem until she met with success. In doing so, she increased in skill, wisdom, and competence in dealing with this issue. Today, she and her children look forward to shopping and have fun on their trips to the grocery store.

ARE YOU RESPONSIBLE FOR EMOTIONS YOU DO NOT CREATE?

HENRY WAS A happily married man with a wife and two children. He worked as a lawyer with two other partners in a lavish, wood-paneled office. One day, Henry came back from vacation to discover that his former secretary had retired and had been replaced by an attractive young woman in her mid-twenties.

At first, Henry kept his relationship with his new secretary strictly one of business, but after a while, he found it rewarding to joke around and then flirt with her. To his surprise, his secretary returned the behavior in kind, and within a few months, Henry was having an affair.

Henry's wife eventually become suspicious of his long hours, late-night phone calls and sudden out-of-town meetings. She hired a detective to check out her suspicions, which unfortunately were confirmed.

When Henry's wife confronted him with the detective's irrefutable evidence, he tried to blame the affair on his secretary. "She seduced me," he said. "She wore skimpy clothing and revealing blouses to work, stayed late to help me finish my work, flirted with me, and threw herself at me."

Henry's wife did not buy his excuses, nor did she stay around to hear the details. When Henry's secretary found out that the affair had been discovered, she resigned and disappeared. A year later, Henry was still single, lived in a one-room apartment, and paid most of his income to alimony and child support. He continues to blame his former secretary for ruining his life.

Some people argue that we are not responsible for our emotions because we do not create them—they just come into our lives independent of our own will. These people believe that anger, fear, sadness, jealousy, disappointment, love, attraction, and other emotions just happen. They are not created by the individual. Because, they believe, we do not create our emotions, they conclude that we cannot be held responsible for them. After all, they claim, how can we be held responsible for something we did not create?

To address this argument, let us consider some possible causes of our emotions. Some researchers believe that our thoughts trigger our emotions:

1. I see the growling grizzly bear running toward me [the perception].
2. I know that angry bears can permanently alter my physical appearance [the thought].
3. Therefore, I fear [the emotion in response to the thought].

Notice that the fear came after the thought. These researchers believe that the precursors of our feelings are our thoughts.

Some years ago I had an experience while hiking in the mountains that seemed to validate this possibility. While hiking out of the foothills after a three-day mountaineering expedition, I walked over a rattlesnake that was directly in my path. A few seconds later, carrying a forty-pound pack on my back, I jumped a couple of feet off the ground. My higher-order mental processes, slowed down by fatigue and exhaustion, finally caught up with me. I interpreted what I had seen and reacted accordingly. After collecting my wits, I discovered that the rattlesnake was already dead when I walked over it.

Others researchers believe that our emotions are biologically motivated. They believe that emotions are not intellectual realizations, but are physiological reactions to certain stimuli. They believe that emotions arise from within the primitive emotional centers of our brain or from chemical substances released by our organs and glands. These researchers point out that clinically depressed individuals have brain scans that differ from nondepressed individuals and that heredity and genetics appear to play an important role in many mental, psychological, and emotional illnesses. Our language is full of idioms and phrases reflecting this interpretation: "in the heat of the moment," "driven by anger," and "overcome by passion."

The answer to the question, Do we create our emotions? is probably yes and no. On the one hand, we know that we can induce many emotions through our thoughts. We know, for example, that we can depress ourselves if we continually dwell on discouraging thoughts, such as our weaknesses, the injustices we have suffered, or dashed expectations. We have seen how people who are paranoid will interpret any situation as being against them and will therefore feel threatened or under attack. The whole body of positive-thinking literature would not be so popular if our thoughts were totally ineffective in altering our emotions.

On the other hand, who has *not* experienced waking up one morning feeling depressed and another morning feeling absolutely terrific for no apparent reason? Who has never battled strong, negative feelings that have swept through their being uninvited, even though they were doing their best to avoid them? Who has never experienced a powerful emotional outpouring, greater than could be expected from mere thought alone?

When it comes to emotional responsibility, we do not need to get hung up on the issue of whether we create our emotions or whether they just happen. The answer to this question appears to be some of both. The important thing is that, as far as emotional responsibility is concerned, the conclusion is the same: *you are still responsible for the way you handle your emotions, whatever their origins.*

For example, even though you do not understand the source of your anger, you are still responsible for the way in which you handle your anger. After all, if you became ill with the flu, would you disclaim responsibility for nursing yourself back to health because you did not create the flu virus or consent to becoming infected?

You are responsible for how you handle your emotions, regardless of whether you generate them yourself or whether they arise from sources unknown.

ARE YOU RESPONSIBLE FOR YOUR EMOTIONAL WEAKNESSES?

WE ALL HAVE physical weaknesses and vulnerabilities. Some of us have allergies, others are prone to headaches; some of us are genetically predisposed to diabetes, others have bad joints; some of us wear glasses, others are prone to heart disease; some of us get colds easily, others bruise easily; and so forth. There are so many varieties of physical weakness and vulnerability that it is rare to encounter a person who does not have *any* physical weakness at one time or another in their life.

Likewise, as imperfect emotional creatures, we all have areas of emotional weakness. Some of us are prone to anger or easy provocation, others are overwhelmed by their fears and avoid taking risks; some of us are easily offended, others feel unloved in life and are vulnerable to those who would take advantage of this fact; some of us are emotionally coarse and insensitive, others are oversensitive and have their feelings easily hurt; some of us have difficulty understanding the feelings of others, others find it difficult to tune in to their own emotions.

Linda was lonely. Even though this was her sophomore year in college, she did not have a single friend. She felt self-conscious and inferior whenever she was around other girls, especially in social situations, notwithstanding her unusually high intelligence. "Other girls are so much prettier than me," she thought, "and they know how to talk to and flirt with the boys."

Linda's roommates always invited her to go along with "the gang" to dances and other social events, but she would either turn them down or immediately leave the event whenever she felt embarrassed, awkward, or inferior. During such occasions, her throat would choke up, her eyes would tear, and thoughts of inadequacy and rejection would dominate her thinking. She often cried herself to sleep.

One day, Linda passed by the campus counseling center. Partly on impulse, partly on a ray of hope, she went in and hesitatingly made an appointment. Although she did not feel much better after her first counseling session, she continued to come in for regular counseling. Over time, her counselor helped her to understand her feelings of inadequacy; look at herself in new ways; see herself as a worthy person with talents, assets, and unbounded potential; and identify and practice the skills she needed to socialize with the boys and build her self-confidence.

Two years later, Linda was no longer lonely. She was a confident young woman with a healthy self-image. She had several friends, went out regularly on dates, and anticipated a bright, exciting future.

To become emotionally responsible, you must own up to your emotional weaknesses. You cannot expect others to take responsibility (or the blame) for your emotional vulnerabilities and weaknesses. They belong to you and to you alone. You must own up to them and avoid blaming them on your upbringing, your genes, or your environment.

If you are easily prone to anger, for example, you should not blame others for "making" you angry, expect them to "walk on glass" whenever they are in your presence, or expect them to read your mind to anticipate what might make you angry. If you are prone to depression, you should not expect others to magically sweep away your depression with a few good words or deeds, nor should you expect others to wallow in your depression with you and shun the good feelings they are enjoying in their own lives.

If this seems harsh or unfair, consider this. You do not expect others to take responsibility for your physical weaknesses, so why should you expect them to take responsibility for your emotional weaknesses? For example, as an adult, you do not expect others to take responsibility for curing your athlete's foot, for providing you with new eyeglasses, for making sure you pass up high fat desserts, or for restraining you from playing basketball when you have an injured knee.

Intellectually, you may be "OK" with the idea of emotional responsibility. But accepting it on an emotional level is actually quite difficult. It is easy to continue to blame others for our emotional weaknesses or continue to expect others to take responsibility for our inadequacies and make up for them. For example, we may refuse to overcome an emotional weakness because "others do not care enough to reach out and help me and share my emotional burdens." We think thoughts such as:

- "If no one cares enough to help me, then I am not going to change."
- "If no one else cares, then why should I care?"

Sometimes we vocalize our thoughts to others as part of a retaliatory power play:

- "Well, if you're going to be that insensitive, then I guess you'll just have to live with me the way I am."

At other times, we set up a "test of true love" proposition:

- "If you really loved me, you would do more to help me."

All of the above declarations are then followed by a mental washing of our hands of responsibility for overcoming our emotional weaknesses and changing our subsequent immature behavior.

Even if the premises to all of the above statements were true, you would still be responsible for your emotional weaknesses. You cannot expect others to "rescue" you from your emotional shortcomings, nor can you wait for others to help you before you assume responsibility for them. They are your responsibility. You must shoulder them. You must take the necessary action to eliminate or minimize them in your life, even if this requires great, sustained effort for a long time.

Besides refusing to change because others "do not care," there are several other ways we can refuse to take responsibility for our emotional frailties. For one, when others commit real or perceived injustices against us, we tell ourselves that we are justified in taking whatever action that naturally comes to mind, whether that action is mature or not. For example, when someone cuts in front of us on the freeway, we feel they deserve the rude gestures we make.

When other family members treat us harshly and insensitively, we feel justified in yelling or lashing back in kind. When things are not going well, we feel validated in being depressed and withdrawing from life.

One of the reasons that the robots found in early science-fiction movies seem, by today's standards, to be so mechanical and stilted is precisely for this reason. These robots did not possess any emotional responsibility-avoidance mechanisms in their speech or behavior. In those days, no one expected a robot to be a "hothead" or to sit down in a corner and sulk because "nobody cares about me." Undoubtedly, the *Star Wars* droids would not have been so popular had they failed to manifest human personalities, complete with their own set of emotional frailties. As humans, we resort to these responsibility-avoidance mechanisms so frequently that we hardly believe that anything is human (or is like us) unless it manifests these very same emotional foibles.

WHAT ARE THE LIMITS OF EMOTIONAL RESPONSIBILITY?

HOW FAR DOES emotional responsibility go? What are the limits of emotional responsibility? Are you responsible for the way you handle your emotions, regardless of your circumstances? Are you justified in giving in to feelings of depression and self-pity when everything seems to be going wrong? Are you justified in screaming and yelling at others when you are under tremendous stress? Are you justified in hating others or in becoming bitter when they commit injustices against you?

The experience of Dr. Victor Frankle, an Austrian psychiatrist and author of the book *Man's Search for Meaning*, offers significant insight into the answers to these questions. During World War II, Dr. Frankle and his Jewish family were captured by the Nazis and imprisoned in German concentration camps. Suddenly, everything that Dr. Frankle held dear was stripped away—his family, his worldly possessions, his friends and professional associates—even his personal liberty. For many years, he was subjected to inhumane physical and psychological conditions. Naked, starved, and living in cold, cramped, pitiful conditions, he became a walking skeleton. Many prisoners died due to cold, disease, forced labor, starvation, and hopelessness. Each morning, their bodies were hauled off to be burned.

Through these unbearably painful experiences, Dr. Frankle reported having discovered something that gave him hope. He learned that he did not have to react to his circumstances with hatred, bitterness, hopelessness, or suicide. He realized that he could instead focus his mind and thoughts on that which gave his life meaning and hope. He discovered that no one—not even the Nazi's—

could take away this last freedom—his freedom to choose how he would react to his circumstances. That, he discovered, was the ultimate human freedom.

Of course, such a realization in no way diminishes the responsibility, accountability, and culpability that those who conceive and inflict such horrors must bear for their heinous acts against humanity. Rather, it demonstrates that, as humans, we are different from the rest of the animal kingdom. We can consciously choose *how* we will respond to the circumstances of our lives. This is what makes us responsible.

Having made that statement, there are a few notable exceptions in which emotional responsibility is limited because of certain physical or mental conditions. Little children, for example, are in the process of developing physically, mentally, and emotionally and are not yet capable of adult mental operations and thought processes. Children, therefore, must be carefully nurtured, loved, and guided in emotional matters as they grow to maturity. They can only be held to a level of emotional responsibility that is appropriate to their age and mental capacity.

Another exception to full emotional responsibility are those who suffer serious physical, genetic, or mental diseases that affect their capability for emotional self-determination. The assignment of emotional responsibility in these exceptional cases is *not* a question of whether the person finds it personally difficult to choose a mature course of action. Rather, it is a question of whether that person has lost—for organic reasons, physical injury to the brain, or genetic reasons—the capability to choose alternative courses of action in response to their emotions. *Difficulty to choose* and *capability to choose* are two entirely distinct and separate issues. Only one's capability to choose can limit emotional responsibility—not one's difficulty to choose a mature response.

Are those who take illegal drugs or who consume alcoholic beverages that, in turn, alter their brain's capability to judge or stay in control, responsible for how they handle their emotions after they become intoxicated or "high?" The answer to this question is a definite "yes." These individuals have deliberately chosen to take into their body substances they know could lead to a loss of normal mental processing and judgment. Therefore, they remain responsible for their actions, even while under the influence of these drugs.

CAN OTHERS AFFECT YOUR PERCEPTION OF EMOTIONAL RESPONSIBILITY?

PERHAPS ONE OF the reasons we have so much trouble taking responsibility for our emotions is that we see so many examples of poor and decrepit emotional behavior in our everyday lives. Books, movies, and television shows, for example, often portray heroes who are involved in admirable causes (such as protecting the environment or fighting government corruption) but who are otherwise emotionally bankrupt. These heroes display anger, outrage, revenge, physical attraction, and intellectual or physical superiority in inappropriate, reckless, and destructive ways. Not only are examples of emotional irresponsibility continually paraded before us, the immature behavior of these individuals is often passed off as typical, normal, or even desirable.

Consider, for example, the Rambo-style action movies in which violence and revenge are seemingly the muscle-bound hero's total repertoire of emotional response. Or consider movies that attempt to capture our attention with passion or graphic violence that go on to portray emotionally reckless and irresponsible behavior that—even in the end—leads to no destructive or negative consequences whatsoever. The image portrayed by these movies is one of heroes and heroines satisfying their emotional and physical urges whenever and with whomever they want, without any serious consequences. The effects that would follow such behavior in real life are often distorted, made light of, or entirely ignored. Considering the destructive and life-altering consequences that follow gross emotional irresponsibility, we could not hold up a more dangerous proposition to the impressionable minds of our young people than the message that "there are no consequences associated with the way you choose to handle your emotions."

Of course, not all movies and books portray bad or poor emotional role models, but it seems to be getting more difficult to find them. The entertainment industry increasingly finds itself on the defensive (at least with people who understand the importance of emotional responsibility) over violence, foul language, sexual content, and consequence-free behavior that is being depicted or advocated in movies, television shows, and music. Many parents are themselves lax or inattentive or fail to regulate what their young children and teenagers watch. Many do not set a proper example themselves.

At least some people are making the connection, whether it can be proven scientifically or not, that if we (1) portray emotionally immature and reckless behavior in a positive light and disassociate it with anything negative (especially real-life consequences), (2) bombard people's minds with it over and over, (3) make it the focus of nearly everything they watch, and (4) make it attractive, "cool," and popular, that eventually young people are going to pattern their thinking after what they see and adopt these beliefs as acceptable and as truth (the way things really are).

An example of a movie that portrays good emotional role modeling is the old Walt Disney classic *Follow Me Boys*. In this movie, Fred MacMurray portrays a musician who finds himself penniless and unemployed in a small Midwestern town. Rather than becoming depressed and engrossed in self-pity, he deals with his situation creatively and constructively. He secures a job as a clerk at the local general store and soon finds himself volunteering to be the first scoutmaster for the town's boys. Throughout the rest of the movie, he faces one difficult situation after another. He meets stiff competition for courting the only eligible girl in town; marries but is childless; faces immature boys in his troop; adopts a rebellious, runaway teenage son; tries constantly to pursue the study of law but is frustrated at every turn; finds himself taken captive while his Boy Scout troop is camping near an army military proving ground, and has his dream of building a permanent scout meeting hall threatened by a frivolous lawsuit.

Nevertheless, through it all, he looks at life positively, turns challenges and limitations into opportunities, and handles difficult emotional situations creatively and appropriately. This is not to say that he is perfect, but he is not flawed in any gaping or glaring way. His heart is right, and he ultimately stays on the path of maturity. In the end, the long-term consequences of his choices are made apparent. The boys he mentored have grown up and become successful, caring adults and leaders. The scouting program he fostered has become a well-established, powerful force for good in the community. Ultimately, the town rallies to create a new, local holiday to honor him for his influence on their lives and on the lives of their children. Such a movie is not only a positive inspiration, it portrays a mature emotional role model by which others would greatly benefit were they to follow suit.

Our entertainment is not the only source of influence on our perception of emotional responsibility. Parents, peers, and others with whom we associate also influence—for good or for bad—our perception of emotional responsibility. If parents, for example, handle their emotions poorly or blame their emotional outbursts on sources outside themselves ("you made me mad, therefore you are responsible for my screaming at you"), then their children are almost sure to adopt similar thinking. If a brother constantly points out supposed faults and "defects" in his sister in order to feel superior, his sister is likely to practice this same kind of behavior with those over whom she has power.

Of course, your upbringing does not absolutely determine your character or what you become. Some children grow up in emotionally abusive homes, but nevertheless become exceptional models of emotional maturity. Even though your partner, other loved ones, and society in general can and do influence your perception of emotional responsibility, you are still free to reject those influences and choose a more constructive course of action. Of course, it goes without saying that if you grow up with undesirable emotional role models, you will have to work much harder to overcome any negative programming that they have modeled and reinforced.

Retraining Your Automatic Emotional Response Mechanisms

To take charge of your emotions, you must first become aware of them. After all, how can you take responsibility for properly handling emotions for which you are entirely unaware? You must recognize and identify your emotions before you can consciously manage them in mature ways.

Zain was a master programmer. From an early age, he demonstrated an unusual genius for anything to do with computers. He felt most at home when he was sitting in front of a keyboard working on a challenging programming problem. Conquering one difficult computer programming problem only made Zain more excited to tackle the next.

Zain's wife long ago accepted the fact that, for Zain, computing was his life, but she still had emotional needs that needed to be fulfilled. When she approached him about going out on the town or sitting down together to watch television, he replied that he was busy, that he did not "feel like it," or that they had just gone out the previous week.

Zain was too preoccupied to be sensitive to his wife's emotional needs. When she became excited about purchasing a small, inexpensive item at the store, Zain told her they really didn't need the item and made her feel silly for wanting it. He often forgot his wife's birthday and anniversary and failed to understand and respond to his wife's emotional ups and downs. Even Zain's children sensed that their father lived in another world.

Zain never gave his emotions much thought or credence. For him, life was pretty much even-keeled, and he did not see any reason for it to change in the future. His computer provided him with his interaction, and it was always logical and emotionally constant.

As Zain grew older, he became increasingly plagued with burnout, depression, and loneliness. Life was feeling more and more hollow. At first, he tried to ignore these uncomfortable feelings, just as he had done all his life. "Feelings just get in the way of logical thought—they are so *irrational.*" But they refused to go away and only grew stronger.

When Zain's feelings began to seriously disrupt his life, his wife persuaded him to seek professional counseling. After a number of sessions, Zain began to understand and accept the fact that he was an emotional— not just an intellectual— creature. He began to tune in to his emotions, express them more openly (but in appropriate ways), and address the emotional needs of himself and his family. Soon thereafter, Zain began to enjoy life in ways he had never really experienced before. Zain was happier than ever, and even his family thought they had acquired a new father.

Being in touch with your emotions is not always a given. You can be out of touch with your emotions for a variety of reasons. Your thinking may be dominated by rushed schedules and weighty responsibilities. You may have been taught to ignore your feelings when you were growing up (boys, for example, are supposed to be tough and are taught that "crying is for sissies"). You may be out of touch with your emotions because you have reacted to certain situations the same way for so long that you now respond to similar stimuli automatically, without even thinking.

How can you respond to your emotions automatically, without conscious thought? In the same way you learned to respond to other things without conscious thought. When you first learned to drive, for example, every driving task—moving the steering wheel, shifting, applying the brake, judging distances, and reacting to hazards on the highway—required your full and complete mental concentration. Over time you gained more and more driving experience. Gradually these actions and thought processes required less and less of your conscious attention until they finally became automatic. Once your reactions to the road became automatic, you could drive down the highway in "autopilot mode," thinking about things far removed from driving. For example, you might drive for miles without later remembering a thing, or you might drive home instead of to the store because you invoked the wrong "autopilot script" when you started your journey.

Automatic processing and responding can occur in your emotional life as well. You might react with anger and harsh words to your youngest child's misbehavior because this is how you have reacted to your anger since your oldest child was born. You might react to disappointment with depression and withdrawal because this is how you have reacted to disappointment from your earliest years.

You might react to jealousy by verbally attacking the person you are jealous of because this is how you have always reacted to jealousy. It each case, your emotional reactions have become automatic through repetition over long periods of time. Responding to your emotions no longer requires your conscious attention or mental processing.

Although *automatic emotional response mechanisms* are common, they do not release you from your responsibility to manage your emotions maturely. Just because you react to your emotions without thinking does not make you any less responsible for the way you manage your emotions. To become emotionally responsible, you must learn not only to recognize your emotions but your responses to them— even your automatic responses—so that you can intervene as necessary to govern your responses appropriately. If you are out of touch with your emotions or with the way you handle them, you will be at the mercy of your emotions and the consequences they bring.

THOUGHTS TO PONDER

- Do you believe that you are responsible for the way you manage your emotions? If so, do you believe that you should be held accountable for any *consequences* that come from mismanaging your emotions?

- Is simply saying "I'm sorry" an adequate accountability for serious emotional misconduct? Is complete and adequate restitution, especially for misconduct that has led to significant suffering and loss, necessary for emotional responsibility? What should be done in situations in which full restitution cannot be made (such as the case of a ruined reputation, serious trauma, or rape)?

- Can others "make" you angry, that is, force you to become angry against your will? Is anger a viable solution to a problem? Are there constructive ways of handling anger? Are there ways to avoid becoming angry? Do parents who become angry at their young children on the slightest provocation generally raise healthy, well-adjusted adults? How does being "quick to anger" damage a relationship? What are the causes of being "quick to anger?" (Hint: Consider at least the following possible causes—a lack of self-control, a lack of knowledge of how to solve problems in more constructive ways, entrenched automatic emotional response mechanisms, insecurities, being quick to judge or being quick to attribute evil intent to the actions of others, and laziness to take a more constructive approach)?

- As emotional creatures, our natural inclination is to act based on our emotions, not on pure reason, unless we have trained ourselves to do otherwise. If some decisions (and subsequent actions) have a greater potential than others to bring us success and happiness or misery and self-destruction, what are the bounds within which we may allow ourselves to make decisions and actions on a purely emotional basis? (For example, is an emotional decision to go out to eat at a favorite restaurant rather than to go to a movie different from an emotional decision to use mind-altering, body-destroying drugs? Should the decision to drop out of school and join a gang rather than prepare for a trade or profession be made solely on an emotional basis?) When can we base our decisions and actions on a purely emotional basis? How important is it to assess the possible long-term consequences of our potential actions and decisions *before* deciding whether to let our emotions completely guide those decisions and actions?

- Is it all right to retaliate in kind when your partner has acted irresponsibly toward you? If your spouse is unfaithful, for example, are you justified in being unfaithful yourself?
- How can you combat the people, entertainment, and other influences in society that popularize or justify emotionally irresponsible behavior? Who should teach emotional responsibility to your children? How can you best help your partner to understand, accept, and value emotional responsibility? Will your example influence your partner's receptivity?

ACTIVITIES FOR SELF-IMPROVEMENT

1. Memorize the following and repeat it to yourself whenever you find yourself getting angry: "There must be an intelligent and mature way of handling this situation." Copy down the following questions in advance and then review them after you have repeated the previous statement: "Am I misjudging the motives and intent of those involved in this situation? How do I know? Have I gathered sufficient information (including gathering information from each of the individuals involved) to understand what really occurred in this situation and why? Am I reacting to my insecurities? Am I getting angry simply for convenience, to avoid the effort required to take a more constructive approach; for example, am I getting angry and yelling at my kids rather than sitting down and talking with and teaching them? What principles would make me more effective in dealing with these situations (for example, learning the principles of good parenting)? Where can I go to learn these principles, increase my wisdom, and develop the skills necessary to deal with these situations more maturely? What can I do to prevent this situation from occurring in the future?" To control your anger when all else fails, find a constructive outlet for dissipating your anger (exercise, go for a walk, watch a movie) or simply grit your teeth and hold your tongue.

2. Are you having difficulty properly managing a troublesome emotion, such as anger, jealousy, hate, envy, rage, or hopelessness? If so, keep a log for several days of when, where, and why you experienced this emotion and what you did to handle it. Then periodically review your log and determine appropriate and constructive

ways you might have used to deal with your feelings in those situations (get the help of others with this exercise, if necessary). Plan how you will carry out these mature actions in new situations as they occur. Evaluate your success in carrying them out and set up new strategies, if necessary. If the problem persists, you may need a deeper understanding of the underlying root causes of your problem, which you can gain by reading good books, talking to others, or getting professional help.

3. People tend to become the most defensive, reactionary, and aggressively hostile toward others on things that trigger or expose their emotional weaknesses. To help you identify and uproot your emotional weaknesses, analyze the situations in your life that evoke (1) deep-seated defensiveness (refer to the ego-defense mechanism of rationalization described on page 12 and the other ego-defense mechanisms described on pages 161 through 162), (2) hypersensitivity (situations where you take serious offense at others or make others "walk on glass" when they bring up certain topics or joke playfully about your behavior), and (3) aggressive or passive hostility towards others (such as making damning accusations about another person's character or giving your partner the "silent treatment" or "cold shoulder" when he or she does not comply with your wishes). Additionally, look for areas in your life where you repeatedly mismanage your emotions and analyze those areas to determine if there are any underlying emotional weaknesses.

When you have identified your weaknesses, work on uprooting them. Use a one-at-a-time selective approach (focus on one weakness at a time until you overcome it or make significant progress) rather than an all-fronts attack (trying to overcome all of your emotional weaknesses at the same time). Make a commitment to demonstrate the determination, persistence, and patience you will need to overcome your weakness. Get the help of others, as necessary, to overcome it.

CHAPTER 5

WHY YOU SHOULD CARE ABOUT EMOTIONAL RESPONSIBILITY

*For good or for ill, you cannot escape the
unrelenting gravity of consequence*

Too often we learn to care about what is important in life by what we suffer, rather than by what we learn from being taught. Although this approach may be fine for acquiring many lessons in life, it is totally inadequate when it comes to making critical life decisions that have serious and far-reaching consequences. We must know what the land mines of life are *before* we enter the battlefield, not after we are blown up.

That is why it is so important to fully understand the good consequences that follow emotional responsibility and the bad consequences that follow emotional irresponsibility—for yourself, your partner, your family, and society in general. Unless you truly understand these consequences, you might ignorantly walk over an emotional land mine that will forever change your life.

The Consequences of Emotional Irresponsibility to Yourself

SOME PEOPLE DO not take emotional responsibility seriously because they do not believe that there are any significant consequences of emotional irresponsibility to themselves. Others acknowledge that consequences exist, but they do not believe that they will personally be touched by them. Still others believe they can outsmart, outmaneuver, or overpower whatever consequences may come their way (if they dare show up at all). Finally, some, like so many Las Vegas gamblers, believe they can "beat the odds."

Unfortunately for them, when it comes to emotional irresponsibility, there are no odds. Negative consequences will *always* follow irresponsible behavior. It is not a matter of *if* the consequences will occur; it is only a matter of *when* the consequences will occur. There is an unbreakable link between emotional irresponsibility and its resulting consequences. Even though these consequences might not appear immediately, they will not be far away. Their bitter arrival cannot be prevented by mere human denial, wishful thinking, or boastful conceit. Emotional laws, like laws of physics, are just that—laws.

What are the consequences of emotional irresponsibility to you personally? The following are a sampling:

Feeling Victimized by Your Emotions

Emotions are powerful forces in your life. If you do not learn to control and channel them, they will control you. When this happens, you will feel subject to their destructive power and influence. You will feel victimized by forces that seem to rule your life. You will feel driven to do things you later regret, such as saying things when you are angry that you later wish you had never said.

Depression and Loss of Hope

When powerful Dark Emotions sweep through your being unchecked, they wreak emotional havoc. As described above, they leave you feeling victimized by forces beyond your control. In this vulnerable state, you may feel sorry for yourself and lose hope that your circumstances will improve. For example, you may deal with your disappointment and frustration by concluding that life is unfairly picking on you and becoming chronically depressed. Unchecked, unrestrained Dark Emotions eventually bring depression and despair.

Increased Vulnerability to Danger

A life overpowered by unmanaged Dark Emotions will leave you groping for true emotional satisfaction. Without true emotional satisfaction, you will be left emotionally vulnerable and susceptible to the lure of dangerous physical enticements. Such allurements include alcohol, drugs, sex, gambling, eating disorders, and other potentially reckless and risky behaviors. Although such allurements appear to provide quick emotional and physical fulfillment, in the long run, they leave you feeling empty and unsatisfied. The thrills and excitement they seem to provide ultimately give way to emotional, financial, and physical destruction as addictions, dependencies, and other serious consequences set in.

Passing Time Battling Dark Emotions
Instead of Enjoying Happy Emotions

Like weeds that multiply to take over a garden, if you do not learn to manage your Dark Emotions, they will eventually dominate your thinking and your behavior. Unmanaged Dark Emotions divide and multiply and spawn other Dark Emotions. Feeling unloved, for example, can lead to feeling rejected. Feeling rejected can lead to self-pity. Self-pity can lead to depression, dejection, and hopelessness. Unless you learn to effectively turn around, counteract, neutralize, and channel these emotions, you will find yourself spending more of your time and energy battling Dark Emotions and less of your time enjoying Happy Emotions.

Emptiness

When you try to satisfy your basic emotional needs through emotionally irresponsible behavior, you end up empty handed. Such behavior cannot satisfy your long-term emotional needs. Irresponsible emotional behavior, like junk food, might appear to satisfy your hunger pangs, but "sugar highs" soon turn into "sugar lows," leaving you with even greater feelings of dissatisfaction. Just as a steady diet of empty calories eventually leads to malnutrition and a serious loss of health, the instant gratification that comes from "doing whatever you feel like doing" disappears as quickly as it arrives, leaving you with lingering feelings of dissatisfaction. Illegitimate ways of satisfying emotional needs leaves you not only empty handed, but "empty hearted."

ISOLATION AND LONELINESS

Uncontrolled, unmanaged emotions drive others away and damage relationships. Just as people do not willingly place themselves in the path of tornadoes, erupting volcanoes, or bolts of lightning, they do not like being around others who are emotionally explosive, abusive, or draining. When others avoid you because you are emotionally immature, you become socially isolated and alone, even though you may be surrounded by large numbers of people.

LOSS OF SELF-ESTEEM AND SELF-RESPECT

Self-esteem is based on personal growth, integrity, meaningful contribution, and worthy accomplishment. If you are emotionally reckless, irresponsible, or abusive, at some point in the future, you will be faced with the damage you have inflicted on yourself and others and your self-esteem and self-respect will suffer. Who can say what the far-reaching consequences of emotional irresponsibility really are? Who can measure the true cost of dashed dreams, shattered hopes, and thwarted human potential?

SADNESS, SORROW, GUILT

These feelings follow the loss of self-esteem and self-respect. Not only do you lose self-esteem when you impose emotional pain on others, you reap sadness, sorrow, and guilt when you finally witness the true consequences that follow your actions.

FAILURE TO REACH YOUR POTENTIAL

When your time and energies are consumed battling unmanaged Dark Emotions and their consequences, precious little time is left to pursue personal development and self-fulfillment. Because it takes time and determined effort to develop talents, character, and complex skills, those who are emotionally irresponsible fail to grow out of their emotional infancy. They remain as emotional toddlers, even though they live in an adult body.

THE CONSEQUENCES OF EMOTIONAL IRRESPONSIBILITY TO THOSE CLOSE TO YOU

EMOTIONAL IRRESPONSIBILITY not only affects you, it affects all those with whom you have contact. It is not possible to contain the effects of emotional irresponsibility within the boundaries of your own life. Other consequences follow, including the following:

DIVORCE OR SEPARATION

Although divorce is much too common and regardless of whether it is morally justified, people find it difficult to live with those who no longer meet their emotional needs, who emotionally manipulate or abuse them, or who inflict intense emotional pain.

DYSFUNCTIONAL FAMILIES AND FAMILY RELATIONSHIPS

When family members are emotionally irresponsible, they fight, quarrel, shout, tear down, and otherwise emotionally injure one another. This kind of interaction results in emotional pain that can lead to lifelong emotional scars. Many of us feel that our noses are too big, our figures imperfect, or our intelligence below average because of the things our siblings told us growing up. Dysfunctional families burden family members with heavy emotional baggage and fail to provide the support and encouragement that is necessary to maximize human potential.

SHATTERED OR THWARTED INTERPERSONAL RELATIONSHIPS

No one wants to be walked over emotionally or be forced to bear the brunt of immature emotional outbursts. Interpersonal relationships are nourished by mutual trust, concern, respect, and sensitivity. All of these are violated when you lose emotional control and force others to be the recipient of your own emotional hostility, insensitivity, rudeness, and recklessness.

LOSS OF THE TRUST AND CONFIDENCE OF OTHERS

Violating emotional trust is destructive, just as violating other forms of trust is destructive. When you use the thoughts and feelings that others have confided in you against them in arguments, when you are insensitive to the emotional needs of others, when you become verbally abusive in stressful situations, when you show that you do not care, when you are emotionally abusive rather than emotionally supportive to those who depend on you, and when you take out your frustrations on others, you violate emotional trust. Those at the receiving end of such outbursts as well as those who witness such behavior will quickly lose their trust and confidence in you.

LOSS OF EMOTIONAL INTIMACY

When others are not sure if you will hurt them emotionally, they will be reluctant to share their feelings with you. People do not share their feelings with those who are emotionally reckless, who trample or ridicule their emotions, or who ignore important emotional needs. Moreover, when you are emotionally irresponsible, those who depend on you for emotional intimacy will go wanting. In their vulnerable state, they may turn to apparent quick fixes, such as drugs, gangs, or sex, in an attempt to satisfy their needs. Such behavior leads to even greater destruction in the lives of all those involved.

CONSUMPTION OF TIME AND ENERGY BELONGING TO OTHERS

When you impose your emotionally irresponsible behavior on others, you rob them of something they cannot replace—their time. When you handle your frustration and anger by yelling, blaming, or hurling accusations, you consume the time and energy that others could have spent in more pleasant and useful activities. More importantly, the emotional hurt you inflict may take days, weeks, or even years to get over. As those who receive such treatment know, it does not take very much emotional immaturity to steal away one hundred percent of another person's free time.

Pollution of the Emotional Environment of Others

When you fail to manage your emotions, you pollute the emotional atmosphere of those around you. Your spouse, children, coworkers, and subordinates cannot easily escape your presence. When you corner them and force them to listen to your insults, outbursts, and verbal abuse, you force them to breathe toxic emotional pollution and effectively make them "secondary emotional smokers." You violate their right to clean emotional air and a peaceful, happy environment.

Failure to Serve as a Source of Emotional Refuge and Support

When medical doctors become ill, their ability to help those who are sick is severely limited. Similarly, when you are emotionally injured, discouraged, or disabled, you cannot easily provide emotional support to your children or your partner. Emotional problems draw you inward, consume your energies, and preoccupy your mind. Just as physical illnesses and injuries require time and careful nurturing to heal, emotional wounds likewise demand time and careful nurturing, to heal. When you are suffering the injuries and illnesses of your own unmanaged Dark Emotions, you cannot easily be a source of emotional support to others.

Being a Curse to Future Generations

All of the consequences listed above affect not just those in your immediate sphere of influence, they affect the generations yet unborn. Children are quick to model the immature behavior of their parents, which they then pass along to their own children and spouses. Because your posterity grows geometrically, not linearly, your emotional irresponsibility curses not only the living, but many generations yet unborn.

THE CONSEQUENCES OF EMOTIONAL IRRESPONSIBILITY TO SOCIETY AT LARGE

TO MANY, THE social consequences of their actions, whatever they may be, are unimportant, questionable, or far removed. But such is not the case. Consider, for example, the following fictitious, but possible, scenario:

> Joe thinks that cheating on his tax return will not affect society. Government is so big, he reasons, that they will not miss a few of his dollars. When Joe makes a joke about it with his friends, they laugh about it too, but secretly they are strongly attracted to the idea. If Joe did it, why couldn't they? Because they already know of someone who is cheating on their taxes, it somehow doesn't seem so bad. Soon Joe's friends are cheating on their taxes too, making jokes about it, and laughing off the seriousness of their actions. The trend soon spreads when popular nightly television sitcoms pick up the same jokes and viewpoints, broadcast them before millions of viewers, and otherwise popularize characters who cheat a little and lie a little. Within a year or two, many people are cheating on their taxes. Because the local, state, and federal governments cannot afford to audit every tax return, they respond to decreasing tax revenues by raising taxes. Dishonest taxpayers feel vindicated in their belief that the government is already taking in too much, so they cheat with even greater determination. Honest taxpayers are burdened even more. As a result, they buy less. The economy lacks stimulation and begins to take a downturn. Because people have less to spend, they spend less. The economy finally stalls and people start to lose their jobs. Before long, Joe wonders why he is in the unemployment line. He can be heard blaming everyone he can think of for his current state of affairs. Everyone, that is, except himself.

The emotionally irresponsible often laugh at the idea that their behavior has any consequences to society as a whole or to the society they will pass on to their children. Nevertheless, just watching the evening news will reveal a different story. The following are a few of the consequences of emotional irresponsibility to society in general:

More Crime and Violence

When natural forces such as fires, winds, and seas exceed their bounds in tidal surges, hurricanes, and forest fires, the result is widespread destruction of physical property and natural resources. Similarly, when millions of people allow powerful Dark Emotions to surge out of control in their lives, an even greater wave of emotional devastation, suffering, and physical violence is unleashed. Those who do not take responsibility for properly managing their emotions allow other forces to dictate their thoughts and their actions—including powerful and violent Dark Emotions that motivate people to lash out, overpower, find instant gratification, take possession, and seek revenge.

Emotional irresponsibility is a precursor to crime. When lawyers look for a motive in a crime, what they are really asking is, "What unrestrained Dark Emotion could have motivated this crime—greed, lust, jealousy, revenge, anger?" Criminals do not properly manage their emotions. They see people or forces outside of themselves as responsible for their emotions and the subsequent actions those emotions "provoke." "He deserved to be stabbed—he taunted me and made me mad." "She asked to be raped because of the way she was dressed." "He should-n't have left his wallet out in the open." Unrestrained, unchecked Dark Emotions lead to emotional, verbal, and physical harm or violence.

War

On a larger scale, uncontrolled and unrestrained passion has been the great motivating force behind many of mankind's greatest tragedies, including two World Wars, numerous massacres, untold armed conflicts, massive starvation, and the repression and enslavement of whole societies by power-crazed dicta-tors. History has repeatedly witnessed the human suffering and tragedy that result when emotional misfits become dictators, holding the power of life and death over millions of people. Unmanaged Dark Emotions, such as a lust for power, hatred, racism, greed, intolerance, and jealousy, have motivated many of mankind's most cruel conflicts.

An Emotionally Sick Society for Our Children

Society is only as emotionally well as the individuals who comprise it. Any number of social welfare programs cannot create an emotionally healthy society out of emotionally irresponsible citizens. We have yet to witness the long-term consequences that will follow the widespread and continuous stream of immature emotional behavior that is being modeled before the eyes of our young people by popular figures in television, movies, magazines, music, and books. These are the same children who will grow up to become your children's bosses, your children's future politicians, and your grandchildren's parents.

HIGHER TAXES, HIGHER PRICES, AND LESS SPENDABLE INCOME

Emotional irresponsibility costs literally billions of dollars every year. The United States federal government alone spends billions of dollars on the so-called "War on Drugs," on social welfare programs designed to pick up the pieces left by emotionally immature people, and on lifetime medical care for brain-damaged or physically deformed babies born to drug addicted or alcoholic mothers. Self-aggrandizing politicians sacrifice the long-term economic health of the nation with their deficit spending to win re-election votes. White collar criminals file fraudulent insurance claims that inflate auto insurance premiums by an estimated fifteen to twenty percent. Prices on consumer goods are inflated because of shoplifting and employee theft.

LESS PRODUCTIVITY

Your emotions are not left behind at home when you leave for the day. They go with you to your place of employment. When you are emotionally ill or are suffering the consequences of unmanaged Dark Emotions, you have less energy and more difficulty focusing on your work. Whatever your trade or profession, work demands focused attention for extended periods of time. When your thoughts are overshadowed by emotional pain, psychological wounds, battered feelings, or struggles with Dark Emotions, your attention is diminished and your energies are drained. This loss of energy and preoccupation with feelings translates into less productivity and increased risk of accidents.

DETERIORATION OF FREEDOM

If we ourselves are emotionally irresponsible, we are more susceptible to electing public officials who are also emotionally irresponsible. Such officials are more vulnerable to bribes, corruption, and blackmail. They are also more interested in serving their own selfish interests than the best interests of the country or of those they represent. Emotionally irresponsible citizens are more concerned with exercising their passions and fattening their wallets than with safeguarding their freedoms. The survival of our nation depends on an educated citizenry who can distinguish truth from lies. Freedom cannot flourish in an atmosphere of ignorance, irresponsibility, apathy, or the inability to distinguish truth from twisted emotional pitches.

PREJUDICE

Those who are prejudiced blame other races, religions, or groups for their problems and believe that the elimination or persecution of these groups will resolve their troubles. Emotionally irresponsible people are particularly susceptible to prejudice because they are already used to blaming outside influences (including others) for their problems.

GREAT HUMAN SUFFERING AND TRAGEDY

Emotional irresponsibility and its consequences encompass the most intense and painful experiences that human suffering, sorrow, and tragedy know. These include divorce, rape, physical violence, sexual abuse, emotional abuse, accidents involving drunk drivers, physical abuse, sexual harassment, depression, crime, and drug addiction. If you are fortunate enough *not* to have personally suffered from someone else's emotional irresponsibility, you probably know someone who has.

In view of the above consequences, you cannot argue that emotional irresponsibility is a "private matter" that does not affect or concern others. It affects you, your partner, your immediate family, your associates, all those with whom you come into contact, your society, your future posterity, your own future, and your destiny.

THE BENEFITS OF EMOTIONAL RESPONSIBILITY

EMOTIONAL RESPONSIBILITY does not come easy. It requires disciplined effort, self-control, and a determination to behave in a responsible fashion. Nevertheless, emotional responsibility will bring you big benefits, including the following:

Increased Freedom, Time, and Energy

Unmanaged Dark Emotions rob you of your time, energy, and freedom. They consume huge amounts of emotional, mental, and physical energy. Little time, if any, is left for pursuing positive, constructive, or self-fulfilling activities. Emotional irresponsibility is enslaving, not liberating. On the other hand, emotional responsibility is liberating and energizing.

Increased Self-Confidence and Self-Esteem

Those who take responsibility for their emotions have greater control over their lives. They have learned to take charge of their emotions instead of letting their emotions take charge of them. They are free to focus their lives on personal growth, development, and meaningful contribution and are free from the devastating consequences of unmanaged Dark Emotions. They mature faster, achieve more, contribute more, and enjoy more.

Enduring Friendships and Relationships

People avoid those who are emotionally out of control. Enduring friendships and relationships are built on emotional stability, sensitivity, trust, and mutual concern. Those who are emotionally irresponsible violate emotional trust, are tossed to and fro by their emotions, are insensitive to the feelings of others, and are consumed by their own problems. On the other hand, those who are emotionally responsible manage their emotions in mature ways. Therefore, their relationships are much more likely to prosper.

Greater Emotional Intimacy

Most of us long for close, emotionally intimate relationships. Even crazed dictators seek out mistresses with whom they share secrets that they will not even disclose to their closest generals. But emotional intimacy, as we have previously learned, is not the same as physical intimacy. Emotional intimacy thrives in relationships in which emotional stability, understanding, sensitivity, trust, and caring are demonstrated and proven over time. Emotional responsibility is requisite to emotional intimacy.

Support in Kind

Few things warm the heart as much as receiving the emotional support and encouragement you need from a loved one during times of trial, suffering, and hardship. When you are emotionally strong and healthy, you are capable of providing loving emotional support to those around you. When you provide that support to others during their times of need, they will remember your kindness and will return similar support to you in your times of need.

Stronger Family Relationships

Family relationships cannot thrive in an atmosphere where contention, insensitivity, emotional volatility, or emotional abuse are present. Family relationships are highly intertwined and interdependent. Those who are emotionally responsible avoid emotionally reckless behavior, are emotionally stable, and are more sensitive to the emotional needs of others. They therefore enjoy stronger family relationships.

A Happier, Safer Society

Our individual choices and actions do make a difference. Society is molded person by person, choice by choice, action by action. When you choose emotional responsibility, you are choosing to make society safer, happier, and more peaceful. When you and others are emotionally responsible, society as a whole moves forward.

THOUGHTS TO PONDER

- Do you think that emotional immaturity is an important problem in our society today? What impact will increasing emotional immaturity have on children, families, and society? What impact will it have on your future? On the future of your children? What are you doing to help stem this societal trend?

- Do you pay taxes to cover the costs of the emotionally irresponsible acts of others? Should government make it easy for people to avoid any significant consequences for their seriously irresponsible actions? Is it fair to make those who are emotionally responsible pay for the destructive acts of those who are emotionally irresponsible? Does Joe have a right to take away what Robert, his neighbor, has worked hard to obtain to pay for the damages incurred by Joe's own emotional immaturity? If not, does government have the right to step in and perform this function on behalf of Joe?

- Is your life's potential being limited by your emotional baggage? Was any of this baggage created when you acted in emotionally irresponsible ways? Is any of what you suffer today the result of your previous emotionally irresponsible decisions?

- Are you an emotional polluter? Do you inflict emotional pain and suffering on your partner and those around you because of your emotional irresponsibility? Do your actions force others to spend time in emotional recovery, grieving and figuring out how they can pick up the pieces of their lives and go on?

- Can you expect to enjoy a happy, fulfilling, lasting relationship if you are emotionally irresponsible? Why?

- How have the emotionally responsible decisions you have made benefited you? Do you enjoy greater or lesser freedom in your life when you act in emotionally responsible ways?

ACTIVITIES FOR SELF-IMPROVEMENT

1. Choose an instance when your acting in an emotionally irresponsible way led to serious consequences in your life. List all of the negative consequences that followed your actions. Was it worth it? Is choosing emotional maturity really harder in the long run than choosing emotional immaturity? Is it easier to discipline yourself

to manage your Dark Emotions properly or to give in to Dark Emotions and suffer the intense emotional pain, anguish, and destruction that ultimately will follow?

2. As you read biographies, watch true-life movies, view documentaries, listen to the news, and otherwise learn about the lives of others, make a conscious effort to identify the benefits and negative consequences that follow other people's emotionally responsible and irresponsible decisions and actions, respectively.

3. Write a paragraph describing the influence you want to have on your future posterity. Will your acceptance of emotional responsibility have any effect on whether that influence is realized?

4. Pick up a copy of today's newspaper. For each news article, jot down whether the incident being reported is beneficial or detrimental to society. For those that are detrimental, read the article and determine if the improper management of emotions was involved in motivating the behavior that produced the detrimental outcome. Calculate the percentage of articles out of the total number of articles that report detrimental incidents due to improper emotional self-management. How might these outcomes have been different if the individuals involved would have properly managed their emotions and emotional needs? How would society be different if people better managed their emotions?

PART THREE

FULFILLING EMOTIONAL NEEDS IN RELATIONSHIPS

CHAPTER 6

WHAT'S SO IMPORTANT ABOUT RELATIONSHIPS?

*Treat your relationships as if everything
depends on them—it does*

Our relationships are probably the single greatest external influence on our emotions and our lives. How we treat others—and how they treat us, talk to us, care about us, and regard us—powerfully impacts our emotions for good or for bad. At one extreme, relationships can be a source of great joy and deep satisfaction. At the other extreme, they can be a source of turmoil, distress, and living hell. In between are relationships with all varying degrees of constructive or destructive interaction.

Relationships are necessary to life. For life to be conceived, we must have a father and a mother. When we are born, we inherit relationships with parents, grandparents, brothers, sisters, relatives, and others. When we go to school, we interact with teachers, peers, and administrators. When we go to work, we establish relationships with bosses, employees, coworkers, suppliers, clients, and customers. Before we can get married, we must persuade another person to enter into a serious, public, and legally binding relationship. To stay married, we must carefully nurture and cultivate our relationship with our spouse. To raise children, we must take on parent-child relationships and eventually grandparent-grandchild relationships.

RELATIONSHIPS ARE PRECIOUS
AND ARE ALL YOU HAVE

IMAGINE WHAT IT would be like to live on a lifeless planet where you had no one to talk to, no one to care for, no one to share memories with, no one to run around with, no one to love, and no means of living vicarious relationships (such as through television or movies). Experiences in this life take on their true significance only as you discuss, share, and relate them to others. After all, if you were the only person riding the attractions at an amusement park, how fun would it be?

What if, for example, people who emotionally abuse others suddenly had no one to corner, manipulate, and use to satisfy their emotional cravings? What if things were suddenly reversed so that they were at the receiving end of their abusive treatment and were powerless to escape the emotional pain, abuse, and torture that they have heaped on others? What if, because of the way they have abused others, they were judged unworthy to have any relationships at all and were sentenced to a lifeless planet in total isolation for the rest of their lives? Perhaps then they would begin to understand the supreme importance of relationships in fulfilling emotional needs and the serious consequences of their actions.

If we truly understood how important positive, healthy relationships are to our happiness, we would treat them more carefully than we now do. It is foolish for us to recognize how dependent we are on our relationships with our bosses at work for our physical survival while being blind to the even greater dependency we have on our relationships with our loved ones at home for our overall happiness and quality of life. Although most of us would never consider blowing up at our boss at work, many of us find it easy to let loose on our spouse and children at home.

Why do we take our family members for granted, neglect their needs, treat them recklessly, and use them for our own selfish purposes? Perhaps it is because we do not fear that there will be any serious or lasting consequences for our actions that will affect *us*. Why else would we treat those outside our homes—friends, bosses, coworkers, and even strangers—with more dignity, respect, politeness, consideration, energy, patience, and good will than we do those of our own household? Logic, if anything, would dictate just the opposite.

Unfortunately, some of us tend to judge and prioritize our relationships based on what they can currently (or potentially) deliver to us in monetary value, social prestige, power, pleasure, or a life of ease. Applying this criteria to our loved ones automatically devalues our relationships with them. Our relationships with our spouse, children, and parents were not designed for these purposes nor meant to compete on these terms. When we devalue our relationships, we find it easy to misuse them for our own selfish purposes. This kind of thinking produces spouses who divorce their companions for younger, prettier women or richer, more powerful men, or people who feel perfectly fine treating their loved ones—on whom they depend for daily food, shelter, or nurturance—with harshness, rudeness, and gross insensitivity.

The harsh reality is that outside of a very small handful of people on the earth, you are very much alone—despite the billions of other earthlings who live on this planet. After all, who is going to care for you or care about you outside of your immediate family?

- When you are ill, who looks after you? Strangers?
- If you lost your wallet and passport in a far away country, who is going to stop and help you? Passersby?
- When you get into trouble or are experiencing rough times, who comes to your assistance? Your bill collectors?
- When you are critically ill in the hospital, who stays by your bedside all night? Your boss?
- When you are in college, who works extra jobs, extra hours, and makes do with less to keep you in school? Your teachers?

The bottom line is that the quality of your life is determined not by the size of your paycheck or by the influence you wield in the outside world, but by the quality of your day-to-day relationships with your loved ones. If this is true, you must learn to value your relationships with your family members more than you value your relationships with your boss, friends, and others, and you must demonstrate that value through your actions, not just your words.

Can we say, for example, that we sufficiently value our relationships with our loved ones when we:

- Shout at and berate our spouse for causing us to be late for an appointment or a social event?
- Unleash a storm of verbal abuse and make exaggerated threats to our children when they get restless at a store?
- Seldom think about or attend to the emotional needs of our spouse?
- Throw emotional tantrums when things do not go our way?

- Use intimidation, threat, guilt-trips, or other forms of emotional manipulation to get others to do our bidding?
- Take others for granted and consume their resources without expressing sincere gratitude and appreciation for their contribution and sacrifice?
- Value our "freedom to express whatever we feel whenever and however we please" more than we value our relationships with our loved ones?

You have little time in life to create and build relationships. Much of your time is already consumed in necessary daily rituals, such as working, sleeping, eating, cleaning, and taking care of others. Precious little time is left to develop and strengthen the relationships that are so essential to your happiness and well-being. Therefore, every interaction you have with your loved ones is important. You only have a few such interactions with them in this life, and you never know when you might unexpectedly lose those relationships through accident, illness, or crime.

RELATIONSHIPS ARE THE MEANS BY WHICH IMPORTANT EMOTIONAL NEEDS ARE MET

RELATIONSHIPS ARE important to emotional health because it is through our relationships that many of our most important emotional needs are met. Love, acceptance, emotional support, understanding, friendship, and valuing of self are just some of the needs that are met only through our relationships. Therefore, when relationships fail, important emotional needs go unmet and serious emotional consequences follow. There is no substitute for solid, loving relationships. Only relationships can deeply satisfy the emotional cravings we so strongly feel.

Peter and Lisa had been married for six wonderful years. They grew up together from the time they were in kindergarten, dated in high school, and married each other their junior year in college.

Pete could not imagine life without Lisa. She was his best friend, confidant, and cheerleader. Her unconditional love healed Pete's childhood wounds and gave him the security he needed to develop his talents, take reasonable risks in his career, and overcome his low self-esteem. Lisa's friendship, companionship, and unselfish interest in Pete's success bonded them closely together.

After marrying, Pete and Lisa continued to court each other. They went out on weekly dates and enjoyed every minute they spent together. They were so closely bonded that they could often discern each other's emotions simply by exchanging glances. Their lives and souls were intertwined as much as two lives could ever be. Life couldn't have been happier.

Then one day a drunk driver took Lisa's life in a reckless, senseless accident. The tragedy devastated Pete so badly that he spent the rest of his life struggling to put himself back together. He felt intense anger, hatred, and bitterness toward the drunk driver who had taken his wife's life and toward a system of "justice" that let a known repeat offender go free on a short prison sentence.

Pete's life was forever changed. Even after several years of professional counseling, he never fully recovered. The light of his life had been extinguished. The unconditional love, friendship, support, intimacy, understanding, and affection that he had enjoyed and relied on for so many years was gone, never to return.

Despite the profound importance of relationships, we often mistreat them, take them for granted, or treat them lightly. We may feel, for example, that our spouse or our parents are obligated to take care of our emotional needs. While freely consuming the emotional resources they provide us, we give very little back in return. We make a scene when our own needs or desires are not sufficiently pampered. We manipulate or coerce them by judging, accusing, demanding, dominating, threatening, or abusing them to get our way. Then we gloat in our own contentment when our needs are fully satisfied and completely forget about the needs of others. We fail to realize that every human being has emotional needs, no matter who they are, how old they are, how beautiful they are, or what their situation in life is.

Perhaps if we more fully understood the damage we do when we neglect or mistreat our relationships, we would be more careful to treat them properly. Perhaps if others visibly bled a little each time they were ridiculed, neglected, manipulated, verbally abused, or made the target of our anger, our behavior would change. If others visibly saw the damage we inflict when we mistreat our relationships, we would reform, if for no other reason than to avoid the social embarrassment and the disapproval of others.

Getting through the challenges of life is difficult enough without having to worry if the source by which our most important emotional needs are met is stable and secure. If we are emotionally mature, we will avoid imposing this fear in the lives of our loved ones. We will become revered and cherished for the love and support we give to others, and we will fulfill our own emotional needs in the process.

RELATIONSHIPS ARE NECESSARY FOR YOUR PERSONAL GROWTH AND FULFILLMENT

LIFE AS A HERMIT is unconducive to building character. Only as you reach out and care for others do you stretch your capabilities, overcome selfishness, and build self-confidence. Others provide you the opportunity to discover, learn, and practice correct values. They give you the opportunity to sacrifice and serve. They give you the emotional support and encouragement you need during severe emotional trials. Finally, they give you the opportunity to benefit from their knowledge and experiences. Without relationships, there would be no such interaction and, therefore, little growth.

Many of your most important emotional needs are met through relationships, such as your need for love, friendship, emotional intimacy, and to make a difference in the lives of others. Unless these needs are fulfilled, your own personal growth will be seriously challenged. Just as someone who is starving is in a poor condition to learn calculus, someone who is emotionally famished is unable to seek after higher-order refinement in their relationships. Those who are emotionally starving are struggling for emotional survival—not to refine their interpersonal communication skills. Unfulfilled emotional needs consume a high degree of energy, leaving little left for personal growth.

Relationships also provide emotional stimulation. Consider how dull life would be were it not for your interactions with others. As young Kevin in the movie *Home Alone* came to realize, living life without relationships can be fun and relaxing for a while, but after a few days of having no one to talk to, play with, or share our accomplishments with, life becomes very boring. Your personality needs others to find expression and definition, and you need the varying personalities of others to add variety, stimulation, fun, and meaningful interaction to your own life.

Finally, others can provide you the support and assistance you need to succeed. You receive a wealth of emotional support, wisdom, and insight from others, not just financial support. Others have experiences that you can draw on, talents that can help you identify and take advantage of opportunities, strengths in areas for which you are weak, and solutions for problems for which you only see frustration. Others can also serve as role models of mature character. All of these contributions are extremely valuable to your personal growth. As Sir Isaac Newton said, "If I have achieved anything, it is because I am standing on the shoulders of giants."

The Consequences of Mistreating Relationships

David grew up as an only child. He was used to getting his own way, and, as far as he was concerned, the world centered around people serving his needs. Because David's parents did not require that he serve others or consider their needs in his choices and actions, his insensitive, self-centered ego grew as tall as his imposing six-foot-two stature.

David was rugged, handsome, and popular in school. He easily charmed the most beautiful women on campus with his romance-novel appearance, quick sense of humor, strong self-confidence, and sporty new car. When Karen became engaged to David, she felt like she was the luckiest girl on earth. After a short but intensely romantic courtship, she married David in a lavish, much-envied wedding.

Soon after the honeymoon, David began to change. He started to openly criticize his wife when she made slight mistakes. He became harsh and judgmental of her idiosyncrasies and weaknesses. He put her down when she did things he thought were stupid. He assumed the role that he previously had taken while growing up and became upset if his wife did not immediately cater to his every whim. He treated his wife rudely, insensitively, and without kindness or empathy. To David, Karen was his personal servant, on call day or night to fulfill his every want and desire.

Karen did not know what to do. David had become the opposite of the person she thought she had married. She was scared and frightened.

David continued to charm and flatter others with his charisma whenever the couple were out in public, as was his style. Others kept telling Karen how lucky she was to be married to David. Because of this, Karen sensed that her family and friends would likely disbelieve her if she were to relate what he was really like, even if she were brave enough to tell them. So she kept things to herself and watched as her husband repeatedly transformed himself from Dr. Jekyll into Mr. Hyde after talking pleasantly with friends on the telephone or getting into the car at the church parking lot after smiling and talking cheerfully with the other church goers.

The year after they were married, Karen delivered her first child. She found temporary relief from her husband's oppressive behavior in her new infant daughter. Her baby needed her, freely gave her love and affection, and did not verbally abuse her.

But the birth of their firstborn child only made things worse with David. He resented getting less attention and pampering. As the infant grew up, David began to include his young daughter as well as his wife in his emotional tirades.

By the time they had two more children, David's behavior had become intolerable. Several times a week, he became emotionally abusive, tearing into his wife and children, making great false accusations, exaggerating, yelling, belittling, glaring, harassing, dictating, putting down, making ugly facial gestures, demanding instant results, manipulating, blackmailing, playing on people's worst fears, making others an offender for a word, treating small indiscretions as capital crimes, trumpeting damming but false evidence, violating trust, making bold and unreasonable demands, radiating hatred and contempt, and otherwise emotionally cornering and tormenting his family.

Karen endured the abuse for the time being. She did not want her children to grow up in a broken home, and she was scared to leave because she did not have any employable skills. Furthermore, she did not believe that there were any laws against this kind of behavior. She continued to live in her emotional concentration camp, with her husband as head of the Gestapo. She felt as if she had been sentenced to a living hell.

Karen grieved that she could not offer her children the stable, loving environment they so desperately needed. She was torn by the obvious damage her husband was inflicting on her children. But she was in an emotionally weak condition, deeply wounded, and barely able to function herself. The years of constant emotional and psychological battering had taken its toll. Emotionally, Karen was mostly a walking corpse. She wished every day that she could die to escape her pain. She was literally fighting for emotional and physical survival.

David told his wife to shape up and stop being a wimp. He denied that he had any emotional problems. Every time Karen asked him to seek out professional help, he became infuriated and immediately abusive. At the same time, he refused to allow his wife to see a mental health professional.

One day, Karen suffered a serious mental breakdown. She was hospitalized for several weeks, tested, and admitted into a mental institution. When her husband's emotionally abusive behavior was discovered, the children were placed in several foster homes, where they struggled to cope with the severe emotional handicaps that had been imposed on them in their prior home.

David divorced Karen, moved out of state, and promptly cut off his alimony and child support. He never admitted to any wrongdoing. Instead, he started going out with and charming other beautiful young women. Soon he married another unsuspecting women, with whom he repeated the same cycle of abuse.

Those who misuse or abuse their relationships destroy the very means by which they themselves can progress and grow. They greatly dim the prospects for their own future emotional fulfillment. The following are some of the other consequences of mistreating relationships.

EMOTIONAL NEEDS GO UNMET

This is serious enough in and of itself and has already been previously discussed.

EMOTIONAL TRUST IS DESTROYED

When you mistreat your relationships, you put your own selfish needs before the needs of others and trample or neglect the needs of others. When this happens, others know they can no longer depend on you as a source of emotional fulfillment and support. When you hurt others, they will no longer trust you with their feelings and their needs. People do not trust others to whom they attribute questionable motives.

YOUR OWN GROWTH IS STUNTED

As previously discussed, when you mistreat others, you cut off one of your own best sources of emotional support, growth, and fulfillment. You stunt your own growth.

YOU BRING UPON YOURSELF DESTRUCTIVE DARK EMOTIONS

Dark Emotions never travel solo. Whenever you give place to one Dark Emotion, ten others soon follow, more destructive than the first. Arguments, shouting matches, and heated interpersonal exchanges produce destructive emotional forces that ultimately bring guilt, remorse, anger, bitterness, loneliness, emptiness, frustration, and a loss of control over life in their wake. Such feelings do not and never will promote personal or interpersonal growth.

Your True Values Are Made Evident

When you misuse your relationships, you are telling others what you really value. If you speak kindly and politely to strangers in public and then turn around and treat those of your family with harshness, contempt, or anger, you are plainly manifesting your true values. Although you may think that you can rationalize away such behavior, your actions will speak louder than your words. Your loved ones, like others, will believe your actions before your professed saintly attributes.

You Become Isolated and Alone

Any form of energy out of control is highly dangerous and often destructive. When others sense that your emotions are out of control or are being driven by unrestrained Dark Emotions (such as passion, anger, jealousy, bitterness, greed, pride, revenge, or selfishness), they will be repulsed and will try to escape your presence or avoid you altogether. When you cause your partner to avoid you or fear being in your presence, you are damaging—not building—your relationship.

You Become a Stumbling Block—or Worse—to Others

When you heap your frustrations, anger, hostility, fear, hatred, jealousy, or selfish desires on others, you impose Dark Emotions on them with which they must cope. They, in turn, must divert their attention and energy away from their current activities to confront and combat these powerful emotions. Not only is this a great waste of human productivity, it is a real trial to those you afflict. What if others are not strong enough to handle your mistreatment? What if others make life-altering decisions while struggling under the influence of your attacks? What if others fail to reach their potential or give up hope as a result of your emotional tirades?

You Threaten the Relationship Itself

Everyone is human. All relationships have their limits. If you act like a shrew or a devil, others may eventually grow weary of your torture and decide that enough is enough. Even though others can and should learn to endure a certain degree of emotional pain and trial through patience, love, and forgiveness in a genuine effort to help you grow, if you show a persistent determination to seriously mistreat or abuse those whom you should love, they may ultimately decide that they must leave you in order to move on with their lives.

Thoughts to Ponder

- Why is it so disturbing to lose a loved one? What do we remember most, for good or bad, about those who have passed away? Why do eulogies typically focus on the emotional contributions that the deceased has made on the lives of others and little (if anything) on their financial contributions? Does this tell you anything about what other people—your partner included—really value in their lives?

- It is a human tendency to cry out until our own needs are met and then forget about the needs of others after our needs are fulfilled. When everything is going well, we focus on enjoying what we have and on keeping our immediate source of satisfaction secure. How does this tendency work against our valuing our relationships with our loved ones? How can we counteract this influence?

- What is more important: the size of your paycheck or the quality of your relationships? What proportion of the quality of your relationships is determined by your partner? How much is determined by you? How did you arrive at this ratio? What can you do to improve the relationship from your partner's perspective? When you make things better for your partner, will this usually make things better for you?

- Some people may think it macho to brag about how they achieved success in life all by themselves, but is this really possible? Is it likely that no one ever helped them along the way? If, as Sir Isaac Newton said, "If I have achieved anything, it is because I am standing on the shoulders of giants," then what about us? Can we truly claim that we have achieved greatness without the help, support, and emotional nurturance of others? What can you do to nurture those who are depending on you for emotional support? Could you unknowingly be the gatekeeper through which a unique world contributor or genius will someday appear? What if Einstein had failed to get any emotional support at critical times in his life?

- How intelligent is it to bite the hand that feeds you, whether it be financially, materially, or emotionally? Who are the hands that feed you emotionally? Are you in the habit of regularly biting them? If so, what should you be doing instead?

- Why do people in television shows that depict close calls with death change their attitude toward their life and their relationships when they or their loved ones are seriously injured or are nearly lost?

● What if the punishment for emotionally abusing our relationships were having those relationships taken away from us? What if hell were being placed on a planet where everyone hated us?

ACTIVITIES FOR SELF-IMPROVEMENT

1. Review the twenty emotional needs identified in Chapter. How many of those needs can be met *only* through relationships? How many are *often* met through relationships? How many are *indirectly* met through relationships? How many do not fall into any of these categories?

2. List five emotional qualities you like and rely on in your partner. Share them with your partner and express your appreciation for what your partner brings and contributes emotionally to the relationship. Do the same thing a week or two later. Repeat this on a regular basis.

3. The next time you think about letting loose on your partner, picture yourself letting loose on your boss at work. Now visualize the consequences. If you are unwilling to threaten your financial security by taking your emotions out on your boss at work, then why are you willing to threaten your emotional security (including your ability to fulfill your emotional needs) by doing the same thing at home?

4. Ask your partner how you can provide greater emotional support. Express your commitment to provide this support and then follow through.

CHAPTER 7

Ten Secrets of Emotionally Fulfilling Relationships

*How well do you care for the emotional
hands that feed you?*

Happy, lasting, fulfilling relationships do not just happen. They are built on meeting the needs of others; building others up; helping others achieve their God-given potential; developing good character in yourself; acquiring proper values; and compliance to emotional law. Emotional law states that you cannot violate the emotional principles upon which happy relationships are based and then expect to have happy relationships. For example, you cannot violate emotional trust and then expect others to feel emotionally intimate with you or to have tender feelings toward you. You cannot dominate others in a relationship and then expect them to want to be around you. You cannot verbally or emotionally abuse your children and then expect them to grow up to become emotionally stable adults. You cannot neglect or ignore the needs of your partner and then expect your partner to care about your own needs or feel close to you.

On the positive side, emotional law dictates that if you interact with others with the purpose of helping them to achieve their greatest potential; if you are emotionally stable, trustworthy, and slow to judge; if you are sensitive and empathetic; if you build up and strengthen those around you; if you treat others with dignity and respect; if you have reasonable expectations; if you respect the agency of others; if you use example, persuasion, long-suffering, and the teaching of correct principles to influence rather than threats or force; if you are more concerned with improving your own character than the character of others; and if you actively help meet the emotional needs of others, you will likely enjoy happy, lasting, and fulfilling relationships.

THE EMOTIONAL FOUNDATIONS OF HAPPY RELATIONSHIPS

HAPPY, ENDURING, FULFILLING relationships have much more to do with motivation and character than with romantic capabilities, verbal expertise, interpersonal wizardry, or charismatic personality. Although all of these attributes can add to an already sound relationship, such attributes cannot serve as the *foundation* of a happy, fulfilling, lasting relationship. Foundations must be rock-solid, stable, and enduring. In relationships, such foundations are made of solid values, good character, and adherence to correct principles.

The survival of a marriage, for example, depends more on the character of the individuals involved than on fleeting physical attractions or romantic expertise. Although many permanent relationships are initially motivated out of romantic or physical attraction, unless they quickly become anchored on the more solid ground of character and values, the relationship will falter. Only relationships that are built on good character, solid values, and correct principles will survive the storms and stresses of life.

How could it be otherwise? How could character *not* be an issue? How could those who are self-centered and immature be patient in their interactions with others? How could those who lie and cheat and steal in other areas of their lives maintain emotional trust and be faithful to their spouse? How could those who are accustomed to getting their way by bullying, intimidating, exerting authority, and manipulating others be sensitive to the needs and agency of their partners? How can those who seldom think about the needs of others practice empathy or show sensitivity?

If happy, fulfilling, lasting relationships require good character, then the following corollary is also true: if you have poor character, do not expect to have happy, fulfilling, lasting relationships. The Law of Harvest applies just as much in your emotional life as it does in other areas of your life.

For a relationship to achieve its highest potential, both individuals in the relationship must be emotionally mature, properly motivated, and of good character. If one person is extremely mature and the other person is extremely immature, the relationship will be severely lopsided. Unless the mature party is capable of living with long-term unmet emotional needs and of successfully confronting and coping with powerful emotional opposition, the relationship is unlikely to survive.

Although he came from a dysfunctional family, William was determined to have a successful relationship with his new bride, Cynthia. "I'm going to do whatever it takes to make this marriage succeed," he thought as he began his married life. William was highly motivated. He had personally witnessed the devastating effects of mistreated relationships in his own childhood, and he wanted to avoid those results in his own married life. Little did he know just how high a price he would have to pay to keep that promise.

A few weeks after they were married, the realities of adult life began to settle in. Like many other married couples, William and Cynthia began to have disagreements over how to spend money, what television shows to watch, who was doing the most work around the house, and who was leaving their dirty dishes on the table.

William loved his wife. He knew that there would be disagreements in his marriage, and he had prepared himself to deal with them. When his feelings were hurt, instead of lashing out in retribution, he expressed himself calmly and respectfully. When he was falsely accused, he controlled himself and refused to make accusations in kind. When he was upset, he avoided blaming, name calling, and making exaggerated and inflammatory statements, such as "You always…," "You never…," "I can't believe how lazy you are," "You don't love me anymore," and "How could you be so selfish?"

When some of William's emotional needs were left unmet due to Cynthia's immaturity, he sought to fulfill those needs in other appropriate ways. If no other appropriate means was available, he endured temporary periods of deprivation and refused to feel sorry for himself. Instead, he focused on his self-improvement and on opportunities for personal growth.

William accepted his wife's current level of maturity and kept his expectations about his marriage reasonable. He celebrated Cynthia's unique strengths and emotional contributions, took advantage of their common interests, and minimized their differences. He did good things for his wife, even when she did not seem to appreciate them, and gave her encouragement and support for pursuing worthy goals.

William did his best to set a good example of mature behavior and to teach Cynthia the fundamental principles of happy, fulfilling relationships. When his wife refused to adopt mature behavior, he did not threaten or blackmail her into conformity; rather, he negotiated reasonable compromises and then waited patiently for her to grow. He repeatedly forgave his wife when he was wronged and continued to treat her courteously and respectfully.

Cynthia could not help noticing her husband's mature example and his focus on self-improvement. His rock-solid love for her deeply impressed her. Gradually, Cynthia became less defensive. She began to openly ponder the principles William had taught her for so long. Over time, she began to see that her perceptions of her husband were really quite narrow and incorrect in many ways. She sensed the deep joy that her husband received from living these principles and began to have a strong desire to experience this joy in her own life. Over time, her immature behavior began to feel uncomfortably childish and selfish—even to her.

Cynthia went through a turning point in her life. She eventually overcame her negative emotional conditioning, her shortsightedness, and her selfishness to develop a deep and fulfilling relationship with her husband.

William had been true to his promise. Although some of his friends told him that he had paid too high a price for his marriage, William thought otherwise. Because of Williams's emotional maturity, a marriage that could have easily become just another divorce statistic instead became a powerful source of emotional fulfillment, intimacy, and joy. "Had I not practiced the principles of happy relationships, I might have ended up just about anywhere else, including places I'd rather not think about."

IS GOOD COMMUNICATION SUFFICIENT?

IF GOOD CHARACTER is absolutely essential to happy, fulfilling, lasting relationships, then what is good character? Your character is made up of the values you uphold and of the principles you follow. The Ten Secrets of Emotionally Fulfilling Relationships that follow will help you develop a good character— the kind of character that will lead to happy, successful, fulfilling, and lasting relationships.

Before you learn these principles, however, you should understand that the Ten Secrets of Emotionally Fulfilling Relationships are *not* clever techniques for pushing the hot buttons of others to make them feel good about you or to manipulate them into giving you what you want. Rather, they are the essential character attributes that you must develop if you want to enjoy happy, successful, fulfilling relationships.

Many self-help books focus their attention on the importance of good communication to happy, successful relationships. Some of these books even assert that techniques for improving interpersonal communication are the yellow-brick road for improving, healing, or saving relationships. If only we knew how to talk to and listen to each other, these voices declare, we could all enjoy the happiness that has previously eluded us.

Although good interpersonal communication is absolutely essential for healthy, happy, and successful relationships, interpersonal communication alone cannot compensate for poor character (that is, the failure to live the principles upon which happy, lasting, successful relationships are based). A thousand of these popular techniques will never equal the power of proper motivation, selfless love, deep sensitivity, genuine empathy, sincere respect, or any of the other principles we are about to discuss.

There are no happy, lasting, fulfilling relationships that are based on selfish motives, verbal manipulation, clever talk, deception, domination, romantic infatuation, lust, or intimidation. Clever communication techniques, emotional "slights of hand," and ploys for manipulating the feelings of others never have and never will compensate for a lack of a mature, solid character that is purely motivated.

Secret 1: Have the Right Motivation

Before all else, you must have the right motivation for interacting with others.

Those who are properly motivated seek to build and lift others up, strengthen them, encourage them, increase their self-confidence, provide them opportunities to develop their unique talents and abilities, love them, teach them true principles, and help them achieve their greatest potential.

What could be a purer motivation than this?

Without a pure motivation, you will not have the power to live the rest of the principles on which happy, successful, fulfilling relationships are based. If you are selfish, for example, your thought processes (not to mention your behavior) will be far removed from concepts such as sensitivity, empathy, understanding, respect for agency, and appreciation. Your attention and your energies will be turned inward toward yourself and your own needs rather than outward toward helping others grow and reach their true potential. Your daily energies will be spent on acting defensively, on competing for what you believe are scarce resources, and on making sure that your own needs and desires are attended to—even if this means trampling over the needs of others.

Those who are properly motivated do not seek to bring others down, to get even, to get revenge, or to make others as miserable as themselves. Rather, they seek to help others grow, build them up, increase their skills and talents, teach them correct principles, encourage them, and care for them. They are quick to forgive and to focus on desired, rather than past, behaviors in their partners. They are long-suffering, patient, slow to judge, and ready to sacrifice and work for the welfare of others. They are free from pride and are not haughty, arrogant, condescending, hypocritical, contemptuous, or self-centered.

Motivation has long been recognized as a critical factor in judging a person's actions. Our courts, for example, judge people's actions not just on what they did, but on their reasons for doing what they did. The accidental taking of life, for example, is treated very differently from the intentional taking of life—even though a life is taken in both cases. This concept is so powerful that in cases involving serious criminal acts, defense lawyers will often try to convince a jury that their defendant's motives were really honorable (or at least understandable) or that the police's motives were dishonorable. They know that in determining guilt and punishment, juries are highly influenced by their perception of the defendant's motives.

As important as having the right motivation is, just having a pure motivation does *not* ensure that everything you do in your interactions with others will be correct or proper. This is a important truth, as many of the most destructive and evil acts that have been committed in history have been committed in the name of doing good. Even today, many continue to justify their wrongdoing in this same way. Those who physically abuse children when they misbehave, for example, often believe that their behavior is justified because they are "teaching" their children proper behavior.

To ensure that your interaction with others is proper, you must not only have a pure motivation, you must compare your proposed actions to sound moral and ethical standards of truth and comply with the rest of the principles on which happy, successful relationships are based.

What are some of the others reasons why it is important to have the right motivation?

"Whom Can I Teach But My Friends?"

As one ancient philosopher pointed out, we seriously consider the advice only of our friends, not our enemies. It is easy to turn away from and ignore the counsel of our foes. To have a meaningful relationship with others, we must believe that they are our friends, not our detractors. The same applies to others. When others believe that our motivation is proper, they are more likely to consider us to be their friends and to receive our love, support, and advice.

"I Cannot Hear What You Are Saying Until I Know if You Care"

This is another way of saying that we must feel good about the other person's motivation before we will open up our hearts, minds, and feelings to them. When we consider entering into a relationship, one of the first things we want to know is if the other person really cares about us or is simply using us. We may ask ourselves, "Is this person genuinely interested in my welfare, or is this person simply putting on a show?" "Does this person really care about me, or is this person using me to achieve his own selfish purposes?" and "Is this person helping me out of love, or out of a desire to make money?"

Selfishness Is Repulsive to Human Beings

As children, we were naturally repulsed by selfishness. When others refused to let us play with their toys, we cried. When our brother or sister took the biggest piece of cake or would not let us play games with them, we called them selfish brats. As adults, we continue to be repulsed by selfishness. We are disgusted when elected officials are caught taking bribes, when company executives exclude themselves from massive employee layoffs, and when spouses become consumed with their own petty needs and desires.

True Love Attracts without Compulsion

Just as we are repulsed by selfishness, we are attracted by love. True love requires the right motivation. When others sense that our love is properly motivated, they will want to be in our presence. True love does nothing through intimidation, threat, manipulation, blackmail, force, or compulsion.

"If You Are My Enemy, I Must Fight or Flee"

When others judge us as their enemy, they have two choices: stay and fight, or flee. Most people choose to flee those they consider to be dangerous or improperly motivated. Staying around not only increases the chances of being harmed, it consumes precious emotional energy with defensive posturing and staying on guard. People wisely do not want to be around those who are interested only in satisfying their own emotional impulses, fulfilling their own needs above the needs of others, and manipulating those around them to get what they want. When others cannot wait to get away from us and dread our presence, we are destroying—not building—our relationships.

THERE ARE NO LASTING, FULFILLING RELATIONSHIPS
WITHOUT PROPER MOTIVATION

Unless others want to be with you and share their lives with you out of their own free will, they will find a million ways to avoid you and shut you out of their lives (by erecting emotional barriers, keeping you at a distance, fleeing your presence, ignoring your counsel, thwarting your manipulations, and acting defensively).

Your motivation for interacting with others cannot be kept a secret forever. It will eventually be made manifest by your actions, decisions, and speech. Although it is true that you can keep your true motivation hidden from others for a time—especially under favorable circumstances (such as during dating and courtship)—it will be revealed later when you are called upon to pass through the acid tests of life (handling differences in your marriage, raising children, paying mortgages and car payments, finding and holding a job, handling disappointments and unexpected setbacks, suffering tragedies, and so forth).

SECRET 2: SERVE AND SACRIFICE
FOR YOUR PARTNER

SACRIFICE IS A willingness to work for the benefit of others, even at the expense of your own immediate comfort, pleasure, or gain. It is doing for others what they cannot do for themselves at the time it needs to be done.

When you sacrifice, you give of your time, resources, and energy to help others survive, grow, and prosper. You endure personal inconvenience, pain, and even suffering to shelter others from danger, support them through their trials, teach them correct principles, and provide them opportunities for growth and development. Sacrifice is giving up, as required, things that are important to you, but of lesser priority, to help others grow and reach their true potential.

Sacrifices can take on many forms. Some sacrifices are financial. Parents, for example, give up tens of thousands of dollars over their lifetime to raise and educate their children. This is money they could have spent on themselves for things such as boats, high-tech electronic gear, dream vacations, new clothes, fancy cars, expensive houses, costly entertainment, lawn care, dining out, maid service, and future retirement. Instead, parents buy diapers, children's cloth-ing, large quantities of food, bicycles, medical services, music lessons, mini-vans, college tuition, and weddings.

Other sacrifices are those of time. Caring fathers and mothers sacrifice their time to play with their children, read to them, take them to activities, help them with their homework, teach them, comfort them, guide them, and befriend them. Children sacrifice a portion of their time to clean their rooms, vacuum floors, put up laundry, do dishes, and help in the yard. Volunteers in churches and charities sacrifice their time to help others in need who are less fortunate.

Still other sacrifices are those of energy. Tired fathers and mothers cook meals, change diapers, bathe and dress children, fix leaky faucets, cut grass, do laundry, mop floors, arrange social activities for their children, attend to sick children, clean dishes, play catch, ride bicycles, and go swimming. Scoutmasters go on hikes, pitch tents, teach skills, supervise outdoor activities, and mentor energetic boys. Caring spouses help lighten the load of their com-panions. Friends lend each other support during difficult times.

Service and sacrifice require that you act when the needs of others are urgent. You cannot wait until it is convenient for you, until you feel like it, or until all of your own needs are met to help others. Needs exist when they exist, and sacrifice is often necessary to address those needs. You cannot be lazy or unwilling to serve and expect your relationships to work. There are no happy and enduring armchair relationships.

SECRET 3: HAVE AN EMPATHETIC HEART

EMPATHY IS THE ability to understand and see life from the mental and emo-tional perspective of another. It is the ability to understand things the way another person understands them—to see life from the eyes of another person.

Empathy is different from sympathy. Sympathy is expressing sorrow over the plight of another person. Empathy is an act of understanding and does not necessarily imply that you agree with the values and choices of the other per-son. Understanding does not necessarily imply acceptance or agreement with that which is understood.

When you practice empathy, instead of immediately judging the person's behavior, you seek to understand the other person's feelings, struggles, situa-tion, and point of view. Empathy is more than just a quick assessment of another person's current mood based on a few verbal interchanges or visual appraisals of the situation. Empathy requires a serious effort to understand the other person's life perspective. Where are they coming from and what have been through? What trials and struggles have they faced? What are their goals and dreams? What failures and successes have they experienced in trying to reach those dreams?

If you do not practice empathy, how will you know what the needs of the other person are or be sure that you are addressing their true needs? A spouse exhausted from a week of work may not need an active night out on the town, but a solid meal and a couple of hours of rest and relaxation. A person who has just experienced a major setback probably does not want a lecture on why things went wrong and how they can be corrected, but a private, personal expression of sorrow and a vote of confidence in his ability to make a comeback and ultimately succeed. If you do not meet the true needs of others, they will think that you do not care about them.

Secret 4: Possess a Sensitive Nature

Sensitivity is thoughtful, considerate responsiveness to the feelings, needs, wants, desires, and goals of others. A sensitive nature is one that is in touch with the feelings of others, that anticipates and addresses their emotional needs, and that treats their feelings with respect, sensitivity, and consideration.

Unfortunately, the term *sensitive* is often associated with the term *oversensitive*, which is used to label someone who is emotionally weak, fragile, easily offended, vulnerable, or lacking in self-esteem. A sensitive person is *not* a person who is weak or easily offended, but a person who tunes into and cares about the needs and feelings of others. Sensitivity is not a sign of weakness or vulnerability, but a sign of maturity and strength. It is an act of caring, not the act of feeling sorry for yourself.

To acquire a sensitive nature, develop the following habits:

Think about the Consequences Your Words and Actions Have on Others

Be considerate in your words and actions and anticipate how others might respond to them. For example, avoid teasing others on highly sensitive issues. When your spouse goes to bed before you do, talk softly, close doors quietly, turn down the television, and get into bed gently.

Be Reluctant to Hurt the Feelings of Others

Avoid making fun of someone else's appearance. Avoid embarrassing others in public. Do not deliberately or maliciously try to make others feel bad or inferior. Avoid resorting to abusive speech, threatening body language, or hateful stares. Do not use others as the butt of your jokes. Do not continuously point out the weaknesses of others or blow those weaknesses out of proportion. If you anticipate that others may misunderstand what you are about to say, try to approach things in another way to avoid misunderstandings. Even when you must confront others with cold, hard facts, do so in a calm, loving, and respectful way.

Stay in Touch with the Feelings and Emotions of Others

Do not wait until others have collapsed or have been overwhelmed by their emotions before you realize that others are in emotional need. Rather, practice empathy. Monitor the speech, body language, and facial expressions of others to better understand their emotions and their needs. Develop an ability to "read" the emotions of your partner. Address not only outward emotional needs, but hidden ones also.

Apologize and Make Amends When You Have Wronged Others

Do not try to deny, defend, rationalize, or justify yourself when you have offended others or hurt their feelings through callousness or insensitivity. Rather, quickly apologize, make restitution, and give special attention to those you have wronged. When others take offense where none was intended, express sorrow for the misunderstanding and avoid similar actions in the future. Seek to maintain good feelings in the relationship. Accept the responsibility to help restore the injured emotions of others when you have wronged them.

Respect the Time of Others

Be careful not to make others wait unnecessarily. Do not forget about others when you are preoccupied in social situations. Plan so that you do not unnecessarily delay others, interrupt others, arrive late at your commitments, or keep others awake at bedtime. Choose appropriate times to engage in decision-making discussions and be focused and attentive when you are engaged in important discussions.

Anticipate and Manage Times of Special Need

Send "get well" cards, write home regularly, give extra attention to family members who are ill or who have special needs, celebrate birthdays, recognize achievements, and give extra love and support during times of trial.

Ensure that everyone is treated fairly and given attention. Go out of your way to make sure that those who are more reserved or shy feel a part of the group and have the opportunity and encouragement to participant in group activities. Do not focus your attention exclusively or dominantly on those who are the most outgoing, interesting, beautiful, handsome, or fun.

Honor Even the Little Requests, if Possible

Honor the little requests of others, as long as they do not violate your own personal values or ethical code. Your children, for example, may want their sandwiches sliced in triangles instead of in rectangles. Your wife may want the silverware drawer organized a certain way. Fathers want their children to pay attention and avoid teasing each other during important family discussions.

Be Considerate of the Fatigue Cycles and Energy Levels of Others

Do not, for example, bring up emotionally disturbing subjects at bedtime or dump difficult problems on others when they walk in the door from a hard day at work. When others are fatigued, recognize their need for recovery and relaxation. Work out mutually agreed-upon times to discuss problems. Express regular appreciation to others for working on your behalf and do things to help them recover, such as provide food, relaxation, and a change of pace.

Secret 5: Manifest a Stable Emotional Disposition

Just as engineers cannot build magnificent skyscrapers on physically unstable earth, you cannot build happy, lasting, successful relationships on emotional volatility or instability.

A stable emotional disposition is one that is steady, in control, reliable, constant, and dependable. It is the opposite of a disposition that is volatile, fluctuating, moody, insecure, unpredictable, out of control, or that requires others to "walk on glass."

To be emotionally stable, you must be in control of your emotions. If Dark Emotions are free to control your speech and your actions, you will be driven by fear, anger, jealousy, selfishness, hatred, frustration, revenge, depression, lust, greed, and other destructive and volatile emotions. You will be emotionally unstable. You will be unable to provide others a stable emotional disposition with which to interact because you yourself will be emotionally volatile and unpredictable.

Emotional stability requires a stable and predictable emotional disposition. You cannot be manic one day, a holy terror the next, and a mild-mannered Clark Kent the next. You cannot compliment others and tell them how terrific they are in the morning and then yell and scream at them in the afternoon. You cannot be fun to be with as long as things are going well and be irritable, sour-faced, or mean when they are not. You cannot talk with others on the telephone with politeness, kindness, and sensitivity and then hang up and verbally tear into those around you. If you require others to walk through emotional minefields when they are in your presence, if you are emotionally unpredictable in your speech and behavior, or if you use others as emotional punching bags, they will lose confidence in you, question your values, and cease to have good feelings about you.

Those who are emotionally stable experience mood swings like everyone else, but they discipline and channel the expression of their emotions in safe ways so that they continue to treat others with respect, courtesy, and sensitivity, even as their moods change from moment to moment and day to day. The emotionally stable value emotional constancy and the benefits it brings to a relationship more than they value the satisfying of unrestrained emotional impulses. They know that they cannot jerk others around with wild mood swings, explosive emotional reactions, and on-again, off-again emotional reactions and then expect to enjoy loving, emotionally intimate relationships.

SECRET 6: HAVE AN HONEST, TRUSTWORTHY CHARACTER

AN HONEST, TRUSTWORTHY character is one that possesses integrity, keeps its word, is true and faithful to vows and promises, and does not deceive, lie, steal, or cheat.

Honesty and trust are important in your relationships for many reasons. For one thing, if others cannot believe what you say, then how will they know when you are speaking the truth and when you are lying? If you give them a compliment, how will they know that you are not simply trying to manipulate them? If you tell them that you love them, how will they know you really mean it? If you say you are sorry, how will they know that your feelings are genuine and sincere?

Whenever others have reason to question your motives, your relationship is damaged. When others find out that the "pure" motives you purport to have are really deceitful, self-serving manipulations to get the things you want, they will be repulsed and offended. Lying, cheating, stealing, and dishonesty are almost always used to cover up wrongful actions and improper motivations.

When emotional trust has been violated, it will not heal overnight. The restoration of emotional trust takes a long time, especially if its violation has been severe and long-term. It can only be restored if the violator shows steady and complete emotional honesty and integrity over a sufficient period of time. You cannot lie, cheat, use, and manipulate others in relationships and then expect to restore their trust in you by giving them a bouquet of flowers or by simply making an apology, no matter how sincere. You must prove, through proper actions over time, that you have truly changed and have incorporated this character attribute into your value system.

SECRET 7: MAINTAIN A REASONABLE SET OF EXPECTATIONS

RELATIONSHIPS OFTEN go awry because one or both parties have unreasonable expectations of the other. For example, one person may expect the other to solve all their problems, remove all stress from their life, or keep their marriage on the same romantic high they experienced during courtship. Newlyweds may expect to enjoy the same high standard of living that they enjoyed while living with their parents (who worked a lifetime to get where they are). Couples may expect their spouse to provide, cater, and pamper their every need, as if they were still a child and their spouse were their father or mother. Certainly there are a million ways for individuals in relationships to have unreasonable expectations of each other.

Reasonable expectations are expectations that are appropriate for the age and maturity level of others, that challenge others to grow but do not expect them to run faster than they have strength, that expect others to treat everyone with basic respect and human dignity, that hold others responsible for their own lives and actions, and that take into account (when making requests) all of the other demands and responsibilities that the other person is trying to faithfully execute.

This definition is best illustrated with examples of both reasonable and unreasonable expectations. The following are examples of *unreasonable* expectations in relationships:

DO NOT EXPECT OTHERS TO PROVIDE YOU A LIFE FREE OF OPPOSITION, STRESS, AND CHALLENGE

By nature, life is full of opposition, stress, and challenge. When properly approached, such challenges can motivate and accelerate personal growth. Opposition gives you the opportunity to test your values and your character, acquire valuable experience, develop new skills and talents, and expand your capacity to empathize, understand, and help others. Rather than expecting life to be free of opposition, stress, and challenge, approach your challenges vigorously with a focus toward growth, experience, learning, and service. Do not expect others to remove you from all opposition, stress, and challenges. If they did, they would be doing you more harm then good.

DO NOT EXPECT OTHERS TO SOLVE ALL YOUR PROBLEMS

Others can empathize with your problems and lend support as they have opportunity and are capable, but the responsibility for dealing with your problems is yours. Although others may lend you help and assistance, do not expect others to rescue you from your problems, assume responsibility for your problems, take over your problems, or get rid of your problems. Each of us must grow in our own capacity and skill to deal with life's problems, stresses, and challenges. That growth cannot occur unless we are active participants in solving our problems. Do not expect others to be knights in shining armor who will come down and rescue you from all of your troubles.

Do Not Expect to Achieve Your Goals Too Quickly or Without Sustained Sweat and Sacrifice

The achievement of worthy goals requires persistence, sustained effort, and personal sacrifice. Getting a college education, mastering a musical instrument, learning mathematics, overcoming a character flaw, writing a book, learning a foreign language, raising children, paying off a mortgage, and saving for retirement all require sustained and disciplined effort over a long period of time. Such goals are not attained with an all-out, showy burst of effort. Rather, they require disciplined, persistent effort to achieve.

Do Not Expect Your Marriage to be Wildly Romantic at All Times

Although keeping romance alive and well in a marriage is important, do not expect your marriage to stay on the same emotional high that you enjoyed during courtship. Courtship is a sheltered time when couples make special efforts to be on their best behavior for a few hours at a time. Courtship activities are fun and relaxed, whereas real life is full of stress, hardship, and responsibility. While keeping the romance alive in your marriage is important, love, commitment, trust, empathy, sacrifice, sensitivity, honesty, mutual respect, unselfishness, and maturity are essential for its survival.

Do Not Expect Others to Have the Same Personality as Yourself

Too often we view things that are different from ourselves or our viewpoint as "bad." We may, for example, view those who have differing personalities or interests as "weird" or "strange." In reality, living in a world that contains people with different personalities is a plus, not a negative. Different personalities provide stimulation and variety in thought, conversation, and interaction. Wise parents do not try to raise their children to have the same personality; rather, they strive to raise their children to have the same set of core values and principles. We are not all striving to achieve the same personality. Common values, not common personalities, bind individuals, families, and societies together. Do not expect your spouse, your children, or others to have the same personality as yourself.

Do Not Expect Others to Achieve Goals in Predetermined, Rigid Ways

Unless certain behaviors are crucial to obtaining a desired outcome, focus on the accomplishment, not on one particular way of achieving that accomplishment. For example, there are many legitimate ways of earning a living, so do not expect your son or daughter to become a doctor, just because you are a doctor. If you assign your children to clean up the kitchen within an hour, do not become angry if they laugh and play as they do so, as long as the kitchen is cleaned up in an hour. By allowing others to determine how they will achieve required outcomes (after making suggestions, if you desire), you will increase their self-confidence, promote self-sufficiency, and increase their problem-solving ability. You might even be surprised when they come up with a new or better way of achieving the same goal faster or more efficiently. Creativity, self-reliance, and self-confidence do not prosper in a harsh, dictatorial atmosphere.

Do Not Expect Others to Run Faster Than They Have Strength

Be considerate of the time and energy of others. If your spouse puts in long hours at work on a particular project, do not expect him or her to begin that wallpapering project you are anxious to start. If your partner works all day and drives your children around to activities all evening, do not expect him or her to also do the cooking, the dishes, and the laundry. If your children are actively working on overcoming a major problem, do not demand that they manifest perfection in every other aspect of their life. In short, if others are already running at peak capacity, do not expect them to fulfill even more demands on their time and energy. To do so is inconsiderate, insensitive, and uncaring and shows a lack of gratitude for what the other person is accomplishing.

Do Not Expect to Live a Higher Standard of Living Than You Can Realistically Support

Trying to maintain a higher standard of living than you can realistically support is dangerous to relationships as well as to your financial health. Financial problems and financial stress has led many marriages to break up. Dealing with the normal financial ups and downs of life is difficult enough. Do not throw your relationship into the trauma room of financial irresponsibility.

Do Not Expect Children to Be Little Adults

Children are still developing mentally, socially, emotionally, and intellectually. Do not expect children to exhibit adult maturity, adult problem-solving capability, or adult emotional capacity. For example, do not expect two-year-olds to understand and internalize concepts such as neatness and picking up their toys unprompted after they finish playing. Do not expect four-year-olds to sit perfectly still for an hour or more on a hard church bench. Do not expect eight-year-olds to remember long lists of weekly chores without verbal reminders or written check sheets. Do not expect children to have the emotional capacity to handle videos, television, and movies meant for older audiences.

Having looked at some examples of unreasonable expectations, let us now consider some examples of reasonable expectations:

Expect Others to Treat You with Respect and to Interact with You in Nonviolent and Nonabusive Ways

Tolerance does *not* extend to tolerance of abuse in any of its forms, nor does it extend to tolerating demeaning, ridiculing, mocking, or destructive language or behavior. You do not have to participate in or be the victim of destructive interaction. If others are verbally venting their anger and hostility, you may have to temporarily leave the room or the house to let them cool off. In more serious cases, when the other person's behavior is severe and persistent and they are unwilling to make serious changes, it may mean restricting or ending the relationship. Others do *not* have the right to abuse you, to treat you as dirt, or to treat you as an inferior or worthless human being.

EXPECT OTHERS TO ATTEND TO THEIR RESPONSIBILITIES

Others have responsibilities to which they should attend. They cannot expect you to drop whatever you are doing to take over their responsibilities whenever they are tired, discouraged, or simply do not feel like working. Part of learning responsibility is learning to do the things that need to be done *when* they should be done, even when it is hard or inconvenient.

This does not mean that you cannot or should not lend support to others when they shoulder heavy responsibilities. But supportiveness does not mean offering others a blank check for unlimited time and energy or becoming someone else's personal slave. You have important responsibilities to carry out too. If you consistently and predictably step in and rescue other people every time they are irresponsible, you are doing them a serious disfavor.

EXPECT OTHERS TO UTILIZE THEIR TIME AND ENERGY WISELY TO ACCOMPLISH THEIR GOALS

Those who have a pattern of laziness or procrastination often put off responsibilities until they escalate into crises. They then become angry when others do not drop what they are doing to help them out. Although there will always be times when unanticipated and unexpected events occur that require the help of others, those who consistently operate in this mode are not growing in character and responsibility. Others cannot waste their time, procrastinate, and indulge in excess leisure activity and then expect you to suddenly rush in to help them meet a deadline or complete an urgent task. Expect others to organize their lives, discipline themselves, plan activities, and make proper preparations so that they are not constantly operating in crisis mode and unnecessarily impacting your life.

EXPECT OTHERS TO HONOR AND RESPECT YOUR PERSONAL PRIVACY

Some people mistakenly believe that, in a relationship, they have the right to know every thought, feeling, and emotion that their companion is feeling, moment by moment. If their partner, upon request, refuses to disclose what they are feeling, they become offended or angry. This, of course, is wrong. To grow mentally and emotionally, people must be given sufficient privacy and personal space to work out their emotions, solve their problems, and grow in self-reliance. What would happen to a plant if you pulled it out of the ground every few minutes to see how the roots were doing?

Others should respect your right *not* to disclose your thoughts or feelings at a particular moment. There are many reasons you may legitimately choose not to do so. You may not trust the other person with your thoughts and feelings. You may be struggling to properly channel your Dark Emotions (such as anger or hostility) that are better left unexpressed during the heat of emotion. The other person may not be prepared to understand your feelings and would simply be confused or hurt by them. Or you may simply need more time to sort through your emotions so that you can look at the situation more objectively.

EXPECT YOUR CHILDREN TO GROW IN RESPONSIBILITY, ACCOUNTABILITY, AND MATURITY

As children grow up, they should be given increasing responsibility in accordance with their age and maturity level. Infants and very young children are innocent and cannot be held morally accountable for their actions. As children grow up, they should be taught how to carry out their responsibilities and be held accountable for completing their assigned duties. If they complete their assigned tasks faithfully, they should be given appropriate praise, reward, and recognition. When they do not, they should receive proper instruction and a reasonable, nonabusive consequence. In this way, children will learn that fulfilling responsibility is important and is followed by consequences that vary depending on their actions.

EXPECT YOUR CHILDREN TO TREAT EACH OTHER WITH LOVE AND RESPECT

Parents do not have to accept constant quarreling, fighting, arguing, and bickering among their offspring. Children should be taught to interact in ways that build others up, not tear them down. They should be taught that disrespectful actions, contention, quarreling, and saying things that tear others down are unacceptable and will not be tolerated and that they should treat each other with love, respect, and consideration. Higher levels of family peace and harmony are possible if correct principles are taught, appropriate standards are established and enforced, and opportunities to serve each other are discovered and carried out.

Reasonable expectations require sensitivity, understanding, love, and compassion. Unreasonable expectations set up goals or standards of behavior that are inappropriate, unrealistic, or impossible to achieve and lead to frustration, anger, discouragement, and loss of self-esteem.

SECRET 8: SHOW A DEEP RESPECT FOR AGENCY

LIFE REQUIRES THAT you make choices. Some choices are major, such as what values you will adopt, what occupation you will pursue, what goals you will undertake, who you will marry, where you will live, and whether you will avoid life-destroying behaviors and influences. Other choices are minor, such as what clothes you will wear, what you will eat for dinner, and when you will mow the lawn.

A deep respect for agency is the recognition that all adult human beings have the ultimate right to choose, without force or coercion, their beliefs, values, and actions.

This freedom to choose is essential to your growth and development. Through making decisions and experiencing their consequences, you learn firsthand what is good and bad. Through making decisions, you increase your self-confidence, become more self-reliant, and decrease your dependency on others for guidance and solutions to your problems. Through making decisions, you manifest and prove your character, your values, and your level of maturity—both to yourself and to others.

Of course, just because you are free to make your own decisions does not mean that you are free to select the consequences of your decisions. You may choose to take mind-altering drugs, but you cannot choose to avoid the physical addiction, the loss of self-determination, and the damage to your body and brain that ultimately follows. You may choose to be self-centered, proud, arrogant, insensitive, and egotistical, but you cannot choose to prevent the loss of friends, the loneliness, the emptiness, and the social isolation that your choice incurs. You may choose to verbally and emotionally abuse your spouse and children, but you cannot choose to escape the devastation, the broken trust, and the loss of your loved ones that follow your behavior. Although you have the freedom to make your own decisions, you do not have the freedom to choose the physical, social, intellectual, emotional, and spiritual consequences that follow those decisions.

When you take away the ability of others to exercise choices through force, coercion, domination, intimidation, blackmail, threat, or improper use of authority, you stymie their growth, incur their resentment, and provoke their hostility. You cannot force others to internalize values—even good values. Values are internalized only when an individual chooses to adopt and live by those values free of force or coercion.

Happy relationships are based on an attraction that is voluntary, not forced. Those who use intimidation, physical force, threats, coercion, blackmail, domination, anger, emotional outbursts, pressure, or manipulation to get their way will repulse others, not attract them. These individuals may get their way for a time, but their apparent gains are hollow and short-lived. The resentment, anger, and repulsion experienced by those they force will further disintegrate their relationship.

Although it is desirable to try to influence others to achieve worthy goals and build solid characters, you must do so through persuasion, example, love, kindness, gentleness, patience, long-suffering, encouragement, suggestion, and empathy. While you can teach correct principles, establish reasonable rules and consequences that are appropriate to the age and maturity level of those involved, and point out the consequences that follow wrong choices, after all is said and done, you must finally allow others to learn for themselves the consequences of their choices—within the bounds of common sense, parental responsibility, and capability (especially in the case of children).

SECRET 9: HAVE A SUPPORTIVE DISPOSITION

LIFE IS NO picnic. From time to time, we all struggle with heavy burdens, unrelenting stress, serious setbacks, disappointments, and feelings of inadequacy and despair. Even day-to-day living can require unusual emotional strength and courage to face difficult challenges, weighty responsibilities, and near impossible expectations. Regardless of our station in life, we all need the emotional support of others repeatedly throughout our lives.

A supportive disposition is one that builds and lifts others up in conversation and deed, that stimulates growth, and that gives extra love and support during times of trial and opposition.

You support others when you address their true needs, express confidence in their ability to achieve worthy goals, work alongside others to lighten their load, point out the good they do, focus on their strengths, give them the benefit of the doubt, assume good motives on their part, speak favorably of them when they are not around, help them to discover their true strengths and talents, praise them, empathize with them, show concern for them, express your appreciation for the good things they do, encourage them, point out creative alternatives and solutions, and stand by them in times of difficulty or special need.

Supportiveness is acting on the answers to questions such as, What can I do to lighten the burdens this person is carrying? What can I do or say to build this person up? How can I help this person feel encouragement, hope, and greater self-confidence? and How can I show this person that I really care?

EMOTIONAL BUILDERS VERSUS EMOTIONAL DESTROYERS

Emotional support exists on a continuum. At one end of the continuum are Emotional Builders. Emotional Builders have a positive, energy-inducing emotional disposition that strengthens, energizes, and builds others up. At the other end of the continuum are Emotional Destroyers. Emotional Destroyers have an energy-consuming emotional disposition that tears others down, provokes Dark Emotions, and drains others of their energies.

To determine where you are on the supportiveness continuum, ask yourself if your emotional demeanor:

- Inspires Happy Emotions or attracts Dark Emotions.
- Lifts others or depresses them.
- Enlightens and enlarges the minds and understanding of others or darkens their minds and causes confusion.
- Inspires the best in others or brings out their worst.
- Gives others renewed hope or snuffs out what little hope they may have had.
- Energizes others or saps their energy.
- Attracts others to our presence or repulses others and burdens them down with heavy emotions.

To enjoy emotionally fulfilling relationships, you must be an Emotional Builder. You cannot treat your loved ones with disdain or contempt or act as if they are stupid, ignorant, or foolish and then expect them to feel emotionally close to you. You cannot treat others as a burden, an irritation, or a bother and then expect them to be your friend. You cannot accuse others, find fault with them, and blame them for every wrong you experience and then expect them to be attracted to your presence. Rather, you must learn to postpone judgment, to speak uplifting words, to build, edify, and strengthen others in all you do and to handle differences with love and kindness. In short, you must learn to be a joy to be around.

Secret 10: Be Obsessed with Improving Yourself, Not Your Mate

After a fight or an argument, we sometimes find ourselves thinking about how our relationship would improve if only the other person would change his or her behavior:

- "If only my husband would be more sensitive and romantic."
- "If only my wife would let me talk more when we are socializing with our friends."
- "If only my parents would stop flying off the handle every time I tell them what I want to do."
- "If only my son would be more responsible and take care of the yard without my having to nag at him."
- "If only my in-laws would stop treating me like a child."

If only the other person would change, then we could feel close to them, get along with them, and really move forward in our relationship with them.

A focus on self-improvement is having a greater concern about overcoming your own character flaws and weaknesses than on making sure others overcome theirs. It is working to improve your own character, regardless of whether others choose to improve theirs and regardless of whether they treat you maturely.

Although relationships will certainly improve when any of its participants act more maturely, waiting for others to change before we change stymies our growth and stalemates our relationships. Happy relationships are enjoyed by those who focus on correcting their own deficiencies and character, not on fixing the supposed "defects" of their partner. This holds true even when only one person in the relationship has such a focus, although the level of happiness in the relationship will naturally be less.

Why Self-Improvement Works

At times it might seem like the best way to improve a relationship is to focus on the perceived or real imperfections of others, but the more sure way to better your relationships is to improve yourself. This is true for the following reasons:

You Will Be More Lovable and More Capable of Loving

When you improve yourself, your own character will grow and improve. As a result, you will have more to offer and bring to the relationship. For example, you will be more capable of looking after the emotional needs of the other person because *you* yourself will be more empathic, sensitive, honest, supportive, sacrificing, and respectful. Not only will you be more lovable, you will be more capable of loving. As others interact with your better character, they will be more strongly attracted to you and your relationship will improve.

Your Motivation Will Be Perceived More Positively

When others see that you are focused on self-improvement, they will be less likely to judge your motivation—and therefore your words and actions—negatively. Before others will trust you and open up their lives to you, they must believe that your motivation is right. If they believe that your motivation is wrong, they will put up defenses and tune you out.

Your Example Will Influence Others to Grow

When others see that you are striving to improve your own character, they will feel a drawing force to improve their own character as well. Role modeling is a powerful way of influencing human behavior, as is testified by its heavy use in television commercials and printed advertisements. Although others may choose to ignore this influence, it will nevertheless be there. Consistent acts of love, consideration, and kindness by one party in a relationship often inspire similar responses in the other party.

Why Focusing on the Faults of Others Doesn't Work

When you focus on the faults of others or when you insist that others change before you will change, you will damage your relationship for the following reasons:

OTHERS WILL SEE YOU AS ATTACKING
THEIR EGO OR CHARACTER

When you criticize others, they may feel that their character or ego is under attack, especially if you criticize them publicly or in the heat of emotion. They will see you as judging, criticizing, and lashing out at them. When others perceive that your motivation is to hurt them, they are more likely to treat you as their enemy, close their minds to your advice, and take defensive or retaliatory actions.

OTHERS WILL SEE YOU AS HYPOCRITICAL

None of us are perfect. We all make mistakes and have imperfections. When your focus is on criticizing or blaming others for your ills, they will likely view you as a hypocrite. "Who are you to judge me?" "What a hypocrite you are to be talking to me about _____ when you yourself do _____." "What right do you have to criticize me when you do things that are far more serious than _____." When others see you as a self-appointed, hypocritical judge, their defenses, contempt, and anger will sharply rise.

OTHERS WILL SEE YOU AS AVOIDING RESPONSIBILITY
FOR YOUR OWN WEAKNESSES

When you focus on the other person as the cause of stagnation or failure in a relationship, you psychologically wash your hands of your own responsibility to improve. No longer do you have to struggle with the difficult task of overcoming your own weaknesses and character deficiencies. By blaming others, you can sit back, relax, and feel free of guilt for not improving yourself.

YOU WILL SUFFER THE CONSEQUENCES OF
DESTRUCTIVE EMOTIONAL EXCHANGES

A disposition to confront others with their faults leads to emotional arguments in which bitter accusations, defensiveness, one-upmanship, ego attacks, misrepresentations, exaggerations, and shouting quickly take over. This disintegration occurs even more quickly when you have a history of finding fault in others and when others carry a great deal of pent-up anger, resentment, and frustration for your fault-finding disposition. No one escapes the aftermath of such destructive emotional exchanges without incurring painful emotional wounds and scars.

How silly it is for us to think that we can improve our lives and our relationships by spending our time and energy trumpeting the faults and weaknesses of others. Our time and energy in this life are limited. When we waste these precious resources by dwelling on the weaknesses of others or by pulling others down, we will have little time or energy left to improve our own character. Overcoming our own faults and weaknesses and internalizing crucial values requires our full devotion. We cannot afford to waste our life in activity that not only will drag others down, but stunt our own personal progress.

THOUGHTS TO PONDER

- In the long run, what is more important to happy relationships: romantic prowess or a good character? Can a person who has a good character also be romantic? Can a person who is romantic lack good character?

- Does the Law of Harvest (you reap what you sow) apply to relationships? Can a person violate the principles on which happy relationships are based and then expect to have happy relationships? Why do some people try anyway?

- Can excellent communication skills in a relationship compensate for poor character? Can a person with poor character simply learn a few romantic tricks or emotional slights of hand and then expect to have happy, enduring relationships?

- Why is it critical to have a pure motivation in interacting with your partner? Are others better able to forgive our mistakes and tolerate our weaknesses if they know that our overall motivation is to help them grow, be successful, and achieve their greatest potential? Can you use your partner for your own selfish purposes and then expect your partner to feel close to you or good about you?

- Are you willing to make sacrifices and be inconvenienced for your partner? Can you be lazy about helping your companion (be stuck to your bed, chair, computer, or TV) and then expect your companion to feel close to you?

- Is it more important to treat others the way *you* think they should be treated or the way *they* want to be treated? Do people ever give gifts *they* want to receive rather than gifts *others* want to receive? Is empathy quick to judge, or is it quick to postpone judgment and gather additional information to understand a situation from the other person's point of view? Does empathy require more than just an understanding of the facts at hand?

- What is the difference between sensitivity, oversensitivity, and hypersensitivity (in answering this question, consider traits such as the propensity to take offense, to be highly defensive, and to wrongly conclude that others are on the attack)? Is sensitivity one of the ways we show thoughtfulness and respect for others?

- Can wild mood swings or other manifestations of emotional instability be justified or deemed desirable on the basis of making relationships more playful, suspenseful, and exciting? What is the difference between emotional variation that is normal and moods swings that are damaging or even destructive to a relationship? (Hint: Consider whether the mood swing leads to behavior that violates emotional trust, sensitivity, agency, and the other principles on which happy relationships are based?)

- Movies have been made about busy fathers or mothers who, for one reason or another, do not keep their promises to their children (to show up at important events, to go on special trips, to be there at performances, and so forth). Can our character be measured in part by how well we keep our promises and by how well we do what we say we will do? What happens to a relationship when we make apologies, promise to take specific actions, and then fail to carry out our promises? Are little promises just as important as big ones? If not, then how can others be expected to distinguish between the two? Why is infidelity such a serious violation of trust? Are mere apologies sufficient to make up for serious violations of trust?

- In general, do today's popular movies lead us to have reasonable expectations about sex, romance, marriage, and relationships? Do our expectations about these things change as we grow older? Should you expect your spouse to assume the role that your mother or father fulfilled when you were growing up? Is it reasonable to expect mutual respect, politeness, and courtesy in all your relationships?

- Are you violating the agency of others when you use emotional blackmail (serious threats, intimidations, strong coercion, accusations, emotional tantrums, and so forth) to get them to comply with your desires?

- Are you an Emotional Builder or an Emotional Destroyer? Does your partner agree? Is it important for your partner to feel emotionally attracted to you? If so, can that attraction be forced or must it be earned?

- Can people who have a focus on self-improvement be held down for long in life, or do they have a bright future, regardless of their present circumstances? Would you rather marry someone who is constantly working to improve their character, intelligence, wisdom, and skills, or someone who is content to get by in life with as little effort as possible? Which person are you? Can you be highly defensive and then claim that you have a focus on self-improvement?

ACTIVITIES FOR SELF-IMPROVEMENT

1. Ask your partner the following question (verbally or written on a sheet of paper): "If you could change one thing about the way I handle my emotions, what would it be?" (If you do this in person, avoid the urge to defend, justify, explain, or take offense at what your partner says.) Then ask, "How does the way I act in these situations make you feel?" and "How does this affect your life?" Follow up by making any appropriate improvements in your character. Repeat this activity every few months.

2. Write down your expectations of your partner. Have your partner do the same for you. Jointly discuss which expectations are reasonable, which are unreasonable, and which would be better met through some other means (review pages 139 through 146 if necessary).

3. During the day, after each interaction with your partner, ask yourself, "Did I uplift and strengthen my partner or emotionally dampen and discourage my partner?" "What did I say or do to uplift my partner?" and "What did I say or do to discourage or depress my partner?" Review the criteria for Emotional Builders and Emotional Destroyers on page 148. Where do you fall on the continuum? Where would you like to fall on the continuum? What are you going to change to get there? How much emotional support do you provide your partner?

4. Create a list of the little and big sacrifices you recently made for your partner. How big is your list? Does it need to be larger? Does it need to have more meaningful entries? Do you detect your partner's needs and fulfill them even before your partner expresses them? Are you willing to "sacrifice" a comfortable, long-held emotional weakness for your partner?

5. Throughout the day, before interacting with your partner, ask yourself, "What is my motivation for interacting with my partner? Am I seeking to lift, to build, and to help my partner grow, achieve success, and find fulfillment, or am I seeking to fulfill my own self-interests?"

6. Analyze several recent contentious interactions to determine if you jumped to conclusions (were quick to pass judgment rather than postpone judgment and gather additional insight). How much time did you spend listening and asking questions to understand

where others were coming from, how they viewed the situation, what they were struggling with, and what they were feeling?

7. Ask your companion to describe what you have done lately to show respect, sensitivity, and thoughtfulness. Then ask what else you could do to further demonstrate these character attributes.

8. Copy Appendix B, or take a blank sheet of paper and turn it sideways (so the long side is horizontal). Draw a horizontal line across the middle of the page and label this line "time." Draw a vertical line close to the left edge of the paper and label this line "mood." From the point where the two lines intersect, create a three-point scale on the vertical line going *both* directions (up from the point of intersection and down from the point of intersection). Label the bottom part of the vertical scale "negative mood" and the positive part of the vertical scale "positive mood." Attach the descriptors "mild," "strong," and "very strong" on the corresponding points on each vertical scale, with "mild" closest to the point of intersection.

Using this scale, ask your partner to plot your mood changes as they occur over a period of time (one or more days). Every time your emotional mood shifts, your partner will plot a new point a little to the right on the page corresponding to one of seven vertical positions (very strong negative mood, strong negative mood, mild negative mood, neutral mood [plotted on the horizontal line itself], mild positive mood, strong positive mood, or very strong positive mood). After the period of time is over, connect all the plotted points from left to right, starting at the point of intersection on the left. The result is a graph of your mood changes over time.

By analyzing this graph, you can reach some tentative conclusions about your emotional stability and volatility. First, how many times did your mood change (how many total points were on the graph)? Second, what kind of pattern did the graph form? If the line graph of your mood changes stayed mainly above the horizontal axis, then your partner likely perceives you as an emotionally stable and positive person. If your graph stayed mainly below the horizontal line, your partner likely views you as an emotionally stable but negative person. If your graph zigzagged above and below the line, but stayed fairly close to the horizontal axis, then your partner likely perceives you as emotionally moody, but not to an extreme. If your graph zigzagged wildly above and below the line and often reached the extremes (very strong positive or negative moods), then your partner likely perceives you as an emotionally unstable and volatile individual. This is the worst pattern to have. Of course, variations of the above patterns are also possible. Repeat this assessment of your emotional stability periodically and take action, if indicated, to become more emotionally stable.

9. Ask your partner to write down all of the promises you failed to keep and how it affected your partner and your partner's feelings toward you.

10. If you find yourself criticizing your companion, remind yourself, "I should be more concerned about overcoming my own character flaws and weaknesses than on making sure my partner overcomes his [or hers]."

CHAPTER 8

THE FIVE GREAT DESTROYERS OF RELATIONSHIPS

Relationships can take years to build,
but only moments to destroy

Unmanaged Dark Emotions in any form can damage a relationship. Nevertheless, some unmanaged Dark Emotions are more destructive to relationships than others. Unrestrained rage, for example, is far more destructive than minor impatience. Because some forms of unrestrained Dark Emotions can bring a relationship down quickly and completely, they must be carefully avoided by anyone seeking happy, fulfilling, and enduring relationships. The following are five, all-time great destroyers of relationships.

DESTROYER 1: SELFISHNESS

SELFISHNESS IS AN overwhelming, unbalanced, disproportionate focus on self. (Notice that this definition of selfishness is *not* "attending to one's own needs" or "caring about oneself." The whole heart of emotional self-reliance and emotional self-management is learning to anticipate and look after the needs of both yourself and others. For example, is it selfish to get an education so that you can make a living? The critical part of this definition has to do with achieving a proper balance between the two.)

Selfishness destroys relationships because it violates so many of the fundamental principles on which happy relationships are based. The motivation of the selfish is exactly the opposite of a proper motivation. Selfish individuals do not make significant sacrifices to help others grow, develop their talents, or achieve worthy goals (unless, of course, they think they will directly gain from such sacrifices). They give little thought or attention to the needs and feelings of others (except when they are trying to manipulate or use them), and thus they do not practice true empathy or sensitivity.

Selfish individuals are impulsive and unstable because they demand instant gratification of their needs, wants, and desires. They bend their actions and values to conform to whatever will help them get the object of their desire. They feel threatened when they perceive that their needs might not be met as quickly as they expect. They use deceit, dishonesty, and manipulation to justify their immature behavior, gratify their impulses, and obtain what they are after (case in point: a partner who is unfaithful).

Selfish individuals expect others to center their lives on meeting *their* needs and whims—no matter how trivial or jaded. They disregard or trample over the agency of others and view others simply as objects to be manipulated. They are grossly insensitive or apathetic toward the needs of their partner. They are more concerned with how much emotional support they receive than with how much emotional support they give. They care more about their own passions than about the feelings of others and the commitments and obligations they have to others. Finally, they rarely practice introspection and deny responsibility for self-improvement by focusing on the faults of others and blaming them when things go wrong.

We cannot be selfish and expect our relationships to flourish. Relationships do not exist for our benefit alone. Those who parasitically milk a relationship for all it is worth, boldly demand more, and then expect their relationship to grow and prosper can instead watch their relationship wither and die.

Destroyer 2: An Accusing or Contemptuous Tongue

Another surefire way to destroy relationships is to have an accusing or contemptuous tongue.

Those who have an accusing tongue are quick to place blame, find fault, and accuse others of being responsible for anything and everything that makes them unhappy in life. They are quick to attribute evil motives, make scathing pronouncements, jump to conclusions, trumpet minor weaknesses, and attack character.

Most participants in relationships occasionally exchange minor accusations, but those who have an accusing tongue characteristically and reflexively blame others for anything and everything that goes wrong in their lives—and they do so with a vengeance. The quickness, intensity, and tenacity with which they accuse others, along with the intense emotion that accompanies their accusations, set them apart as accusers.

Those who have a contemptuous tongue view their partner with undisguised contempt, strong disapproval, or disgust. They demean their partner in word, body language, and gestures and treat their partner with derision, ridicule, mockery, and disdain, as someone who is stupid, ignorant, disgusting, worthless, unworthy of attention, or less than a human being.

As with selfishness, those who have an accusing or contemptuous tongue violate the fundamental principles on which happy, fulfilling relationships are based. Their motivation, emotional stability, empathy, and sensitivity are inherently suspect. They charge the emotional atmosphere with unrealistic expectations, focus on failures rather than on successes, and hold others up to standards of absolute perfection. They make themselves judge, jury, and lynching party for even the most minor of infractions. They attack character, destroy self-confidence, damage self-esteem, and dim prospects for achieving worthy goals. No wonder we often refer to such individuals as shrews or devils.

Destroyer 3: Pride and Ego

By PRIDE AND ego, we do not mean taking satisfaction in a job well done or having a healthy sense of self-worth and self-esteem. These are desirable and beneficial.

By pride and ego, we mean an exaggerated sense of self-importance or worth, imagined superiority, putting oneself above others, arrogance, conceit, contempt of others, defensiveness, unteachableness, excessive concern about one's image, unwillingness to admit to mistakes, placing more importance on appearance than substance, and vanity.

Pride and ego destroy relationships because they are manifestations of selfishness. Pride and ego halt personal growth and promote intolerance, contempt, and disdain of others.

The proud are often insecure and are thus emotionally unstable. They find it hard to feel remorse and make sincere apologies when they injure or hurt the feelings of others. Their motivation is ego-protection and self-aggrandizement, and they are heavily focused on receiving the praise and admiration of special groups or individuals. They viciously attack others when they feel threatened or frustrated and thereby violate emotional trust and trample over empathy and sensitivity. They expect others to constantly prop up their fragile egos. Their defensiveness and distorted perceptions of reality completely choke personal growth and self-improvement. In short, they violate all ten principles upon which happy, lasting, fulfilling relationships are based.

Those who are unfortunate enough to live with the proud often feel like they are interacting with the other person's pride, rather than with the other person. To stay on good terms in the relationship (or, in many cases, to have any relationship at all), they must baby, pamper, and coddle the proud person's ego. Those who live with the proud expend huge amounts of physical, mental, and emotional energy avoiding "crossing" them or offending their pride. Given these punishing demands, it is easy to see why the proud and egotistical drive others away.

SUPPORTING PRIDE: EGO-DEFENSE MECHANISMS

FOR THE PROUD to preserve their distorted self-perceptions and exaggerated self-esteem, they must rely on ego-defense mechanisms. Although everyone uses ego-defense mechanisms from time to time, the proud rely on them extensively. The following is a list of their frequently used ego-defense mechanisms:

PROJECTION

Projection is blaming others for your own mistakes and shortcomings. It is ascribing to others feelings, thoughts, or attitudes present in yourself. It is accusing others of the very things for which you are guilty of yourself or secretly harbor. The proud often accuse others of doing the very things for which they themselves are guilty. Some of their most vicious attacks and harshest criticisms are unleashed on those they perceive as having faults that they themselves possess.

RATIONALIZATION

Rationalization is an attempt to make your behavior seem more logical, reasonable, and justifiable and therefore more worthy of approval by your own conscience or by others (this ego-defense mechanism was discussed in detail in chapter on page 12). The proud, for example, rationalize their use of force, threat, and intimidation to get another person to do their bidding because they believe they "know what is really best for the other person" and therefore "are helping the other person to grow."

Denial

Denial is a refusal to perceive, face, or accept unpleasant realities. The proud deny wrongdoing when confronted with damning facts or evidence of their culpability. They refuse to take responsibility for their destructive actions. Instead, they deny that they have done any wrongdoing and refuse to admit that their actions have led to anything bad.

Identification

Identification is increasing your own feelings of self-worth by identifying with an outstanding person or institution. The proud and the egotistical often seek membership in prestigious or exclusive organizations. They love to mingle, be seen, and be identified with the "right people" and the "right crowd." They like to compare themselves to important and well-respected individuals or historical figures. They seek to raise their own status by associating with popular and prestigious people.

Displacement

Displacement is taking out your frustrations on those who are emotionally less dangerous or threatening than the source of your frustration. The proud and the egotistical are quick to unload their frustrations on those they perceive as less powerful and less capable of inflicting harm in return. While the proud would not consider blowing up at their boss or making a scene in front of their peers, they think nothing of tearing into their spouse and children and throwing fits of rage at home. The proud and egotistical handle stress and frustration by taking it out on safer, "unimportant" others.

DESTROYER 4: EMOTIONAL VOLATILITY AND INSTABILITY

LIVING WITH AN emotionally unstable person is like trying to live on an active volcano. You never know when that person will violently explode with red hot accusations and searing facial expressions and body gestures.

Those who are emotionally volatile and unstable are emotionally unpredictable. They do not provide others with a solid, stable, consistent emotional character with which to interact. They swing wildly and frequently between Happy Emotions and Dark Emotions, often on the slightest provocation or without apparent cause.

Those who live with the emotionally volatile never know what to expect. When they come home, for example, they may want to first dangle their hat or some other article of clothing on a stick through the door to see if it will be shot at, welcomed, or ignored. They often feel like their relationship is completely at the mercy of the other person's emotions and resent having their own emotions jerked around from moment to moment. Trying to have a relationship with those who are emotionally volatile and unstable is like trying to stay on-board a wild roller coaster without a seat restraint that never stops and has no final destination.

The emotionally volatile are quick to destroy relationships because they violate so many of the basic principles on which lasting, happy relationships are based. Like chameleons, they change their motivation from that of caring to that of being selfish or of wanting to hurt, retaliate, or lash out. The emotionally volatile do not make the sacrifice to control their Dark Emotions. Their interactions with others are reactionary rather than empathetic. They are insensitive and apathetic to the hardships and consequences their explosive character imposes on the lives of others. Because they are at the mercy of their emotions, they cannot serve as reliable sources of emotional support.

Emotional volatility and instability undermine emotional intimacy and closeness. Just when the relationship appears to be stabilizing and getting more intimate, something big or small triggers their volatility, which, in turn, dashes emotional intimacy and trust to pieces. Those who live with the emotionally volatile endure a repeating cycle. They gradually build up hope for an emotionally intimate relationship during their partner's period of temporary emotional stability. Then their partner rips their hopes and dreams for a happy relationship to shreds during volatile emotional outbursts. For those who live with this unending cycle, emotional recovery is painful. Only the most stalwart of emotional giants can endure such relationships for very long.

Even milder forms of volatility and instability can damage a relationship. Those who are characteristically hot-tempered, quick to take offense, moody, impatient, impulsive, insecure, or driven by their emotions injure their relationships and its potential.

DESTROYER 5: ABUSIVE LANGUAGE OR BEHAVIOR

ONE OF THE most potent and lethal destroyers of relationships is abusive language or behavior. Abuse of others can take many forms, including physical, verbal, sexual, and emotional abuse. All forms of abuse have the following characteristics:

Abusive behavior is degenerative behavior that forces others to suffer imposed or self-destructive consequences against their will (or against their ignorance or innocence) that seriously impact their well-being, their happiness, and their future ability to mature, grow, and be happy. Abusive behaviors are severe in their impact, intensity, and duration. They impose grave consequences on the lives of others.

Because the scars of abuse are massive, defacing, and often permanent, civilized societies have made most abusive behavior illegal (verbal and emotional abuse are often treated more lightly in today's society than other forms of abuse, even though their consequences can be just as serious). Abuse imposes deep pain and suffering on its victims for which victims frequently cannot escape or forget.

Emotional abuse, although not widely recognized or understood, is a serious form of abuse with highly destructive consequences. Emotional abusers verbally and emotionally assault their victims, make great false accusations, scream, distort, exaggerate, demean, dominate, threaten, trumpet damning but false evidence, force their victims to "walk on emotional glass," reject, make fun of, glare, harass, dictate, manipulate, blackmail, make ugly facial gestures, demand instant results, make bold and unreasonable demands, treat small indiscretions as capital crimes, make their victims an offender for a word, laugh devilishly at their victim's supposed mistakes or failures, play upon their victim's worst fears, and otherwise emotionally corner and torment their victims. Those who are the victims of emotional abuse often feel as though they are caught in a living hell or are being tortured at the hands of a sadistic warden in a wartime concentration camp.

Abusers will often use their positions of power, strength, position, or authority to corner or blackmail their victims. For example, a physically abusive husband may threaten to kidnap or kill his children should his wife leave him and may tell her that she could never make it on her own or support herself and the children were she to leave. A verbally abusive wife may know that her husband will never divorce her because of the children or because of the impact a divorce would have on his life. Abusers often target those who are easy to take advantage of or are helpless to escape their abuse, such as young children or emotionally or financially dependent spouses.

THE FUNDAMENTAL LAW OF RELATIONSHIPS

TRUE BONDING IN relationships occurs *only* when others are drawn to you of their own free will and choice because they are attracted to your solid character, your love, and your good works. This is the Fundamental Law of Relationships. This law was illustrated in the story of William and Cynthia. Indeed, your relationships will rise no higher than the highest level of character you attain as an individual.

If you are not willing to live this law, you cannot expect to have happy, lasting, successful relationships. For example, if you have not internalized the attributes of love, sacrifice, and service in your character, then you are not prepared to enter into happy, lasting, successful relationships. Neither can you neglect, trample over, use, or abuse others and then expect to have happy relationships. Only those who live this law will enjoy the happiness and fulfillment they seek in their relationships.

THOUGHTS TO PONDER

- Consider how much time and effort go into building a bridge, skyscraper, or other major structure. Now consider how quickly these structures can be brought down by a terrorist's bomb. Why is it that things of great worth take so much time and effort to build, yet can often be destroyed in an instant by irresponsible, reckless, or premeditated terroristic acts? Does the same hold true for relationships? If so, what are the "bombs" that can "blow up and destroy" a relationship in short order?

- How do those who are defensive, unteachable, and prideful damn their personal progress? Why are these individuals always the last to see or acknowledge their self-defeating characteristics (if they ever see them at all)? How does that blindness further contribute to the vicious cycle of self-perpetuating, stunted growth? How can people rid themselves of these self-damning qualities?

- Why is it that your relationships with your loved ones cannot rise higher than the level of character you attain?

- What percentage of broken relationships can be attributed to unmanaged, unleashed, or improperly managed Dark Emotions? What does this tell you about the importance of properly managing Dark Emotions in your life?

- What is the opposite of selfishness? Does its opposite require the total denial of one's own present and future needs and welfare? If not, how can we achieve the proper balance between attending to our own needs and the needs of others? How can we know when we should make a sacrifice to help others? How do you feel when you make voluntary sacrifices of time, money, labor, friendship, emotional support, and love to help those who cannot help themselves?

- Is self-hate a Happy Emotion or a Dark Emotion? Does it promote and lead to positive behavior and constructive outcomes? Is it a manifestation of true humility? If not, what is it a manifestation of?

- What is the difference between constructive criticism (feedback) and an accusing tongue? (Hint: Consider the timing, intent, purpose, intensity, how the criticism is delivered [tone, phraseology, body language, word emphasis], what is said and done before and after the criticism is made, the frequency in which criticism is given, the intent of the giver, the state of maturity of the receiver, and so forth.)

- Is marital infidelity a manifestation of "romantic adventure" and "newly discovered love," or is it a manifestation of lust, self-gratification, and selfishness?
- Do you value emotional stability? If so, are you emotionally stable for those around you? Do you easily fly off the handle, get upset, or express your Dark Emotions unrestrained?
- Should emotional abuse (as defined on page 164) be treated as seriously as other forms of abuse? What are the immediate and long-term consequences of emotional abuse?

ACTIVITIES FOR SELF-IMPROVEMENT

1. How often do you get angry at others? How often do you become offended at your partner? How much time do you spend holding and nursing grudges toward others? Do you frequently feel that others are attacking your actions, your good name, your decisions, your opinions, your judgment, your goals, your looks, or your dreams? Do you often feel like others are treating you unfairly?

    If you answered, "quite frequently," "most of the time," or "yes" to the majority of these questions, (1) you could be a victim of emotional abuse and are reacting to the abusive treatment you are receiving, (2) you yourself have a significant need for growth and improvement, or (3) something more complex is going on. In any of these three cases, it is recommended that you seek professional help.

2. Create a list of the ego-defense mechanisms described on pages 161 through 162. For the next two weeks, have your partner place a mark beside each ego-defense mechanism you used in your interactions. Review your list afterwards to see which ego-defense mechanisms have the most marks. Work on overcoming these ego-defense mechanisms by taking responsibility for your actions and decisions (see chapter).

3. Create a list of the characteristics of emotional abusers found on page 164. Ask your partner to check off the items on the list that you have displayed in the last week. If any of the items are checked,

seek immediate professional help from a competent and qualified mental health professional.

4. How quick are you to accuse others when things go wrong? For the next week, ask your partner to record every incident in which you blame others when things go wrong or in which you automatically assume that others are to blame rather than giving them the benefit of the doubt. Review the list at the end of the week and, if indicated, make a plan for monitoring your thoughts and language and consciously intervening when you find yourself beginning to accuse others of wrongdoing.

PART FOUR

HANDLING EMOTIONAL
STRESS AND TRIALS

CHAPTER 9

WHY ARE THERE TRIALS AND OPPOSITION IN LIFE?

Opposition is a catalyst for the development
of compassion and character

The greatest trials you will endure as a human being are highly emotional in nature. The untimely death of a loved one, the breakup of an important relationship, separation, divorce, being victimized by crime, suffering a serious accident, living with a verbally abusive companion, losing your job, failing to reach your goals despite intense effort and perseverance, physical injury or loss of health, and unexpected setbacks are all examples of intensely emotional experiences.

Learning to successfully confront and cope with emotional opposition is necessary not only for personal emotional survival, but for happy, lasting, fulfilling relationships. Opposition will come. Like John Wesley Powell's expedition down the Colorado River, emotional rapids cannot be avoided. Your options are to prepare yourself in advance by developing the appropriate skills or subject yourself to impersonal forces that can emotionally dash you to pieces.

If you cannot successfully pass through the emotional rapids of your life, you will be emotionally injured or incapacitated. In such a condition, you will not be prepared to look after the emotional needs of your partner. In addition, you will be more vulnerable to the powerful influence of Dark Emotions— forces that have the potential not only to destroy your peace and your relationships with your loved ones, but to destroy your life.

WHAT ARE THE FORCES OF EMOTIONAL DARKNESS?

THE FORCES OF emotional darkness are events or conditions that impose emotional pain, deprivation, and suffering in your life. They are incidents that disrupt your emotional stability, dispel your inner peace, threaten your security, and destroy the fruits of your labor. They are forces that impose fear, attack self-confidence, drain motivation, dash hope, and cause you to question your belief in ultimate justice and fairness. The forces of emotional darkness are forces that work to tear you down, destroy your happiness, chew you up, and spit you out. They are forces that inflict emotional pain, opposition, and suffering.

The forces of emotional darkness can arise from many sources. They can originate from internal sources, such as from mismanaged Dark Emotions, or from external sources, such as a controlling boss or spouse. They can arise out of ignorance of correct principles, such as the principles of emotional health and fitness, or from the adoption of faulty beliefs and values. They can originate from your own actions and choices, such as failing to meet the needs of your spouse or eating an unhealthy diet, or from the actions of others who are abusive, criminal, irresponsible, uncaring, or immature. They can arise from a series of unfortunate or unexpected events, such as a downturn in the economy or the sudden hospitalization of a loved one, or from weighty responsibilities, such as raising children or pulling off a complex deal with a potential client. They can originate from stressful environments, such as uncomfortable work conditions or high-crime neighborhoods, or from dysfunctional relationships. They can arise from fatigue, poor physical health, political or societal conditions (such as limited opportunity or freedom), or from your inner insecurities, fears, poor self-esteem, immaturity, low self-confidence, or bad past experiences.

The emotional pain inflicted by the forces of emotional darkness is real. It can be just as debilitating as physical pain and injury. Emotional pain can take the form of grief, rejection, loneliness, depression, hopelessness, lack of love, anxiety, fear, frustration, disappointment, and many other painful emotional states. Intense or chronic emotional pain can lead to overloaded emotional coping mechanisms, distorted judgment, mental and emotional disorders, reduced physical health, and loss of happiness.

The forces of emotional darkness are not once-in-a-lifetime visitors. They will confront you repeatedly throughout your life. They may be with you constantly, as with ongoing financial pressure or being married to an immature spouse. Or they may descend on you suddenly, like an unexpected wind shear that smashes you to the ground with tornadic force. Few, if any, lead charmed lives devoid of serious emotional opposition. Most of us run headlong into the roaring hurricanes of emotional darkness repeatedly throughout our existence here.

WHY IS THERE OPPOSITION AND SUFFERING?

WHEN TRAGEDY strikes, you may ask yourself, "Why did this happen to me?" When you have to sweat and toil every day to eke out a living to sustain yourself and your family, you may wonder, "Why does life have to be so hard?" When you watch how things naturally break down, wear out, rust, and decay, you may ask yourself, "Why does the universe seems to go from a higher state of order to a lower state or order?" Finally, you may wonder, "Why does life have to have so much opposition, so much suffering, so many struggles, and so many painful events?" The answers to these questions are fourfold:

OPPOSITION AND SUFFERING EXIST BECAUSE MAN HAS THE AGENCY TO ACT FOR HIMSELF

In your existence here on planet earth, you are free to use your vocal chords and your body from moment to moment as you wish. Even though you may choose not to follow a certain course of action because of its severe consequences (such as clubbing a stranger over the head to take his money), you still have the ability to choose that course of action (and indeed, some do). Your freedom to think, reason, and consciously choose alternative courses of action is one of the outstanding and distinguishing hallmarks that separates you from the rest of the animal kingdom.

Even though you have your agency, agency does not stand alone. Agency is inextricably linked to personal responsibility. Where one is, there is the other. Where one is not, there the other is not. Agency—your ability to choose your actions in a world of opposites or alternatives—is what makes you personally responsible for your actions. You could not be responsible for your actions if you did not have agency.

This fact is fairly self-evident. If you did not have the ability to choose or if you had no alternatives from which to choose, you would be forced, despite your will, to take a predetermined course of action. Do we put cats, dogs, birds, and other animals on trial and hold them personally responsible for following their instincts and genetic programming? Of course not. We do not put animals on trial because we believe that they cannot choose any other course of action other than that which has been programmed into their instincts. Man is responsible for his actions because he possesses the conscious ability to choose from a range of opposing alternatives. Agency could not exist if man could not choose evil over good, crime over civility, abuse over love, and self-depravity over self-improvement. Even though we sometimes resist the thought, man could not progress if he did not also have the option to retrogress.

Unfortunately, not everyone chooses to progress. Some misuse their agency. Their immature behavior, irresponsible choices, and deliberately malicious acts bring consequences of emotional, mental, physical, financial, and other forms of suffering not only to themselves, but to others.

In short, you are holed up on earth with billions of your fellow beings, held captive by the impracticality of escaping the earth's gravitational field and by the empty, lifeless vacuum of space. When anyone abuses their agency through irresponsible behavior, that person as well as others will suffer in one way or another. In general, the greater the position of power, authority, or influence of the offender, the greater the number of people who will suffer. Adolph Hitler's abuse of agency resulted in far more destruction and suffering than that of a person who fishes without a fishing license. Although they both have negative consequences and deserve sanctions, the consequences are far more severe, destructive, and widespread in one case than in the other.

When you misuse or abuse your agency, you may affect fewer people than those who are in positions of great authority, but the pain and suffering you inflict on others is just as real and can be just as profound in their conse-quences. Those at the receiving end of intense emotional abuse, for example, often feel like they are being held captive in a concentration camp or are being tortured at the hands of a sadistic Gestapo. Those who live with people who pollute the emotional atmosphere with their quick tempers, contemptuous attitudes, and destructive interactions are robbed of emotional support, stabil-ity, and peace and can be just as unhappy as anyone else. If we fully com-prehended the suffering, pain, and sorrow we inflict on others when we abuse our agency, perhaps then, we would change our reckless, irresponsible, and immature behavior.

Of course, just because you have your agency does not mean that you should be free of accountability for your actions. Agency is inextricably linked to personal responsibility, and personal responsibility is meaningless without personal accountability. Just because man has agency does not refute the need to establish and enforce societal sanctions against seriously irresponsible, immature, and damaging behaviors. The enforcement of laws protecting the security, stability, and future of society and the fundamental rights of men and women is absolutely essential. For one thing, societal-imposed consequences are necessary to deter the many who would otherwise take advantage of, overpower, and enslave others, and to punish those who do. If you do not believe this, just observe how quickly businesses are looted en masse by dozens of "normally law-abiding citizens" when hurricanes, floods, or riots sweep through our cities.

OPPOSITION AND SUFFERING EXIST BECAUSE WE LIVE IN A PHYSICAL UNIVERSE IN WHICH THINGS NATURALLY DECAY

In our current state of existence, things naturally go from organized to disorganized, from clean to dirty, from young to old, from new to worn out, from energetic to exhausted, from shiny to rusty, and from healthy to diseased. The earth does not spontaneously grow wheat, fruits, and vegetables, nor does it naturally protect the food we grow from drought, insects, and disease. Neither does it spontaneously bring forth beautiful, comfortable homes with electricity, indoor plumbing, furnaces, and air conditioners. If you desire these things, you must work with your hands and your mind to obtain them. If you just sit back and do nothing, you will soon become hungry, cold, and sick. You must work against naturally resistive forces of nature just to exist.

Although your ability to perform at least some form of physical labor is a natural endowment, your ability for mental labor is not so readily conveyed. Mental skills, such as balancing books, managing a business, diagnosing illnesses, analyzing complex problems, and designing computer chips, require knowledge and skills that are not a part of the brain matter that is genetically passed on from one generation to the next. Knowledge and mental skills are acquired through disciplined study, education, training, apprenticeship, and personal experience. Unless you are highly gifted, they are not a part of your natural ability or instinct.

Because things naturally decay, because you were not born with innate job skills, you cannot simply stand still and exist. Rather, you must battle the resistive forces of nature in order to raise (or purchase) food, obtain shelter, acquire possessions, care for your family, and carry on a comfortable, civilized existence. You must labor to exist, and every kind of legitimate work requires that you battle resistive forces of one kind or another.

Opposition and Suffering Exist That Is
of Your Own Making

Not all opposition and suffering can be blamed on others or on the resistive forces of nature. Some is of our own making. How can we create our own opposition and suffering? In many ways. One way is by failing to prepare for our future needs, due to procrastination, denial, disorganization, neglect, laziness, or rebelliousness. For example, we may neglect to put antifreeze in our car's radiator and experience serious engine failure when winter arrives. We may fail to prepare for a trade or a profession and suffer financial hardship, limited opportunity, and a stressed-out marriage later on. Or we may procrastinate getting ready to leave for an appointment and then become emotionally caustic or verbally abusive when we are late and cannot find our keys.

Another way we create our own opposition and suffering is by behaving in emotionally irresponsible ways. When we act immaturely, we impose not only destructive consequences on others, but Dark Emotions as well (the ones we are harboring). These Dark Emotions generate Dark Emotions in those we offend, who often react in kind and return the favor. When we scream and shout at others, for example, they often become angry or upset themselves and in turn make life unpleasant for us.

Another way we create our own opposition and suffering is a result of the Law of Harvest. When we sow irresponsible behavior, we must reap the negative consequences that follow (see chapter). These negative consequences are a form of opposition and suffering we could have otherwise avoided.

All irresponsible behavior is ultimately self-defeating. For example, when we treat others contemptuously, we damage our relationship with them and drive them away. When others subsequently avoid us, we reduce our chances of having meaningful relationships and therefore of having our emotional needs met. When our own needs go unmet, we make ourselves vulnerable to emotional manipulation, dangerous enticements, and even more dangerous Dark Emotions. By our own actions, we have created our own opposition.

A third way we create our own opposition and suffering is by adopting false values and beliefs. When we choose to believe in things that are not true, we set ourselves up for deception, disappointment, failure, injury, hurt, accidents, and other serious consequences. A teenager, for example, who believes he can sniff dangerous inhalants without incurring any serious or permanent injury will suffer irreversible brain damage, lung damage, nervous system damage, and possibly even death. A woman who believes that the best way to attract and keep a man is by allowing him to have sex with her while they are dating has set herself up for serious pain and disappointment when he "tires" of her and moves on to "more exciting" prospects, leaving her with sexually transmitted disease, pregnancy, disrespect for self, disillusionment, and financial hardship. Those who value money or their jobs more than their loved ones should not be surprised when their loved ones have little feeling or emotional attachment for them, become estranged from them, or leave them.

A final way we create our own opposition and suffering is by having a proud, egotistical, or unteachable character. To learn from our mistakes (as well as the mistakes of others), we must be teachable, devoid of pride, and be willing to recognize our weaknesses, acknowledge our dependencies on others, and accept our need to change. Unless we do, we will be doomed to repeat our mistakes and will continue to suffer their consequences. Unfortunately, this is one of the most pervasive and crippling forms of self-affliction.

OPPOSITION AND SUFFERING EXIST TO HELP YOU DEVELOP YOUR COMPASSION AND YOUR CHARACTER

One of the most important purposes of this life is to develop your character so that you and others might experience greater joy. You develop your character when you internalize correct values, develop self-mastery, and increase in your love and service to others. Correct values include love, service, sacrifice, empathy, sensitivity, stability, honesty, integrity, responsibility, faithfulness, supportiveness, caring, self-mastery, sound judgment, love of truth, teachableness, respect for agency, a reasonable set of expectations, and a focus on self-improvement.

If you will allow it, life's opposition, pain, and suffering will make you a better person. It will refine your character, increase your wisdom, deepen your compassion, and broaden your appreciation for all that is good.

Thoughts to Ponder

- People readily recognize that it takes careful training and preparation to successfully scale a cliff, kayak a white-water river, or parachute out of an airplane. Why, then, do they have such a hard time recognizing that it takes careful training and preparation to successfully navigate the emotional rapids in their lives?

- Would all of your troubles in life (including emotional opposition) disappear if you suddenly became rich? Are emotional challenges simply the offspring of economic challenges? Is money the best tool for confronting and combating the forces of emotional darkness? Can happiness be bought?

- Would the way we treat each other change if, like chameleons, we turned different colors according to the degree of emotional pain we were suffering?

- Of the four causes of opposition and suffering, the one that people have the most trouble acknowledging is "opposition and suffering that is of our own making." Why is it easier to blame others or outside forces for our pain, suffering, or "misfortunes?" Are "misfortunes" that are of our own making really misfortunes or are they simple and straightforward examples of the Law of Harvest?

Activities for Self-Improvement

1. List the most serious emotional challenges that you are currently facing. Classify each challenge into one (or more) of the four causes of emotional opposition described in this chapter (be honest!). Look at the items you categorized into the "opposition and suffering that is of your own making" category. How many of these items would cease to be emotional challenges if you were emotionally more responsible and mature? How much longer do you want to continue suffering these consequences?

2. Ask your partner to describe his or her most serious emotional challenges and opposition. What can you do to help lighten a burden, alleviate pain, and lift spirits? How important is it to love and empathize with those who are experiencing extreme emotional opposition?

3. When sore trials come your way, ask yourself, "What principles and insights can I learn from this situation?" "How can I turn this situation to good?" and, if you dare, "How much (if any) of my current troubles are of my own making?"

CHAPTER 10

Ten Potent Weapons for Battling the Forces of Emotional Darkness

Only light can overcome darkness

If the principles of happy, loving, emotionally fulfilling relationships are valid only when things are going well and your life is free of stress, then what value would they have? If becoming emotionally aware and responsible does not help you to manage, endure, and cope with the trials, opposition, and disappointments of life, then they would be weak principles indeed. To accomplish difficult life goals and create and enjoy happy relationships, you must learn to successfully battle the forces of emotional darkness. Unless you can diffuse, divert, and conquer the forces of emotional opposition, you will be emotionally devastated or overridden by them, become discouraged, and cease striving to reach your goals.

Dark Emotions Cannot Be Conquered through Dark Emotions

Tina's life was falling apart. Her ex-husband Jim was going to court to win expanded visitation rights to see their nine-year-old daughter,

Jennifer, even though Jennifer hated her father. Jennifer cried and resisted getting in the car with her father every time Jim arrived to take her away for the weekend. If Jim won his request, Jennifer would be forced to spend equal time with her father, an idea she found terrifying.

Tina knew that her ex-husband drank excessively and that he was emotionally and verbally abusive when he drank. She also knew that because of his drinking problem, he was a walking time bomb, capable of committing far more serious acts of violence or abuse. Tina had petitioned the courts to have Jim's visitation rights terminated, but she was turned down because she could not prove that her ex-husband had any serious problems.

Jim was a successful business executive with deep pockets. Due to Jim's false testimony and his lawyers' sly legal maneuvering, Tina was awarded minimal alimony and child support and none of her ex-husband's large estate. Jim came out of the divorce financially unscathed.

Tina's ex-husband made sure the divorce was as painful as he could make it. He instructed his lawyers to drag out the divorce as long as possible and to do everything they could to embarrass Tina, humiliate her, and hurt her financially. He accused Tina of being unfaithful to him and of deliberately sabotaging their marriage to get rich off his estate. The lengthy legal battle cost Tina thousands of dollars that she did not have. She was heavily in debt.

Shortly after the divorce, Tina found out the real reason her husband had divorced her. He was having an affair with a young legal assistant at his firm who he wanted to marry. When Tina confronted Jim about the affair, he angrily denied it and claimed that his relationship to his assistant was strictly one of business.

Jim lashed out once again to hurt Tina, this time over the issue of visitation rights. He didn't really care to see his daughter more often, but he knew that Jennifer meant more to Tina than anything else in the world and that Tina feared that he might harm or abuse Jennifer. He enjoyed toying with Tina's fears and even told her that he might disappear with Jennifer to another part of the world.

The stress of what her ex-husband might do to his daughter was too much. Tina suffered a mental breakdown and was hospitalized for a short time in a psychiatric facility.

Shortly after being discharged, Jack informed her that he was now seeking full custody over Jennifer and that her mental breakdown and subsequent hospitalization proved that she was mentally ill and emotionally unfit to care for their daughter. That same day, Tina lost her job in a corporate downsizing. Later that week, Tina's mother, on whom she had relied so heavily for emotional and moral support throughout the divorce, passed away from a sudden stroke.

When the ferocious jaws of emotional opposition reach out to snap you up, you need more than just a positive attitude to see you through. You need real power to escape their grip. The forces of emotional darkness are real, and their ability to inflict emotional pain and suffering is real. They are so powerful that unless you can effectively draw upon counteractive, neutralizing, and healing sources of energy, you will be at their complete mercy. In the battle for your emotions, you cannot declare neutrality or sit on the side lines. Your choice is either to prepare yourself to draw upon available sources of strength or be emotionally eaten alive.

In giving battle to the opposition, you must first recognize that the forces of emotional darkness cannot be conquered through the forces of emotional darkness. Dark Emotions do not conquer other Dark Emotions. Hatred does not dispel hatred, anger does not dispel anger, hurt does not dispel hurt, revenge does not dispel injury, and bitterness does not dispel tragedy. Throwing a snowball back into a raging blizzard only adds to its destructive forces. Only the warming rays of the sun can change a destructive blizzard into a gentle rainstorm. Darkness cannot be conquered by darkness. Darkness can only be conquered by light.

Ten Potent Weapons for Battling the Forces of Emotional Darkness

To successfully battle the forces of emotional darkness, you must have a deep understanding of correct principles, possess strong self-discipline, and be skilled in applying counteracting and neutralizing measures. These things are embodied in the following Ten Potent Weapons for Battling the Forces of Emotional Darkness. They are the weapons of choice in emotional combat and in bodily one-on-one emotional warfare.

Weapon 1: Find Purpose and Meaning in Life

An enemy with a purpose is an enemy indeed. An enemy that does not know what it is up to cannot focus its strength and is easily overtaken. So it is with your life. When your life has purpose, it has greater focus, greater meaning, and greater power. Without purpose, you have no real destination and, therefore, no real direction.

Living life without purpose is like riding an electric bumper car in an amusement park—you are constantly in motion, but never really getting anywhere. While your life is full of activity and excitement, it lacks substance and meaning. You feel like you are driving across the same worn-out territory again and again.

When you have purpose, you know what you are striving for and can therefore lay out tangible plans for accomplishing your goals. Plans give you a frame of reference by which you can judge priorities and make decisions. They break difficult tasks into smaller, more manageable tasks and provide milestones by which you can measure and celebrate your progress. A purpose gives you something tangible to strive for every day.

Purpose brings greater enthusiasm and self-esteem. When you see yourself progressing toward your goals, you feel good about yourself. Feeling good about yourself and your progress toward your goals generates new enthusiasm for reaching your goals.

Purpose brings meaning. Your life's meaning is working to accomplish your worthy goals. Without purpose, there is no meaning, and without meaning, you will not have the motivation, resolve, or determination to live by your values and endure through difficult times. Without meaning, it is easy to give up on yourself and on life.

Although purpose is a principle of power, not all purposes bring you power to combat the forces of emotional darkness. Only worthy purposes can do that. A *worthy* purpose is one that builds up your character and the character of others and that helps others achieve their true potential. A *dark* purpose does just the opposite.

If your purpose, for example, is to accumulate wealth, recognition, influence, and power by whatever means possible—even by dishonesty, deceitfulness, or taking advantage of others—then you will be contributing to—not working against—the forces of emotional darkness.

A worthy purpose builds others up through encouragement, love, support, sacrifice, and the teaching of correct principles. A dark purpose works to bring others down—to injure, hurt, enslave, dominate, take advantage of, or deceive. A dark purpose keeps others in ignorance and destroys their ability to make wise decisions and take control of their bodies and their minds. It hinders growth, enslaves bodies and minds, undermines motivation, engages in self-destructive behaviors, and disregards correct principles. It serves selfish interests.

One of the most powerful ways to combat the forces of emotional opposition is to have a *worthy central purpose* in your life. A worthy central purpose is a worthy goal to which all other goals are subset or supportive. It is what you want to become and achieve in your life. It is your ultimate desired destination. A worthy central purpose will focus your physical, mental, emotional, social, and spiritual energies into a laser-sharp beam. It will help you avoid despair and maintain "The Big Picture" in your life.

Larry had just turned 45. "What is life all about?" he wondered. "I go to work every day, put in my eight hours, bring home a paycheck, make another payment on the house, send the kids off to college, fix the car, cut the grass, buy groceries, and handle crises. Is this all there is to life?" Larry was having a mid-life crisis.

Larry pondered these questions for many weeks. Inside, he felt there must be a deeper meaning to life, a higher purpose for his own existence. He decided to find out what that purpose was.

Up front, Larry decided to keep an open mind, to think for himself, and to disregard prejudices and preconceptions—his own as well as those of others. He knew that truth cannot be measured by what is popular, politically correct, or in vogue. Truth must be accepted on its own terms, for what it is. He knew that truth stands independent of man and remains unaffected by whether man accepts it or not. It cannot be altered to suit the mind of man.

Larry also recognized that truth cannot be compartmentalized. Truth has no artificial boundaries. It encompasses all aspects of life. Therefore, he would search for truth in every area of his life—spiritual, emotional, intellectual, physical, and social. Truth is reality—the way things really are, were, or will be. Larry reasoned that the more truth he could learn, the less vulnerable he would be to deception and the more power he would have to govern his life and control his destiny.

Larry eventually found the great truths he was looking for. He discovered spiritual truth that gave his life new meaning and helped him understand his divine potential and destiny. He discovered truth in the emotional realm, including the principles on which emotionally fulfilling relationships are based. He learned about the history and nature of man, including the importance of freedom, the proper role of government, and the consequences of ignorance and apathy. He learned truths about his physical body, such as how to keep it physically fit and healthy and how to avoid addiction, disease, and injury. He learned truths about people and societies, including the importance of family, friends, community service, and caring.

Larry finally discovered that the purpose of his life was to progress and grow in wisdom, truth, and character and to help others achieve their greatest potential.

Larry's worthy central purpose energized his life. He finally knew what he was about and what he was trying to accomplish with his life. Larry's new conviction changed his life. He became active in his religion. He spent more time helping his wife and kids. He gave voluntary service to others. He improved his character and developed his talents. He strengthened his family and his community. He overcame his weaknesses and turned them into strengths. For the first time in his life, Larry felt alive.

Selecting your worthy central purpose is something that requires serious thought, careful consideration, and deep reflection. Ponder the following questions as you choose your life's central worthy purpose:

- What kind of person do I want to become?
- What kind of character do I want to develop?
- When I reach the end of my life, what do I want to have accomplished? What do I want to have contributed?
- What will be of most value to me and others in the long run?
- What heritage do I want to pass on to my family and posterity?
- What truths should I seek in making this decision?
- What do spiritual sources of truth teach me about the purpose of life?

WEAPON 2: DEVELOP A LONG-RANGE PERSPECTIVE

HAVE YOU EVER watched ants build a new home? Grain by grain, speck by speck, they carve out a complex labyrinth of tunnels. In the process, they create a mound of dirt many times their own height. Ants do not create their new home instantly, but by repeatedly carrying out the simple act of dislodging and carrying a single grain of dirt to the surface. They continue this activity without discouragement, even though humans may accidentally destroy a portion of their colony with a lawn mower or shovel. They work undaunted until they achieve their goal.

In this respect, we should be more like ants. Things of great value take a long time to achieve. Overcoming a weakness, getting a degree, mastering a trade or profession, learning a musical instrument, raising responsible children, writing a book, establishing your own business, paying off a mortgage, giving meaningful service, overcoming serious obstacles, and making a difference for good in the lives of others are not achieved overnight. They take time to achieve. If this is so, then you must develop an equally long-range perspective; otherwise, you will become discouraged and give up on your goals before reaching them.

Those who possess a long-range perspective are able to see the significance and progress that even small efforts make toward the accomplishment of long-term goals. They work toward their goals even when progress consists of tedious, minute steps that are difficult to measure on a day-to-day basis. They judge events based on their long-range eventualities, not on their short-term pizzazz.

Those who have a long-range perspective are better able to handle frustration. They do not look at their short-term losses as signs of long-term defeat. Rather, they view them as minor irritations that "come with the territory," as challenges to be handled creatively, or as events that must simply be endured for a period of time. Parents who take a long-term perspective in raising their children are less likely to overreact to their children's short-term mistakes, such as spilled milk, broken lamps, and wrecked cars, and are more likely to motivate their children to achieve long-term goals themselves.

Those who maintain a long-range perspective have realistic expectations. They understand that worthwhile accomplishments take months or even years to achieve. Unlike impatient novices who throw temper tantrums and curse at the ground when their seeds do not produce a bountiful harvest by the end of a week, they have faith that their harvest will eventually come if they persist in following correct principles and processes. Their emotions are not tossed to and fro by unrealistic expectations, apparent contradictions, and fleeting feelings.

Finally, those who maintain "The Big Picture" avoid concluding that they are being picked on or are being unfairly and undeservedly singled out in life for special persecution. Instead of asking, "Why me?" "What did I do to deserve this?" or "Why am I always so unlucky?" they see events that are out of their immediate control as impersonal chance happenings and as opportunities to develop their character, do good, and prove their values.

The following suggestions will help you take a long-term perspective:

DETERMINE YOUR OVERALL WORTHY CENTRAL PURPOSE

How can you take a long-range perspective if you do not know what you are trying to accomplish? How can you determine how you will achieve a goal that does not yet exist? How can you focus your energies on a nonexistent mental objective? How can you take into account "The Big Picture" when you do not even know what your big picture is?

IDENTIFY AND UNDERSTAND THE PROCESS

After you have identified your worthy central purpose and goals, determine what process is required to achieve those goals. Ask yourself questions such as, "What milestones will I have to accomplish?" "What skills, knowledge, and character attributes will I have to acquire?" "How long does this process take?" and "What sacrifices will I have to make?" By understanding the process ahead of time, you will not be caught off guard or be unduly alarmed when life actually requires that you make these sacrifices.

TRUST IN THE PROCESS

Do not be confused if you are doing everything right and you still suffer temporary setbacks or are confronted by apparent contradictions. Have faith that if you properly care for the orchard, the trees will eventually produce. If, for example, your children occasionally act immaturely, do not despair or think that all is lost. Instead, maintain a long-term perspective—remember the progress your children have already made, the progress your children will yet make, the struggles you faced when you were their age, and your love and commitment to your children. Have faith that if you adopt correct principles and follow correct processes, you will, in the long run, be successful.

REMEMBER "THE BIG PICTURE"

Whenever you feel yourself becoming frustrated, angry, or discouraged, stop and ask yourself the following question: "How important will this be ten years from now?" Frustrations become greatly magnified when seen from the narrow perspective of current emotions. Therefore, evaluate frustrating events in terms of their impact on your fulfilling your overall worthy purpose and goals. If the event is *not* important in this perspective, then take it in stride, endure it gracefully, or handle it in some other constructive way. If the event *is* important, then determine if it is something that you have control over or if it is something that you can do nothing about. Then, handle it accordingly.

BE LESS CONCERNED WITH SHORT-TERM PROGRESS
AND MORE CONCERNED WITH LONG-TERM GROWTH

When you take a short-term perspective, you become more concerned about the demands, needs, and pressures of the moment than about taking strategic action to achieve long-range goals. Often, it is easier and more socially rewarding to measure progress by short-term gains than by long-term growth. For example, you may feel that because your child is an "A" student, that all is well. Only later do you learn that your child has been experimenting with drugs and participating in gang initiation rites.

PERIODICALLY REFRESH YOUR VISION

An image on a television set is created when an electron beam traces horizontal lines one by one across the face of your television tube. Because the phosphors inside the tube glow for only a fraction of a second, the electron beam must scan the entire face of the screen many times a second to produce a non-flickering image. Like images on television screens, a long-range perspective must likewise be constantly refreshed or it will quickly fade from consciousness. You can refresh your long-term vision by regularly reviewing your overall worthy purpose and goals, by reading books or other materials that strengthen your motivation, by attending to your spiritual renewal, and by interacting with those who are excellent role models of maturity.

WEAPON 3: SEEK OUT AND ADOPT
CORRECT BELIEFS AND VALUES

YOU ACT ON the basis of your beliefs. For example, you attend college or trade school because you believe that it will lead to a good job and a better life. You wash your hands before eating because you believe that it will help prevent illness. You go to work in the morning because you believe that it is essential to your physical and financial well-being. You drink water because you believe that it will satisfy your thirst. Your beliefs are the basis of your actions.

Even though you act on the basis of your beliefs, not everything you believe is necessarily true. Some of your beliefs may be false. For example, you may believe that smoking will not harm your health, that you are strong enough to take mind-altering drugs without getting addicted, that you can sustain a marriage based on physical attraction alone, that you can drink and drive safely, that you can cheat on your spouse without incurring serious consequences, that you can emotionally abuse others without damaging your relationships and your own character, that you can lie on your income tax return without doing any real harm, or that you can raise happy children by simply giving them everything they want as they grow up.

Some incorrect beliefs are highly dangerous. They lead to permanent, life-altering or life-threatening consequences. For example, those who believe they can "experiment" with drugs without incurring any real harm lose control over their mind and body, damage their brain, subject themselves for the rest of their lives to flashbacks, catch communicable diseases, cause accidents, and serve jail time. Some will die from drug overdose. Many find out too late that their beliefs in a certain area are faulty.

You cannot overcome the powerful forces of emotional darkness in ignorance. You must possess correct knowledge and believe in correct principles. Only light can overcome darkness. Light is truth, knowledge, intelligence, and wisdom. Therefore, you must seek out and accept truth, knowledge, and wisdom wherever you find it.

In seeking truth, you must not allow personal prejudice, upbringing, bias, tradition, professional training, financial pressures, your job, friends, family, other people's perception of truth, or popular societal beliefs to deter you from recognizing or accepting truth. You must be willing to accept the truth no matter where it is found, in all areas of your life—physically, emotionally, socially, intellectually, and spiritually. Only truth can save you from the evil manipulations of others and from the consequences of ignorance and false belief. The more truth you discover, accept, and live by, the more power you will have to overcome the forces of emotional opposition and achieve your worthy goals.

Correct beliefs and values not only shield you from the destructive consequences of falsehood, they give you hope, courage, and strength to endure extreme emotional trials. The following are some examples of powerful beliefs that will help you combat the forces of emotional darkness:

BELIEVE IN THE ULTIMATE TRIUMPH OF GOOD OVER EVIL

If you do not believe that good will ultimately triumph over evil, then how can you hope for a better future or view the apparent triumphs of the forces of evil as temporary? If good will not ultimately prevail over evil, then what motivation do you have to resist evil? What if, for example, during World War II, Allied leaders had decided that Nazi Germany was simply too powerful a force to resist and that a Nazi takeover of the world was inevitable? How would this have affected the Allied resolve and determination to fight?

Believe in the Law of Restoration

Believe that while life may not be fair, eternity is. Believe that every good act you do in this life, no matter how small, will be returned unto you in kind and that every good deed you cast out upon the water will ultimately come back to you greatly enlarged. Believe that every effort you make to develop your character, to be true to correct values, to help others grow, and to improve the world will ultimately be rewarded, either here in this life or in the life to come. Believe that, in the long run, no one really gets away with anything, that everyone will eventually get exactly what they deserve, and that people will ultimately be treated the same way they have treated others.

Belief in the Law of Restoration will help you persist in the face of opposition, knowing that none of your efforts to improve or to do good will ever be wasted. It will also help you avoid despair when you suffer injustices and watch the guilty seemingly go free or unpunished.

Believe That You Can Take Greater Control over Your Life

It is not easy to believe that you can take even greater control over your life than you now do. You may already feel that you are working hard, handling frustration, and facing difficult opposition. Who would dare suggest that you could take better control over your life? Anyone who would do so must certainly be unthoughtful, unknowing, unappreciative, or wrongly motivated.

Notwithstanding your feelings, most likely there are aspects of your life that you could take better control of, that you could better manage, or that you could improve upon. To find out if there is some aspect of your life for which you could take better control, ask yourself the following questions: "Am I living each of the Ten Secrets of Emotionally Fulfilling Relationships?" "Do I anticipate and properly address the emotional needs of myself and others?" "Have I done all I can to take care of my body and arrange my environment to combat negative emotions and inspire me to pursue worthy goals?" "Am I doing all I can to seek out, identify, and embrace truth?" "Have I determined my worthy, central purpose in life?" "Have I rationalized away control over my life by saying, 'I am already doing enough,' or 'I cannot do anything more until my spouse changes,' or 'Nobody's perfect'?" "Do I believe that I am a victim of fate, upbringing, past experiences, or present circumstances?" and "Do I see myself as a helpless victim, powerless to take actions that would make my life successful?" If you have not done all you can to fully address each of these questions, then, by definition, you are not doing all you can to take control over your life.

By believing that you can take greater control over your life, you will open wide the door to self-improvement, free yourself to discover creative ways of solving your problems, and focus your mind on finding solutions to your problems rather than on placing blame for them or feeling sorry for yourself. There are a thousand ways to explain failure, but only a handful of ways to explain success.

BELIEVE THAT YOU CAN RISE UP FROM THE ASHES OF APPARENT DEFEAT STRONGER THAN EVER BEFORE

Sometimes you might feel that the forces of emotional darkness have won a final victory in your life. You might feel that the forces of emotional darkness have lunged out of their hiding place, grabbed you by the throat, and are trying to choke you to death. You might feel worn out, defeated, and exhausted. Or you might just feel beaten up, wounded, and discouraged. You wonder *how* you can go on. You may wonder *if* you can go on.

Or perhaps you feel that you have given in to emotional immaturity when you were weak, tired, and vulnerable, or that you have repeated immature behavior you have exhibited many times before. You feel disappointed in yourself, guilty about your actions, and discouraged about your ability to change. You think, "Why should I try again when I have just proven that I cannot live up to my desired ideal?"

The forces of emotional darkness try to discourage you and convince you to give up your struggle to reach your goals. They do this by attempting to make your situation look hopeless. If you become convinced that things are hopeless, then victory on their part is assured. Because of this, you must not believe that their apparent conquests are final, however overpowering or conclusive they may seem. Setbacks are only permanent if you allow them to be. Like the mythical phoenix of old, you can rise up from the ashes of apparent defeat stronger and more powerful than ever before.

How is this possible? By using your setbacks and trials to refine your character—to increase your sensitivity to the feelings and suffering of others, to deepen your empathy, to broaden your concern for your fellow beings, to probe more deeply into areas of knowledge that you lack, to better understand

and overcome your weaknesses, and to motivate you to do good. Although the forces of emotional darkness can make your life miserable for a time, they cannot stop you from using your suffering to build your character, increase your wisdom, do good deeds, or radiate a positive influence on the lives of others.

Believe in the Power of Love

Love is one of the greatest influences in the universe. It ultimately accomplishes more good than any other influence. Therefore, the best thing you can do for others is to truly love them. True love is purely motivated—its only desire is to help bring joy into the lives of others by helping them reach their true potential. True love is unselfish. It respects the agency of others. It influences others through persuasion, example, encouragement, friendship, patience, long-suffering, forgiveness, the teaching of correct principles, and the application of consistent, fair, and appropriate consequences for good and bad behavior.

Tina [the woman described earlier in the chapter with the spiteful ex-husband] finally reached rock bottom. Everything important in her life had been stripped away. Her abusive and unfaithful ex-husband was taking legal action to take away her precious nine-year-old daughter, the main source of her emotional support had suddenly died, her own health was faltering, and she had lost her job.

Tina could easily have given in to self-pity, become embittered, or withdrawn to a dark corner, never to be seen again. But she knew that such actions would only be a slow form of emotional suicide.

Instead, Tina believed in the Law of Restoration and in the ultimate triumph of good over evil. She believed that if she was creative in trying to solve her problem, endured well whatever her situation required, and did everything she could to turn her experience to good, that she would have all of the things that she had been deprived of at some point in the future. She believed that whatever she cast out upon the waters would ultimately come back to her, only greatly multiplied, if not in this life, then in the life to come.

Drawing upon family, friends, and spiritual resources, Tina courageously fought to turn her situation to good and to rise out of the ashes of defeat stronger than before. With the help of others, she hired a detective and a lawyer. Together, they documented her husband's true character and presented the evidence in court, where she was awarded full custody of her daughter.

Tina's great courage inspired others to show greater emotional courage in their own trials. She eventually used her experience to give support and guidance to other emotionally abused women at a local women's shelter.

Tina's refusal to become embittered, to give up, or to fight Dark Emotions with Dark Emotions strengthened her character, boosted her self-esteem, and brought her inner peace. She learned to value more deeply the things of true importance in her life and to more fully appreciate the blessings she had already received.

Tina's character radiated a positive energy and a certain light that touched those around her. Men of similar character were strongly attracted to Tina, and within a couple of years, she had remarried to a man who was her equal in character, love, and devotion. She went on to have three more children and to enjoy a deeply fulfilling relationship with her second husband.

Although Tina knew that the Law of Restoration may not have been completely fulfilled for her in this life, she knew that even the fierce winds of emotional opposition could not hold her back from improving her character, strengthening others, and making the world a better place.

BELIEVE IN GOD AND THE POWER OF PRAYER

Believe that God has placed you here for a purpose, that He is the Creator and Controller of the universe, that He is the Father of your spirit, and that you are one of His children. Believe that just as earthly parents love, care for, and make sacrifices for their children, your Heavenly Father loves you, knows you, and has established a plan by which you may progress and find eternal happiness, if you so choose. Believe that God will bless you and help you as you seek to do good. Call upon Him in prayer, ask for His guidance, pray for His intervention and support, seek for His comfort, and thank Him for the blessings He has given you. Pray for strength to endure and overcome whatever trials He may allow in your life. Ask to be guided to greater truth and for the humility to recognize and accept the truth when it is presented. Believe that He will hear your prayers and answer them in ways that would be best for your long-term growth and blessing. Believe that God will ultimately hold all men and women responsible for their thoughts, intentions, and deeds and that He will ultimately reward those who do good and punish those who do evil.

Weapon 4: Practice Creative Problem Solving

Sometimes you may suffer unnecessary emotional pain because you do not solve problems that confront you that are solvable. These problems can create stress, deplete your energy, test your patience, divert attention away from your goals, and bring you pain and suffering. Life is difficult enough without having to endure problems that are solvable on top of those you already have.

If many of your problems are solvable, then why do they go unresolved? There are several possible reasons. First, you may have given up trying to solve the problem. You may have become so frustrated and battle weary that you are convinced that a solution does not exist. Or you may believe that the problem is out of your control or that you have already exhausted every possible solution.

Second, you may lack essential knowledge. You may not yet possess the critical understanding you need to overcome the problem. Parents who are ignorant of effective parenting techniques often resort to screaming or other ineffective disciplinary tactics with their children, even though there are other effective alternatives that do not exacerbate the problem or inflict long-term negative side-effects. Students who do not know how to study effectively are seriously handicapped in their academic work. Drivers who are ignorant of the principles of defensive driving are more likely to suffer automobile accidents and personal injury. People who do not have adequate social skills have greater difficulty succeeding in their jobs, establishing friendships, and avoiding feelings of loneliness and inferiority.

Third, you may lack self-discipline. Sometimes you know what you need to do to eliminate a problem or a barrier, but you do not discipline yourself to take the necessary action to resolve the problem. For example, you may know how to exercise and eat healthier, but you do not want to give up your fast-food lunches or your evening snacks in front of the television. You may know that you need to treat your spouse with greater sensitivity and concern, but you are stressed out and do not want to think about it. You may know that you need to control your spending, but you continue to buy exciting things anyway.

Fourth, you may lack adequate problem-solving skills. You may not know how to break large problems into smaller, more manageable ones; identify critical and noncritical aspects of problems; reflect on analogous problems that already have solutions; identify and turn to sources of information that may help you solve your problem; ask others how they have solved similar problems; and apply principles of logic and reasoning. Although these skills do not guarantee your success in solving a problem, they greatly increase the odds of doing so.

Harry and Carol lived in a small house with three small children. Even though they needed more space for their growing family, they could not afford to move into a larger house on Harry's meager salary. Living in their small quarters with three active youngsters meant high tensions and pushed-to-the-limit emotions. The house was cluttered. Everyone seemed to be walking over things just to get around. Toys, clothes, and coloring books were scattered everywhere.

One day, Harry decided that something had to be done. "What can I do?" Harry thought. "I need a larger house, but I cannot afford one. I wonder if I could get more usable space out of my current house."

One night, while lying on his back on the living room couch as he played with his son, he had a sudden insight: "When you turn the house upside down, there is plenty of space. Look at all that wasted space up there near the ceiling." Harry realized that space is three-dimensional. Space is volume, not square feet, the usual standard for measuring the size of a house. He leapt up and walked around from room to room, visualizing how he might use the space near the ceiling.

Before long, Harry was turning his realizations into reality. He removed the particle-board shelving in the pantry that was vertically spaced too far apart for efficient storage and installed new wire shelving from floor to ceiling that was spaced just right to accommodate specific cans and containers. This doubled the number of shelves in his pantry and allowed storage space elsewhere in the kitchen to be cleared out, much to his wife's delight.

Next, Harry analyzed his garage. He installed wire shelves high up the walls on three sides of the garage, which tripled the existing shelf space there and allowed many items in the house to be moved out into the garage.

Finally, Harry installed shelves high up in each of his closets and in the utility room above the washer and dryer.

To make it easy to access those shelves, Harry bought several sturdy, folding step stools and placed them strategically throughout the house where the children could not access them.

Harry then bought several inexpensive, modular cabinets with hinged doors at a local lumber store, which he assembled and secured to the walls in each of the children's rooms. He bought extra pre-made shelving from the same place to make extra shelves so that he could maximize the use of the space inside each cabinet. In addition, he made inexpensive but attractive toy chests for all of the children with their names on each one. All of these efforts allowed his wife and children to get the toys, clothes, and other clutter off the floors.

Having finished with the shelves and cabinets, Harry next built a sturdy bunk bed out of wood from the plans he found in a book at the library. His two sons were so excited about their new bed that they fought over who was going to sleep in the top bunk. He even modified the plans by adding pull-out drawers underneath the lower bunk for added storage.

Finally, Harry bought several inexpensive, cardboard file storage boxes from an office supply warehouse, which he used to organize and store seldom-used items such as holiday decorations and winter clothing. Because the boxes had lids and were uniform in size, they stacked neatly and compactly in closets, underneath stairwells, and on his new shelving. He labeled the boxes and created an index so that he could easily find whatever he was looking for.

Harry's wife was so inspired by his creative handiwork that she organized the entire house, throwing out (or donating) the things that they no longer needed and storing away everything else. Now, she had a place for everything and everything was in its place. She trained the children to clean up and put things back where they belonged before dinner every day.

When everything was completed, Harry and Carol were astonished at the results. With all of their newfound floor space, they felt as if they were living in a mansion. Not only that, they now had everything they owned at their fingertips, which greatly reduced their day-to-day frustration when they tried to find the things they needed. Harry could even find specific tools and the Christmas lights when he needed them. Moreover, having a clean, well-organized house made both of them feel much better and be less embarrassed when friends dropped by unexpectedly to visit.

Even the children behaved differently in their cleaner, more spacious environment. With plenty of room to play, they quarreled less, were more relaxed, and showed a greater respect for their possessions.

Carol was very proud of her husband. Because of his creative problem solving, she and her family had extinguished a lot of frustration. On top of everything, they were living a happier, more enjoyable life.

The following are some suggestions for how you can solve more of your problems:

Become Strong Where You Are Weakest
in Your Problem-Solving Skills

Determine which of the four causes of failure to solve problems— giving up, ignorance of correct knowledge and principles, lack of self-discipline, and inadequate problem-solving skills—you are weakest in and then work to turn your weakness into a strength. Study books on problem solving, work on self-discipline, identify and learn key principles in the areas in which you are struggling, take classes, attend seminars, and talk to others so that you can draw upon the wisdom of dozens of lives, not just your own.

If you lack knowledge on how to properly discipline your children, for example, read parenting books, attend parenting classes, and talk to others about how they raise their children and handle misbehavior. If your problem is a lack of space, then watch home improvement shows, study remodeling books, ask others how they solved their space problems, determine how you can take better advantage of the existing space in your house, or make plans to save for a bigger house.

Distinguish the Problems You Control
from Those You Don't

Although some problems are clearly out of your control, such as being delayed at the airport by bad weather, other problems, such as spending more money than you earn, are definitely under your direct control. Distinguish problems you control from problems you do not control so you can devote your full energies to solving problems you can do something about.

Identify and Understand Key Principles

All knowledge is not equal. Some knowledge is more key than other knowledge. Key knowledge embodies principles that are very powerful in their application. Principles describe how things are related, particularly cause and effect relationships. Key principles are principles that embody the greatest power in their application. For example, although there is a great body of knowledge about investing, understanding the principle of compound interest can help you achieve a more comfortable retirement if you apply it early and consistently throughout your working life. Therefore, the principle of compound interest is a key principle in the great body of knowledge about investing.

Learning the key principles in a given subject is the fastest way of bringing power into your life. For example, understanding the key principle of emotional needs may help you understand that your toddler's disruptive behavior is a sign of an unfulfilled need for love, affection, or attention rather than a lack of self-control.

SET THE PROBLEM ASIDE AND TRY AGAIN LATER

It is possible to work on a problem so intensely that you lose the ability to see the forest for the trees. If you have given a problem your best shot and it still refuses to budge, try setting it aside for a while and engaging in some other totally unrelated activity. Take a walk, get some work done around the house, eat, play with your children, go out with your friends, read a good book, watch a good movie, or sleep on it. Give your fatigued brain cells time to recuperate and your subconscious mind an opportunity to exercise its creativity.

MINIMIZE THE EFFECTS OF PROBLEMS THAT ARE BEYOND YOUR CONTROL

If a problem is not under your control, minimize or counteract the effects that it has in your life. Make the best of your circumstances. Avoid feeling sorry for yourself. Decide that you will accomplish great good within the constraints and boundaries you have been given. In the height of his political career, before he became the 32nd President of the United States, Franklin Delano Roosevelt was stricken with polio. Many of his closest political advisors told him that his political career was over. They strongly suggested that he quietly bow out of politics altogether. Nevertheless, Roosevelt was determined to succeed. He eventually overcame his depression, invented a metal leg brace that allowed him to "walk" (while balancing himself precariously on the arm of his assistants, unbeknownst to the crowds), and successfully campaigned to become President of the United States. Even though Roosevelt could not cure or escape the physical devastation brought on by his illness, he found ways to minimize the negative influence it had on his life and achieve his goals anyway.

PRACTICE SITUATION MANAGEMENT

Avoid deliberately placing yourself in situations that will provoke or exacerbate your problem. For example, if you are trying to lose weight, avoid stocking your refrigerator with a lot of junk food. If you are trying to give up smoking, avoid hanging around those who smoke. If you are a recovered alcoholic, avoid driving by old familiar bars or liquor stores, stay clear of the wine and beer aisles in the supermarket, and socialize with nondrinkers. Use situation management not only to avoid problems, but to pursue activities that will strengthen your motivation to accomplish your goals. Join a health or exercise club. Attend uplifting artistic or athletic performances. Make friends with people of good character. Transform your environment into an inspiring place to live.

AVOID PROCRASTINATION

Anticipate and handle problems as they occur, before they multiply or pile up. Avoid letting problems grow into nightmarish proportions because of laziness, inconvenience, disorganization, or rationalization. Small actions taken now can often save you incredible effort, distress, and inconvenience later on. Consider, for example, how ignoring a small leak in your roof can lead to extensive damage and repair, how ignoring patterns of irresponsible behavior in your children now can lead to more serious irresponsibility later on, and how failing to perform regular maintenance on your car can lead to major future breakdowns alongside the road. When ignored, small problems can compound and multiply into larger, more serious problems. The problems you are facing today may be second- and third-generation problems simply because you did not attend to their smaller predecessors at an earlier date.

TACKLE PROBLEMS WHEN YOU ARE FRESH

Problems are often best tackled early in the day. Why wait until the end of the day to tackle your problems when you are physically, mentally, and emotionally exhausted? Solving problems when you are exhausted leads to poor decision making and hostile interpersonal interactions. By approaching your problems when you are fresh, you will resolve them more quickly or more easily cut them down to size.

DON'T RUSH DIFFICULT, COMPLEX DECISIONS THAT HAVE FAR-REACHING CONSEQUENCES

Why? Because you may be able to gather additional relevant data with just a little more time or because your circumstances may change before you make a decision. The consequences of impulsive decision making are usually unpleasant and can even be life-altering. Try to buy additional time for making critical decisions. For example, ask for more time to think about the decision or show why you need more time to make the decision. Use the extra time to gather additional relevant information and to enlist the wisdom of others in solving your problem. Many newlyweds, for example, make impulsive or unwise financial decisions they later regret because they do not consult with their older, more experienced parents who are more familiar with scams and can offer sound consumer advise.

TAKE INSPIRATION SERIOUSLY

In explaining how they came up with their inventions, inventors often reference sudden flashes of inspiration that came to them at unexpected or odd moments (such as while they were sleeping, taking a shower, or taking a walk). Even though skeptics may discount inspiration, you should not. Inspiration is too valuable an asset to be discounted or treated lightly. Therefore, be prepared to capture inspiration whenever it occurs. For example, carry a pencil and paper or small notebook with you to write down your thoughts and insights. You will be surprised at just how many great ideas you capture. One of them may even help you solve your problem.

DETERMINE IF THE PROBLEM HAS AN ORGANIC OR BIOLOGICAL BASIS

Some mental, emotional, physical, and psychological illnesses have organic, biochemical, or hereditary components. These factors may contribute to, or wholly cause, the problem at hand. Ignorance of these biological factors can lead to frustration and ineffectiveness in understanding and treating the problem. Although our knowledge of the brain and its relationship to emotions and mental processes is still very limited, if you suspect that a problem might be motivated by biological or organic factors, seek out competent medical, mental health, and nutritional guidance immediately.

MAINTAIN A PROPER PERSPECTIVE

Sometimes you may get discouraged or feel like you are a failure because you cannot solve a major problem, despite your most valiant efforts. When this happens, keep in mind that difficult problems often take a long time to solve. Recognize that some problems may be unsolvable, such as a permanent loss of health due to disease or accident. Remember also that true success is not found in solving every problem that comes your way, but in the growth of your character and in the service you render. If you are genuinely striving to increase your knowledge of the truth, to live by worthy values, to develop your character, and to help others achieve their greatest potential, then you are successful, regardless of whether you are able to solve all of your problems.

WEAPON 5: BUILD UP AND STRENGTHEN YOUR EMOTIONAL SUPPORT STRUCTURES

YOUR EMOTIONS are subject to change. You may feel on top of the world today but down in the dumps tomorrow. You may feel confident and secure now, but anxious and insecure next week. Emotions can be influenced by external forces (such as unexpected events, tragedies, disappointments, and accidents), internal forces (such as unfulfilled emotional needs, emotional weaknesses, strong desires, and physiological factors), and other people (who exercise their agency for better or worse). None of us are so strong emotionally that we are immune from these influences. All of us have times when we need the emotional support of others. Individual toothpicks are easily broken, but when several are taken together, it is difficult to break any one of them.

When emotional storms unleash their downpours, your emotional support structures are the precious lifelines that can pull you out of danger and onto safer ground. Because of this, prepare your lifelines ahead of time so that they will be ready for you to call upon when you need them. Do not attempt to walk an emotional tightrope or scale a sheer emotional cliff without a safety net and rope.

Emotional support structures are constructive activities, attitudes, beliefs, habits, values, environments, and relationships that give you strength and lift your emotions without incurring any negative or destructive consequences (getting high on drugs or alcohol, therefore, is disqualified).

The following suggestions will help you to build up and strengthen your emotional support structures:

Establish Physical and Environmental Support Structures

Soldiers do not fight well when their basic physical needs, such as food, water, and rest, go unmet. Similarly, you do not fight the forces of emotional darkness well when you are sleepy, exhausted, running faster than you have strength, or living in a depressing environment. Physical support structures, such as a healthy, rested, properly nourished body and a supportive physical environment, provide you the extra energy, clarity of mind, and inspiring surroundings you need to focus your full mental and physical powers on the problem at hand. Proper physical self-management is a foundation for proper emotional self-management.

Build Strong Interpersonal Relationships

Many of your most important emotional needs, such as love, affection, emotional intimacy, acceptance, support, friendship, and companionship, are met only through relationships. Relationships can restore emotional needs that the forces of emotional darkness deplete. Just knowing that others care about you, are there for you, and are working to lighten your load is empowering and revitalizing. Remember, the forces of emotional darkness are strongest when you must endure them alone.

Develop Your Talents

Most of us will never become famous painters, Olympic gold medalists, or renowned concert pianists—no matter how hard we try. This is not because we are stupid, undisciplined, or unmotivated (although a lack of discipline and motivation can certainly prevent the realization of great contributions on the part of those who do have talent). Sometimes, we may not possess enough native-born talent in a given area to excel above our peers. But just because we cannot become *world famous* painters or gymnasts does not mean that we cannot become excellent painters or gymnasts if we want to, or that we do not possess talents or skills that *do* come more naturally to us. Although you may not be a world-renowned scientist, you may have a gift for conversation, an outstanding sensitivity to the needs of others, the ability to make others laugh, or the gift to help others feel loved. Talents do not have to be things that make you famous or wealthy to be important or valuable. If you develop your talents and then use them to bless the lives of others, you will eventually experience a deep satisfaction and joy when those you have served express their appreciation and love for you.

BECOME MORE SELF-RELIANT

Take responsibility for your own welfare and reduce unnecessary dependence on others for your support, growth, and overall well-being, Anticipate needs and prepare for the future. If you are prepared, you are less likely to suffer physical and emotional hardships when unexpected events—such as downturns in the economy, natural disasters, accidents, or unemployment—take place. Self-reliance promotes a feeling of being in control. It builds self-confidence, reduces anxiety, enhances self-esteem, promotes stability, and increases your security. Become more self-reliant by working to get out of debt, starting an investment account, getting a degree, developing a new skill, growing some of your own food, and setting aside reserves of food, water, and other essentials your family might need in an emergency.

WEAPON 6: DEVELOP AND PRACTICE THE DISCIPLINE OF SUCCESS

YOUR INTENTIONS, good as they may be, can be easily overcome by discouragement, distractions, and other forces unless they are followed up by self-discipline, persistence, and determination. To achieve your goals, you must be disciplined to do the right things at the right time and be disciplined to avoid doing the wrong things the rest of the time.

How can you develop and practice the discipline of success?

DO THE RIGHT THINGS AT THE RIGHT TIME

Sometimes you fail to achieve your goals because you fail to take action when action is needed. For example, you tell yourself that you will take time to play with your son when you have finished everything else for the day, that you will take advantage of educational opportunities when your schedule is less hectic, that you will stop overeating when you have a less stressful job, that you will get organized when you have nothing better to do, and that you will show love, sensitivity, and patience when you are not under so much pressure. You say, "I'll do it later," "I'm too tired," "It's too boring," or "I don't feel like it right now" and thereby rationalize away your taking action when action is needed. Only hard work, intelligent action, and determined self-discipline will make your dreams come true.

EXERCISE

Aside from bringing you better health, physical exercise can help you learn greater self-discipline. The skills necessary to discipline your physical body—making time to exercise, overcoming inertia, motivating yourself, visualizing the benefits of exercising, and working out even when you would rather be doing something else—are the same skills that can help you be disciplined in other areas of your life. Before beginning any exercise program, consult with your physician.

WORK ON IMPORTANT GOALS DAILY

Small actions performed repeatedly over long periods of time can produce big results. A dripping faucet will eventually fill a reservoir. Suppose, for example, you want to write a book. If you wrote only *one page* a day (with one day off each week), you would complete a three-hundred-page book in less than a year. If you only wrote *one paragraph* a day, you would still complete your book in less than five years (at five paragraphs per page). If you only wrote a *single sentence* a day, you would complete your book in twenty years (at four sentences per paragraph). If you continued writing the rest of your life, even at this extremely slow rate, you would still complete two or three books in your lifetime—a worthy contribution indeed! And if you wrote slightly faster, at the rate of one paragraph a day, you would complete *ten to fourteen* books in your lifetime.

SPEAK CONSTRUCTIVELY, NOT DESTRUCTIVELY

A wise man approached a stranger and said, "Speak, that I may *see* you." Your true self is revealed by your words and actions, not by your appearance. People who cannot control their tongues injure their relationships, pollute the emotional atmosphere, and cut off the support they so desperately need to achieve their goals. Speech can build, uplift, and edify, or it can curse, blame, and abuse. Make your tongue one that is welcomed, not feared or hated. Use your power of speech to encourage, compliment, express appreciation, enlighten, show confidence, and communicate love. As you lift others, you will be lifted as well.

CONTROL WHAT YOU THINK

Thoughts precede actions. But they can also provoke certain emotions. Correct thinking—focusing on the bright side of things, postponing immediate judgment, giving others the benefit of the doubt, exercising your sense of humor, and seeing people's potential rather than their weaknesses—promotes Happy Emotions. Unmanaged or uncontrolled thoughts, such as comparing yourself to others, harboring unrealistic expectations, envying what others have, feeling sorry for yourself, putting yourself down, or criticizing others, promote Dark Emotions. Think correct thoughts. Refuse to dwell on the negative. Look for hidden opportunities. Enjoy the beauty around you. Avoid focusing on nits. Your emotions (and your partner) will be glad you did.

BE PERSISTENT

Another aspect of self-discipline is persistence. Persistence is striving for your goals even when progress is slow, even when you get tired, even when you become bored, and even when you are faced with opposition. Without persistence, you will give up on your goals prematurely when you become fatigued, bored, or frustrated. Some people, for example, conclude that they cannot learn to play the piano when, in reality, they do not want to pay the price of daily practice and weekly instruction over a period of years to learn to play.

WEAPON 7: BE EMOTIONALLY COURAGEOUS

ONE OF YOUR most important weapons in fighting the forces of emotional darkness is emotional courage. Emotional courage is refusing to give in to Dark Emotions, even when you feel that your situation is hopeless, even when your emotional support structures have been kicked out from beneath you, and even when you have to go it alone. It is daring to be the actor, not the reactor, even though your feelings are pressuring you to behave immaturely. It is the guts to forge ahead boldly, bravely, and defiantly against opposition and oppression, even though you may be scared, fearful, or shaken. It is the will to do the right thing at the right time.

Without emotional courage, you will not attain your goals. Why? Because the forces of emotional darkness, like the forces of nature, will periodically come together in fearful, intimidating displays of power. They may present you with great apparent contradictions, taunt you with the futility of your efforts, overpower you with a sense of hopelessness, deprive you of important emotional needs, or snatch away your emotional support structures. Emotional courage defiantly pushes ahead in these circumstances and refuses to give in to these Dark Emotions.

The following are some ways in which you can show emotional courage:

STAND UP AGAINST ABUSIVE BEHAVIOR

The virtue of tolerance does not include the acceptance of self-destructive or abusive behavior. If you feel you are the victim of abuse, seek out appropriate family, community, and professional medical and mental health help immediately. Trained professionals can help you receive the support, protection, and other resources you need to handle your situation safely and appropriately. Most forms of abuse are violations of the law and can be dealt with from a legal point of view as well. Many forms of abuse require temporary or permanent separation of the abuser from the abused. Whatever the case, abuse must be taken seriously. Most abusers will not change their behavior on their own. Therefore, if you are the victim of abuse, seek out appropriate help immediately.

WALK BY FAITH AS NECESSARY

Walking by faith is trusting in correct principles and processes and in the power of God to help you succeed, even in the face of apparent contradictions. Avoid demanding proof that you will be immediately rewarded and recognized for every worthy deed you perform or every worthy value you adopt. Instead, maintain a long-term perspective. Stand up against those who seemingly cannot view life more than a few minutes into the future, who demand overwhelming proof or compelling evidence of the truthfulness of worthy principles but are unwilling to put them to the test for themselves. All truth will stand the test of time, but this means that, on some occasions, a long time will be required. For example, even though avoiding smoking has always been a principle of good health, the destructive consequences of smoking have only been publicly acknowledged in recent times. Some truths can only be known by those who practice them and will never be known by those who doubt them, who do not want them to be true, or who are unwilling to put them to the test themselves.

Avoid Judging Life before Its Time

Life is not over until it is over. Endure your hard days without despair. Today may be stormy, but given time, the sun will return. Do not conclude that what you are facing today will continue on forever, even if you cannot possibly imagine how things could change. It is not always given us to see the end from the beginning. Therefore, do not pretend that you can accurately judge your life or your future circumstances from your present emotional viewpoint.

This principle was portrayed in the movie classic *It's a Wonderful Life*, starring James Stewart as George Bailey. In the movie, George Bailey, who inherited his father's savings and loan business during the 1930s, suffers a tragic turn of events when his unscrupulous business competitor steals a large cash deposit that George's partner misplaces on the way to the bank. The resulting scandal threatens to put George in jail, destroy his business, ruin his reputation, and bring suffering and hardship to his family. After failing to raise enough money to avert the scandal and exhausting every other means he could think of to resolve the crisis, George decides that he is worth more dead than alive because of his life insurance policy.

After George contemplates committing suicide by jumping into an icy river, his guardian angel beats him to it, knowing that George will jump in after him to save him. After they are both out of the river and dried off, the angel proceeds to show him just how different the townspeople and the community would have been were it not for his life and his good deeds. In the end, George realizes the positive impact he has made, the people whom he has helped throughout his life rally to save his business, and George comes to know for himself that mortal man cannot fully see the good that comes from a life well-lived.

Cling to Correct Beliefs

To maintain your motivation in the face of fierce opposition, you must believe in correct principles. If you do not believe in the Law of Restoration, for example, you will not be able to fight off the crushing realities of apparent contradictions, senseless tragedies, or serious crimes and injustices. If you do not believe that the good you do will be returned unto you in kind some day, you will return an eye for an eye and a tooth for a tooth. If you do not believe that making sacrifices and suffering losses to live by worthy values will ultimately bring you greater joy and happiness, you will not make these sacrifices. If you do not believe that good will ultimately triumph over evil, you will have little motivation to fight against evil, especially when it seems invincible. Without correct beliefs, courage and persistence are but fleeting fancies.

Develop a Sense of Humor

Laughter releases stress, eases tensions, and cuts fear down to size. Don't take life's ironies, miscarriages, and inconsistencies personally. Instead, learn to laugh at them. Learn to see (and express) the humor that exists in almost any situation. Do not take yourself or your problems too seriously. Lighten up.

Weapon 8: Model after the Emotionally Mature

Modeling is observing the behavior, actions, and character of another person and then emulating that person's character or behavior in your own life. It is thinking, acting, and saying what that person would think, act, or say in your present circumstance. Modeling has a powerful effect on behavior. Children model the behavior of their parents, often to their parent's embarrassment. Teenagers model after peers or popular entertainment figures. Movie stars often start trends or fads when people model after their style of dress or the way they wear their hair. Mentors and teachers model appropriate behavior at work and school. Heroes and heroines become models in novels and history books.

Modeling is a natural human tendency. Therefore, it is a powerful natural force that you can harness in your battle against the forces of emotional darkness. For example, by observing others acting courageously and maturely in the face of great trials or opposition, you will see that it is possible to live by correct values and principles in your own life, and you will learn new ways of handling challenges and behaving maturely. You will also see the long-term advantages and benefits that mature behavior has brought those for whom you are modeling. All of these things will strengthen your resolve to act maturely in your own life.

The following suggestions will help you tap into the power of role modeling in your own life:

IDENTIFY LIVING ROLE MODELS

Identify one or more people who are emotionally mature. This could be a friend, spouse, parent, teacher, colleague, or other person. Although nobody is perfect, some people display unusual emotional maturity in one or more areas of their lives. Identify the best examples of maturity you can find in each of these areas.

OBSERVE HOW YOUR ROLE MODELS MANIFEST EMOTIONALLY MATURE BEHAVIOR

After you have identified one or more role models, observe how they react to the challenges, opposition, apparent contradictions, setbacks, tragedies, unfulfilled emotional needs, fatigue, disappointments, and missed opportunities. Watch how they take responsibility for their own lives, anticipate emotional needs, demonstrate important emotional values, exercise self-discipline, and are actors, not reactors, to their circumstances.

ASK YOURSELF, "HOW WOULD MY ROLE MODELS ACT IN THIS SITUATION?"

After you have observed how your role models act, emulate their mature behavior in your own life. Ask yourself, "How would my role models interpret this situation?" or "How would my role models act in this situation?" or "What would my role models do if they were personally present?" Then try to act the way your role models would act in your particular situation.

EMULATE EMOTIONALLY MATURE BEHAVIOR WHEREVER YOU FIND IT

Model after emotionally mature behavior, no matter where you find it or in whom you find it. Every day, you probably come in contact with people who possess at least one attribute of emotional maturity that you can emulate. For the purpose of modeling, focus on their mature attributes and ignore any immature characteristics they might have. For example, model after the deep sensitivity displayed by your spouse, the happy disposition of a coworker, the persistence of a friend who is struggling to overcome a problem, and the self-discipline of a physical fitness devotee. When doing so, ignore whatever imma-ture characteristics they might have. By picking and choosing attributes to model after in those around you, you can tap into the power of modeling on a daily basis.

Model After the Emotionally Mature Who Are Not Personally Present

Many great examples of emotional maturity have already lived their lives or exist as fictitious characters in books and movies. Fortunately, vicarious modeling can be just as powerful as modeling after the living. Take advan-tage of this power by identifying and emulating worthy role models in tele-vision documentaries, biographies, historical accounts, and great works of fiction. Their mature examples can give you yet another means of combat-ing the forces of emotional darkness, even though they are imaginary or are not personally present.

Weapon 9: Be an Actor, Not a Reactor

Emotional responses can become automatic. If you are not careful, you can go through life on emotional autopilot, reacting to life's events without even being aware of the long-term consequences of your actions. Your automatic emotional response mechanisms can become so entrenched that you may even come to believe that you cannot possibly change the way you respond to cer-tain situations.

Of course, man is not an animal that must react to circumstance by instinct or genetic programming. Your responses do not *have* to be automatic. You can reprogram your automatic response mechanisms. Because you possess agency, self-awareness, and the capability for higher-order intellectual processing, you can choose how you will handle your emotions. You can be the captain of your emotional destiny.

Being an actor, not a reactor, to life's circumstances is a powerful weapon against the forces of emotional darkness. If you are not a helpless victim of your emotions or of your automatic response mechanisms, then you have great freedom and control over your life. Does this not lead to greater hope, increased optimism, and renewed energy?

To become an actor, not a reactor in your life:

INTERRUPT YOUR AUTOMATIC RESPONSE MECHANISMS

Computers have a built-in capability called an *interrupt* that allows other programs and hardware to literally interrupt the program that is currently executing to receive immediate attention. For example, interrupts allow a computer to respond to users typing on the keyboard or moving the mouse. Without interrupts, the computer would not be a very useful device and would be impossibly difficult to program. In this respect, the human brain is also like a computer. Its automatic, habitual, and unconscious thought processes can also be interrupted by deliberate, conscious thoughts. Like a computer, you have the capacity to interrupt your automatic thought processes and interject new programming into your thinking.

One way to change your automatic emotional responses is to continuously monitor your thoughts, speech and actions, especially when you are interacting with others, to identify the first moments when you start to execute an immature script. You may notice, for example, that your first reaction to anger is to raise your voice, become more aggressive, and display angry facial expressions. When you become aware that you are beginning to think or react immaturely, consciously intervene with a mature thought or response (think, for example, how your mature emotional role model would act in this situation). Examine your emotion and see if it was prompted by faulty thinking or improper motives (for example, did you become angry because of an unrealistic expectation or a selfish desire to control others to get what you want?). Replace your defective programming with correct thinking. Repeat the process until your new, more mature programming becomes automatic.

Another technique is to force yourself to wait a few seconds (or longer, if necessary) from the time you perceive a disturbing event until the time you respond to it. Use the time during this forced delay to "cool off" and determine a mature response.

BUY ADDITIONAL TIME TO RESPOND

When you are confronted with an emotionally difficult situation, you may need to buy additional time to think through an appropriate response. Do this by telling others, "I hear you," "I'm thinking," or "Let me think about this for a few minutes." Alternately, use body gestures such as a nod or a posture of reflective thinking to let others know that you are deeply involved in thought and are not simply ignoring them. Use the extra time to reflect on how your mature role model would handle the situation and on what principles you should follow.

REMOVE YOURSELF FROM THE SITUATION

If you feel you need to, temporarily remove yourself from the situation so that you can emotionally detach yourself from your circumstances and really think things through. This will also give others time to do the same. Politely excuse yourself with, "Please excuse me, but I need to think about this somewhere else for a while," "I need to go outside for a breath of fresh air," or, if everything else fails, "I need to go to the bathroom." Be sure that you do not walk off in a huff or with a grand display of emotion. While you are away, do something safe and constructive to release your negatively charged emotions—take your dog for a walk, go for a swim, take a nap, work in the garden, work on a hobby, go window shopping, watch a movie, or engage in some other stress-reducing activity.

CHECK YOUR MOTIVATION

If your motivation for interacting with others is improper—to lash out, get revenge, put down, attack, hurt, undermine, take advantage of, control, or dominate—then do not expect to have the power to be an actor—not a reactor—to the situations that confront you. Dark motivation and Dark Emotions are intimate companions. Where there is dark motivation, there will be Dark Emotions. Just as you cannot turn out all the lights and then expect to see in the dark, you cannot possess an improper motivation and then expect to be an actor—not a reactor.

IDENTIFY AND ELIMINATE YOUR EMOTIONAL HOT SPOTS

If certain events in your life trigger an immature response, then analyze your reactions and determine their underlying causes. You may discover, for example, that your Dark Emotions arise from unrealistic expectations, inappropriate judgments, inaccurate assumptions, distorted perceptions, or selfish desires. Replace any offending thoughts and improper motivations with their correct counterparts. Set up mental flags in your mind that will be triggered whenever you encounter your hot spots so that you can consciously interject predetermined mature responses.

Ask what would your role model do? Visualize how your mature emotional role model would act in your situation. Then act that way yourself. Use the extraordinary power of human modeling to help you behave more maturely.

WEAPON 10: WORK TO TURN EVERY EXPERIENCE TO GOOD

ONE NIGHT AFTER working late, Robert walked to his car in his employer's parking garage. Just before getting in, two men wearing ski masks suddenly hit him over the head with a pipe and stabbed him repeatedly in the chest with a knife. They removed Robert's wallet and took the forty-two dollars it contained.

Robert's vicious attack would have been fatal if a security guard making his rounds had not found Robert lying unconscious in a pool of his own blood. Had the guard arrived a few moments later, Robert would have bled to death.

An ambulance rushed Robert to a nearby hospital, where a team of doctors operated on him for eleven hours to save his life. The blows to Robert's head had shattered a portion of his skull, causing sharp bone fragments to penetrate into and hemorrhage Robert's brain. Other blows had cracked his jaw, broken his ribs, and damaged his kidney. The knife used in the attack cut through Robert's stomach and small intestine. It was a miracle he had even survived.

The attack left Robert in a coma. The injury to his head and brain was so severe that the doctors doubted that he would ever regain consciousness. Even if he did, his brain injuries were so severe that he would be unable to speak, control his limbs, or even understand what was going on around him.

Anna, Robert's wife, was devastated by her husband's sudden attack. For days, shock, anger, bitterness, hatred, depression, and deep anguish swept through her like a pounding surf. She had been very close to her husband from the moment they had first met. They were intimately bonded to each other, not just maritally, but emotionally, mentally, and spiritually.

Robert's children, a five-year-old daughter and a three-year-old son, loved their father dearly. Whenever he arrived home from work, they would race to the door, throw their arms around him, and beg him to play.

Their father was their greatest pal. He played with them, read them bedtime stories, and tucked them into bed every night.

Now, there was no father figure. No one came home and walked through the door every evening, eager to play with them. Instead, there was silence and emptiness. The children were upset and confused. They cried every night and asked their mother where their father was and why he could not play with them or read them bedtime stories. Anna could not give them a satisfactory answer. She could not explain to them why anyone would want to hurt their father. She could only cry and hold her children in her arms.

Robert's extensive hospitalization, operations, and other medical treatment soon exhausted his medical insurance. He had been operated on seven times since the attack and had been seen by dozens of medical experts and specialists. The doctors told Anna that Robert would need hospitalization for the rest of his life.

Anna had never felt the need to work before the tragedy. Robert made a good salary, and she enjoyed being a full-time mother and wife. Moreover, she had no special skills or training to offer in the job market. She had no other choice but to sell their home and move into a small apartment. Financially, Anna was broke.

A few days after the attack, the police caught and arrested two teenage suspects. They were later tried and found guilty of attempted murder, but because they were minors, they were given light sentences and were expected to be set free in a few short years. When asked in the trial why they had attacked Robert, they answered that they each needed twenty dollars to pay for their next drug fix.

Anna greatly struggled to deal with her emotions, the loss of her husband, and her new financial reality. She and her family had been victimized by two reckless, cruel young men who did not care about the consequences of their actions and cared only about themselves. These young men had forced their way into her life, the life of her husband, and the lives of her children, inflicting indescribable pain and causing irreparable and irreversible damage. Yet they were barely aware of the great suffering they had caused and did not seem to comprehended the horrible depth and magnitude of their crimes.

Anna refused to give in to the great Dark Emotions and intense emotional opposition that tore at her heart. She sought after the support of family, friends, religious leaders, and mental health professionals. She prayed, meditated, and read the accounts of others who had survived similarly difficult tragedies. She tried to focus on what she did have—her health, her two children, the love and support of friends and family, her relationship with God, her faith in the Law of Restoration, her memories of her earlier life with Robert, and financial support from a local television station's fund-raiser. Although these things could not bring back her former life or in any way make up for the deprivations that she had suffered, they did help her to cope with her pain and losses and ultimately press forward in her life.

Through her tragic experience, Anna developed a profound understanding of the importance of individual responsibility and of the severe consequences that follow irresponsibility. She learned that the teenagers who had attacked her husband had grown up in third-generation welfare homes to unwed single-parent mothers. Their mothers had been drug addicts themselves from a young age and had been abusive to their children.

Though knowing the personal histories of her husband's attackers did not in any way excuse their crimes, Anna saw how a seemingly unimportant choice made years ago by a single young woman could ultimately ripple out to affect the lives of dozens of innocent others. One irresponsible person could start a chain reaction that could ultimately rain misery, pain, and destruction on countless others who were far removed in space or time from the original irresponsible act.

Anna wanted to teach this insight to others, especially to young people who were at the crossroads of their lives. Perhaps it would help motivate them to lead mature and responsible lives and would prevent a multitude of similar tragedies. She set out on a campaign to motivate others to live more responsibly. She became a spokesperson to young people on the dangers of drugs and the importance of treating their bodies with respect and self-control. She spoke to adults on television and radio talk shows about the far-reaching consequences of parenthood and about the devastating consequences of neglect and abuse. She organized a national support group for victims of drug-related violence. She wrote a book on the topic of individual and family responsibility and gave frequent lectures and speeches on the subject. She used her creative talents to help others become more conscious and knowledgeable about the ultimate consequences of their choices. Because of her personal and tragic experiences, many listened.

Anna undoubtedly saved countless others from tragedies similar to her own. She helped numerous young people and adults alike to take responsibility for their bodies, their actions, and their lives. Because she conquered the forces of emotional opposition in her own life, Anna altered destinies, prevented untold human tragedy, and blessed the lives of thousands.

Trials are part of life. Death, tragedy, setback, injustice, persecution, unreasonable expectations, crime, stress, and other difficulties can strike anyone at anytime. These hardships are exactly that—hardships. But no matter what your trial, you can turn your experience to good. You can use your experience to build your character, to demonstrate your commitment to worthy values, to develop a deeper appreciation for what really matters most in life, and to motivate you to conquer evil with good in your own sphere of influence. Trials and tragedies themselves may be out of your control, but your reaction to them is not.

What can you do to turn your experiences to good?

LEARN FROM THIS EXPERIENCE HOW *NOT* TO TREAT OTHERS

Too often, we treat others the same way we have been treated. If our spouse yells at us, we yell back at them. Although this may feel natural and justified, it does not really teach others what we think it does ("how it feels to be mistreated"). Instead, others become even more offended, defensive, and aggressive in protecting themselves and in wanting to eliminate the source of pain and emotional danger that is threatening them. Fighting Dark Emotions with Dark Emotions only intensifies the emotional exchange of gunfire.

Instead, learn from your suffering how *not* to treat other people and then avoid treating others this way. After all, who knows better at this moment in time how it feels to be treated in this way? You know the suffering, sorrow, and life-altering consequences that follow such behavior. Therefore, let your experience motivate you to resolve never to subject another human being to this same pain. Instead, fight darkness with light. Act the opposite of how you were treated:

- You are treated rudely and insensitively. Rather than returning the gesture, you use your experience to learn (or remind yourself) of the importance of treating others in kind, sensitive ways. You subsequently resolve never to treat others insensitively and to make the opposite behavior a part of your character. Later, at the dinner table, you teach your family the importance of treating others respectfully and sensitively. You show by example how this is done. As a result, you and your family treat each other and outsiders with more kindness and sensitivity.

- Your needs are grossly neglected by your spouse. Rather than retaliating by acting in kind, you reflect on the importance of being aware of and responsive to the emotional, spiritual, physical, intellectual, and social needs of your loved ones. You ponder the consequences that follow long-term unmet needs. You resolve that, no matter how others may treat you, you will always do your part to be caring and responsive to the needs of others. You ask your spouse what you can do to better meet his needs and follow up with tangible actions. You are careful to thank anyone and everyone who helps meet your needs, no matter how small or trivial their actions. You make a sustained effort to understand the needs of those around you and to act appropriately to meet those needs. You teach this principle to your family so they can grow from your knowledge, experience, and example. Over time, others notice that you are more caring and sensitive to their needs. They, in turn, become more sensitive to your needs.

- Your possessions are stolen from your apartment. After your initial shock, you ponder the importance of honesty, respect for the property of others, and personal integrity. You reflect on the personal hurt, financial loss, and suffering this crime has brought to you. Instead of becoming embittered, you file a police report and then renew your commitment to be completely honest in your dealings with others, to return the things you borrow promptly, and to treat the property of others with greater care and respect. When politicians are caught cheating, lying, or defrauding taxpayers, instead of winking at their so-called "indiscretions," you vote for someone else.

If every time you are wronged, you develop a higher character and become more strongly motivated to serve others and do even greater good, then evil is overruled and you have truly turned your experience to good.

LET OPPOSITION AND SUFFERING REFINE YOUR CHARACTER

When the proud suffer, they react by taking offense, casting blame, and lashing out. When the emotionally mature suffer, they allow their experiences to build their character. Rather than letting Dark Emotions (such as rage, anger, bitterness, discouragement, and despair) fester and multiply until they have completely ravaged their emotional being, they instead use their experiences to identify and learn correct principles, to better comprehend the consequences of irresponsibility, and to increase their empathy for those who are suffering through similar experiences.

In the midst of your trials, ask yourself questions such as, "What am I supposed to be learning from this experience?" "How can I use this experience to improve my character?" "What principles of emotional maturity are being violated here?" "Why are they important?" and "What consequences follow their violation?"

USE YOUR EXPERIENCE TO DEVELOP GREATER SELF-DISCIPLINE

Sometimes we do not discipline ourselves until we have to. We do not get out of the bed in the morning until we have to go to work, we do not exercise until we are overweight, we do not save for retirement until we are almost retired, and we do not fully appreciate our relationships until they are taken away from us. Only when our pain reaches a certain threshold, or when serious consequences threaten to destroy our peace, do we suddenly find the motivation to discipline ourselves and attend to important actions and principles.

Waiting until we are on the verge of self-destruction before we discipline ourselves to take important actions is not a very desirable way of approaching life. Unfortunately, some of us refuse to learn important principles until we are frightened into action by impending doom or consequence. Our trials, if we will allow them, can sometimes serve as needed boot camps for kicking us in the rear and getting us in line.

AVOID DWELLING ON THE NEGATIVE

Avoid dwelling on past trauma, past mistakes, and past tragedies. After you have extracted whatever wisdom you can from an experience (and have made proper restitution, if you were the offender, to God and to all those you have hurt, injured, or offended), put your experience behind you and get on with your life. Avoid wasting time seeking revenge or determining fine lines of blame. If you have been seriously wronged, do what you can to support, change, and uphold the law and cooperate with authorities. Then let those who are responsible for administering justice take care of the matter. Avoid dwelling on your experience for the rest of your life. Learn whatever you can from it, do something good with it, and then put it behind you. Keep the lesson, but throw away your bad memory of the experience.

APPRECIATE WHAT YOU HAVE

One way emotional opposition strikes is by depriving us of the good things we are enjoying or are anticipating enjoying. Although deprivation is never easy, we can use it to develop a greater appreciation for all that life has given us—not just recently—but over our lifetime. We can appreciate the big things in our life, such as our spouse, our children, our extended family, our friends, our faith, our freedom, our education, our knowledge of truth, and our current level of health. But we can also appreciate the seemingly small things in life—the things we often take for granted—such as a smile, a hug, a beautiful day, a word of encouragement, a cold glass of water, an expression of appreciation, a warm coat, and a cozy bed. By focusing on just how generous life really has been to us, our burdens will be lightened and our hearts will be gladdened.

REACH OUT TO THOSE WHO SUFFER SIMILARLY

Alcoholics Anonymous and Mothers Against Drunk Driving were both formed by individuals who had suffered the tragedies their organizations are designed to counteract. These organizations have helped save the lives of many thousands and turn around the lives of many more. Those who are stricken by traumatic events or who suffer innocently at the hands of others have a strong need for empathy, love, understanding, and support. Who better to offer that empathy and give that support than those who have gone through a similar experience themselves? You can make a difference in the lives of others and turn your experience to good by helping others to avoid this tragedy and by lending your support to those who are currently suffering through one.

SEEK OUT HELP

If you are the victim of crime or abuse, seek out immediate help from qualified physicians, mental health professionals, social agencies, and law enforcement officials. You are going through a very vulnerable, difficult, and trying time. You need the support, clear thinking, proven interventions, and relief that competent professionals can provide. Seek support as well from close family members, good friends, and trusted religious advisors. Your loved ones know you best and are often in a position to give you the empathy, support, and love you need.

THE BATTLE OVER YOUR EMOTIONS IS REAL

THE BATTLE OVER your emotions is no imaginary fairy tale. It is real. Whether you realize it, you are immersed in this battle every day. There is crime, divorce, abuse, war, injustice, opposition, contention, rudeness, insensitivity, tragedy, set-backs, natural disasters, selfishness, oppression, and suffering enough in this life.

The forces of emotional darkness are unavoidable. They will visit you repeatedly throughout your life. You cannot wish them away, deny their exis-tence, avoid them, or nullify their effects through mere positive thinking. Because of this, you must prepare now to successfully confront and overcome their destructive power. Unless you find your life's worthy central purpose, develop a long-range perspective, seek out and adopt correct beliefs and val-ues, practice creative problem solving, build up and strengthen your emotional support structures, practice the discipline of success, demonstrate emotional courage, model after the emotionally mature, become an actor, not a reactor, and learn to turn your experiences to good, you will likely end up as the con-quered instead of the conqueror.

The forces of emotional darkness are waging a battle for your emotions, your heart, and your mind. Their aim is to take possession of the whole of them. In this they will succeed unless you can wage a powerful counteroffen-sive of your own. With the knowledge, values, and key principles you have just learned, you are better prepared to do just that.

THOUGHTS TO PONDER

- Did famous and infamous people throughout history have a purpose (consider, for example, Mother Teresa, Gandhi, and Hitler). How are our motivation and our goals an outgrowth of our purpose? How does having an overall worthy central purpose help you evaluate and make decisions in your life? (Can it, for example, help you know if you are allowing your emotions to have too much influence in making a decision?) When you near the end of your mortal existence, what overall worthy purpose would you like to have accomplished in your life?

- How does losing sight of your long-range goals, being impatient, or wanting to achieve your goals faster than is realistic undercut your motivation, increase your frustration, and lead you to abandon your goals? Should you expect some failures and setbacks as you work toward your worthy long-term goals? If so, should you feel that life is being unfair when these setbacks occur?

- If you learn from a failure, is it really a failure? Should you view your "failures" as failures or as learning experiences that can teach you important lessons and provide you valuable feedback? Which perspective is emotionally empowering? Which one is emotionally debilitating? Should a student give up learning calculus simply because he misses a few problems on a homework assignment? Why not? Why then do we often demand from ourselves perfect first-time performance?

- Is the ability to handle difficult, complex, and persistent problems a necessary skill for success? If so, should you be surprised when complex problems confront you? How important is it to be adaptable, flexible, and creative in minimizing or overcoming challenging obstacles? How important is persistence?

- Have you ever misjudged the amount of work, the complexity, the struggle, or the raw determination that was required to achieve a significant goal (for example, have you ever personally remodeled a room in your house)? Is remembering "The Big Picture" important during those times? How critical is it to pace yourself (take needed breaks and work regularly at a consistent but reasonable pace)? How can a journal help you see your progress and remember the other times in your life that you successfully overcame challenges?

- Do people act according to their underlying beliefs? If so, then to affect people's actions (without the use of force), what must you first do? Can you progress beyond the level of truth you uphold? If not, then how important is it to seek out and embrace truth in all aspects of your life? How can false beliefs lead to suffering, tragedy, and even death?

- Do you believe in a Higher Power? If so, do you believe this Power will ultimately hold men and women accountable for their actions and the desires of their hearts? Can there be individual responsibility without personal accountability? How can a belief in the ultimate triumph of good over evil and in the Law of Restoration bring you peace when you suffer a great injustice or apparent contradiction (in which evil seemingly triumphs over good)?

- The outcomes of wars are often determined by the quality of the logistical operations supporting the troops behind the battle lines (consider Operation Desert Storm in the Persian Gulf or Napoleon's disastrous invasion of Russia). Does having emotional support structures make you less vulnerable to emotional discouragement or defeat? What can you do to shore up your underlying emotional support structures?

- Why is self-discipline in the *execution* of plans just as important to success as proper planning and preparation? Are successful people willing to do what unsuccessful people avoid or refuse to do? In life, who wins most often: the hare or the tortoise? For example, who ends up with a larger retirement: the person who saves for retirement consistently throughout his life (taking advantage of the principle of compound interest) or the person who waits until ten years before retirement and then makes double the monthly deposits?

- Are you willing to go it alone emotionally to achieve your goals? What if no one else cares about whether you achieve your goals and they fail to give you any emotional support? Are you still willing to push forward under *these* circumstances? What does it mean to walk by faith? Is walking by faith necessary to the achievement of difficult goals? Why is walking by faith so difficult?

- Should you be distracted or diverted from your goals by people who demand overwhelming proof or compelling evidence of true principles before they will (supposedly) live them in their own lives? Are such people sincere seekers of truth? Why is it dangerous to judge the far-reaching consequences of your actions (or your life) before its time? How can a healthy sense of humor help you maintain balance and perspective in your life?

- When people talk about the power of example, they are really talking about the power of human modeling. How do advertisers make extensive use of human modeling to influence people to buy their products? How does seeing others who have faithfully endured difficult challenges help you with your own trials?

- Is it possible to react emotionally to situations without your conscious attention or thought? Are you responsible for your automatic emotional response mechanisms? Can your automatic emotional responses be reprogrammed? If so, by whom?

- How can any good come out of tragedy? What kind of character must you have for this to occur? On a lesser scale, what can being mistreated teach you about how you should treat others?

- In a free society, is success largely a matter of luck? If not, then what is it a matter of? Would it surprise you, for example, to learn that only a very small percentage of the wealthy receive their wealth through inheritance? If this is true, then how did the vast majority of the well-to-do become wealthy?

- Why is it easier to explain our failure to succeed as bad luck, unfortunate circumstances, injustice, or being wronged by others than to believe in personal responsibility and acknowledge that we are free to learn, develop skills, work, sacrifice, persist, and overcome challenges? What is the difference between those who are "unfortunate" and those who are "irresponsible?" Should you support any political philosophy or proposal that is based on the following belief: "People are not responsible for their actions and decisions (because they are too stupid, too unfortunate, too incapable, and so forth); therefore, it is the role of government to tax those who are responsible to fund programs that will allow those who are irresponsible to avoid the consequences of their actions and decisions?" Is it "insensitive" to hold others accountable for their actions?

- Should the government uphold the Law of Harvest in the lives of its citizens, or should it try to circumvent it? What happens to human motivation when the government doesn't strive to uphold this law (for example, when those who work hard and make sacrifices applying correct principles do not fare any better than those who don't due to governmental laws and taxes)? How does this change in human motivation affect the country's economy, strength, and future potential? Should government tax hard-working, responsible citizens so that it can support those who want a life of ease or luxury on someone else's back? Should the American Dream be an opportunity and an earned accomplishment, or a "right" and "guarantee" by the government (which must then tax productive, responsible citizens to make the Dream happen for those who are unwilling to make it happen for themselves)? Should we give in—in the name of "charity," "caring," or "sensitivity to the needs of others"—to the demands of irresponsible people who are looking for free handouts or a free ride in life? How does a government that refuses to support the Law of Harvest affect the emotional lives of its responsible citizens (consider the motivational issues just discussed and the greater burden of stress due to increased taxes and a poorer economy)?

- Is it better to give "unfortunate" people who can work (or be trained to work) something for nothing, or to help them become more independent and self-reliant through training, education, and the insistence on personal responsibility? What relevance does the Chinese proverb, "Give a man a fish and you feed him for a day; teach a man how to fish and you feed him for a lifetime" have on this issue? Is it charitable to help others avoid individual responsibility? (For example, is it charitable to help those who refuse to fish?) Who are the truly needy? Why is it so important to the emotional and economic health of a nation to distinguish between the truly needy and those who are simply looking to avoid individual responsibility? How is individual responsibility linked to personal growth, success, and fulfillment?

ACTIVITIES FOR SELF-IMPROVEMENT

1. Choose your own worthy central purpose. Review the questions on page 185, spend time in deep thought and meditation, and ask others what they would do differently if they had their lives to live over again. Then write a brief statement of your life's purpose. Revisit your purpose regularly and revise it as needed or as it becomes more clear to you.

2. When you are feeling discouraged about achieving your goals, think about how long it took others to achieve similarly worthy

goals (for example, consider how long it takes engineers to build a skyscraper or bridge, farmers to tend and harvest crops, writers to pen a novel, parents to raise healthy and well-adjusted children, and entrepreneurs to start and build a successful business). Recognize that worthy accomplishments require sustained effort over long periods of time. Remember that consistent, daily efforts do make a big difference. Measure and track your incremental progress, celebrate the accomplishment of milestones, and maintain "The Big Picture."

3. Choose a difficult problem you are facing. Determine if the problem is within your power (completely or partially) to solve. Apply any of the problem-solving suggestions on pages 197 through 201 that you have not yet utilized. For example, seek out the advise and counsel of two new people you think might be able to help.

4. Select one of the suggestions for success listed on pages 203 through 205 that you are having trouble implementing. Commit yourself (privately and publicly) to exercising self-discipline in this area for a day or a week. Then exercise that discipline consistently throughout that period of time. How did you feel afterwards? Do you want to enjoy these feelings again? Repeat this activity again and again until you have made this "success discipline" a habit.

5. Think of a problem in your life for which you are *not* making significant headway. Now list specific things you can do to build and strengthen your emotional support structures (see pages 201 through 203) in areas of your life *unrelated* to the problem (for example, clean up and organize your environment or get in better physical condition). How can strengthening your emotional support structures in nonrelated areas help you tackle this problem?

6. Walk by faith. Avoid demanding an immediate reward for every good deed you do in your life or praise for every positive step you take. Laugh at apparent contradictions. Take *reasonable* and calculated risks to achieve worthy goals. Strengthen your faith in correct principles when you are confronted by opposition by reaffirming to yourself: "I believe in the Law of Restoration," "I believe in the Law of Harvest," and "I know that if I follow correct processes, I will eventually achieve my desired outcome." Remember, all that evil forces have to do to succeed is to convince you that your good efforts are meaningless, trivial, or futile.

7. Consider the people you know. Who are good emotional role models (people who are emotionally aware, responsible, courageous, and who properly manage their emotions)? Tap into the power of emotional role modeling by following the steps listed on pages 209 through 210.

8. Ask your partner to identify one of your undesirable automatic emotional response mechanisms (why must you ask your partner?). Follow the steps listed on pages 211 through 213 to reprogram this emotional response mechanism.

9. Describe how you turned a bad experience or a tragedy to good. As you went through the process of grieving, what did you do to look at the situation differently? How did you let your experience refine your character? How did you let it stimulate you to help others?

10. When opposition comes, rather than looking for people to blame, work on finding creative solutions to overcome, circumvent, or minimize the effects of your problems. If your trial is something that you must endure, allow it to refine your character.

YOUR EMOTIONAL QUEST

Knowledge is power only when it is wisely applied

Congratulations! At this point, you should have a good understanding of the emotional foundations of loving relationships.

This important milestone calls for a moment of reflection. Consider, for example, what you now know.

- You now know why emotional awareness, responsibility, self-management, and courage through trials are necessary to personal and interpersonal happiness and success.
- You now know how emotions can influence critical life decisions, how to distinguish Happy Emotions from Dark Emotions, and what your partner's (or your children's, friend's, or boss's) top twenty emotional needs are.
- You now know what emotional responsibility is, the good and bad consequences that follow emotional responsibility and irresponsibility (respectively), how to take responsibility for your emotions, and how to identify and overcome your emotional weaknesses.
- You now know why relationships are so critical to fulfilling your emotional needs, how to identify and satisfy emotional hunger, and the Ten Secrets of Emotionally Fulfilling Relationships.
- You now understand why there is emotional opposition and trial in your life, how to avoid The Five Great Destroyers of Relationships,

and how to apply Ten Potent Weapons for Battling the Forces of Emotional Darkness.

This indeed is a great accomplishment! So, what comes next?

This is a question only you can answer. Emotional awareness is not enough! You must put your knowledge into action. Knowledge is powerless unless it is appropriately and intelligently applied.

So, what are you willing to *do* to enjoy more loving relationships with your spouse, your children, and your loved ones? More specifically:

- "How much change am I willing to undergo for my partner (or future partner)? For my children? For my posterity? For the future of society? For myself?"
- "What am I going to do to become emotionally more responsible, stable, and courageous?"
- "What actions am I going to take to apply what I have learned to better manage my emotions and take greater charge of my emotional life?"
- "What am I going to do to understand and fulfill the emotional (and other) needs of those around me?"
- "What am I willing to sacrifice to enjoy happier, more fulfilling relationships with my partner and loved ones?"

Because of what you have learned, you now possess greater power to foster and maintain loving relationships than ever before. Release that power. Apply the principles. Reflect on the *Thoughts to Ponder*. Carry out the *Activities for Self-Improvement*. Review the many suggestions for emotional growth found throughout this book. Ponder the benefits. Reset your priorities. Set goals and execute a plan of action. If needed, seek professional help or assistance.

By so doing, you will have a much surer foundation on which you can enjoy your own loving and lasting relationships.

EMOTIONAL NEEDS SELF-ASSESSMENT

Instructions: Using the scale below, rate how well each of the following emotional needs is being met in your life.

> 1=Completely Met
> 2=Mostly Met
> 3=Neither Met or Unmet
> 4=Mostly Unmet
> 5=Completely Unmet

___**To feel loved:** To feel that others care about you; to feel understood and accepted; to feel recognized as a valid, important, worthwhile human being; to feel supported during times of trial; to feel emotionally close to another human being; to feel that you are treated with kindness, respect, patience, and sensitivity; to feel special and appreciated; to feel that your needs will be cared for and looked after.

___**To love:** To care for others, to help others in need, and to sacrifice for the welfare of others.

___**To feel accepted by your partner:** To feel that your partner views you as an important human being, listens to you, seriously considers your opinions, and respects your unique talents and abilities; to feel included in your partner's life and activities; to feel accepted despite your weaknesses; to believe that your partner's body language, posture, and actions are friendly.

____**To feel accepted by your peers:** To feel that you are accepted as a member of the group, that you are treated equally as "one of the gang," that you are valued by the group as an important member, and that you are included in important group activities.

____**To feel affection:** To feel "mothered;" to feel emotional warmth; to receive hugs, smiles, sympathetic words, and friendly gestures; to be treated kindly, lovingly, and sensitively.

____**To feel emotional intimacy:** To feel that your partner understands your dreams, hopes, fears, aspirations, and struggles; to feel that you can share important feelings and confidences with your partner without worrying that those feelings will be mistreated, misjudged, divulged to others, or otherwise misused; to feel that your partner knows you so well that he or she can "read" your emotions and respond to your changing emotional needs, often even without your expressing those needs.

____**To feel emotional support:** To be lifted up when you are feeling down or discouraged, to receive encouragement, to have your self-confidence strengthened, to have your burdens lightened, to know that you can turn to your partner and receive help during times of need.

____**To feel companionship and friendship:** To have someone with whom you can socialize, confide, and have fun; to share your interests, dreams, challenges, and frustrations with those who care about you and are empathetic toward you.

____**To feel understood:** To feel that the other people who are important to you understand you—who you are, where you are coming from, what your background is, what trials you have endured, what setbacks you have experienced, and what victories you have celebrated; to feel that others understand your total life situation and what you are currently going through.

____**To feel valued:** To feel recognized and appreciated for your contributions and for who you are; to feel that your ideas, suggestions, and efforts are appreciated and are important; to be given credit and recognition for your ideas, inventions, creativity, and contributions; to be treated with courtesy, respect, and dignity.

____**To feel hope:** To believe that your goals are attainable and that you are progressing toward your goals; to feel that your future is bright, that things will shortly improve if they are not going well, and that your deepest dreams will someday come true.

___**To succeed:** To achieve at least some of your important goals, hopes, and aspirations; to feel successful in what you do and to feel that your efforts are moving you closer to your goals.

___**To avoid failure:** To avoid feelings of inadequacy, incompetence, disappointment, and defeat; to avoid damaging your self-esteem; to avoid the social embarrassment and the stigma that often accompanies defeat.

___**To feel in control:** To feel that you are in control of your life, not other people or other forces; to feel that you possess the power to reach your goals and that you are in control of your destiny, the opposite of feelings of helplessness.

___**To experience variety and stimulation:** To experience a variety of emotions; to avoid boredom; to experience excitement, stimulation, variety, and fun.

___**To feel balance:** To experience emotions in their proper proportion; to avoid undue obsession with any one aspect of life; to lead a balanced life—physically, emotionally, intellectually, socially, and spiritually.

___**To feel good about yourself:** To feel that you are progressing in skill, wisdom, and character; to feel that you are basically good; to feel that you are acting with integrity [in accordance with your personal code of ethics]; to feel positive self-esteem.

___**To make a difference:** To feel that you have made a difference in the lives of others; to feel that you have made the world a better place.

___**To be fairly treated:** To be treated equitably, to work in a system that is fair and impartial, to be given comparable opportunities as others.

___**To feel safe and secure in your relationships:** To feel safe from emotional abuse, emotional manipulation, emotional instability, and emotional volatility.

___**To feel safe and secure in your environment:** To feel safe and secure in your person, possessions, source of income, position, and lifestyle.

___**To live in an emotionally stable environment:** To live with others who are emotionally predictable and stable; to have emotionally stable relationships; to avoid those who manifest wild mood swings, unpredictable emotional reactions, and disturbing emotional volatility.

EMOTIONAL STABILITY ASSESSMENT

Instructions: Have your partner plot your mood changes over time by drawing a point on the graph (on the next page) every time he or she thinks your emotional mood has changed. Then connect the points together in a line graph. (See pages 156 through 157 for further instructions on how to take this self-assessment and interpret the results.)

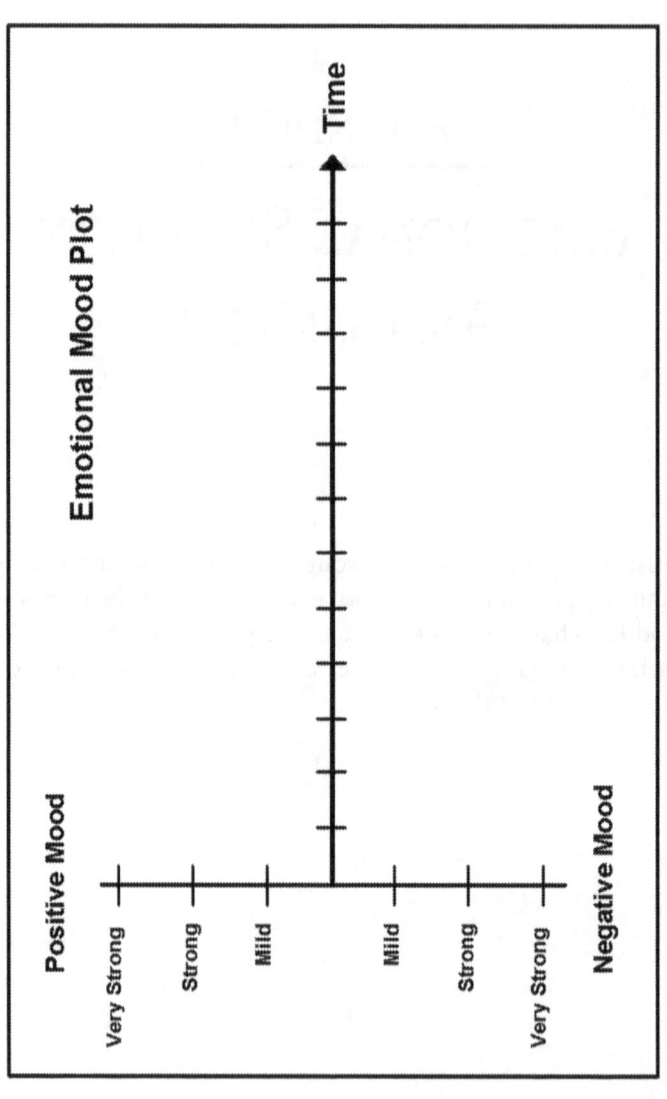

INDEX

E

I

M

Q

R

0-595-34100-4

www.ingramcontent.com/pod-product-compliance
Lightning Source LLC
Chambersburg PA
CBHW061340280526
45784CB00001B/80